KU-600-650

SHORTLIST

Prague
2009

WHAT'S NEW | WHAT'S ON | WHAT'S BEST

www.timeout.com/prague

Contents

Published by Time Out Guides Ltd
Universal House
251 Tottenham Court Road
London W1T 7AB
Tel: + 44 (0)20 7813 3000
Fax: + 44 (0)20 7813 6001
Email: guides@timeout.com
www.timeout.com

Managing Director Peter Fiennes
Financial Director Gareth Garner
Editorial Director Ruth Jarvis
Deputy Series Editor Dominic Earle
Editorial Manager Holly Pick
Assistant Management Accountant Ija Krasnikova

Time Out Guides is a wholly owned subsidiary of Time Out Group Ltd.

© Time Out Group Ltd
Chairman Tony Elliott
Financial Director Richard Waterlow
Group General Manager/Director Nichola Coulthard
Time Out Magazine Ltd MD Richard Waterlow
Time Out Communications Ltd MD David Pepper
Time Out International Ltd MD Cathy Runciman
Production Director Mark Lamond
Group IT Director Simon Chappell
Head of Marketing Catherine Demajo

Time Out and the Time Out logo are trademarks of Time Out Group Ltd.

This edition first published in Great Britain in 2008 by Ebury Publishing
A Random House Group Company
Company information can be found on www.randomhouse.co.uk
10 9 8 7 6 5 4 3 2 1

Distributed in US by Publishers Group West
Distributed in Canada by Publishers Group Canada

For further distribution details, see www.timeout.com

ISBN: 978-1-84670-105-4

A CIP catalogue record for this book is available from the British Library

Printed and bound by Firmengruppe APPL, aprinta druck, Wemding, Germany

The Random House Group Limited supports The Forest Stewardship Council (FSC), the
leading international forest certification organisation. All our titles that are printed on
Greenpeace approved FSC certified paper carry the FSC logo. Our paper procurement
policy can be found at www.rbooks.co.uk/environment.

Time Out carbon-offsets all its flights with Trees for Cities (www.treesforcities.org)

Prague Shortlist

The **Time Out Prague Shortlist 2009** is one of a new series of guides that draws on Time Out's background as a magazine publisher to keep you current with what's going on in town. As well as 2009's key sights and the best of its eating, drinking and leisure options, it picks out the most exciting venues to have opened in the last year and gives a full calendar of events from September 2008 to December 2009. It also includes features on the important news, trends and openings, all compiled by locally based editors and writers. Whether you're visiting for the first time in your life or the first time this year, you'll find the *Time Out Prague Shortlist* contains all you need to know, in a portable and easy-to-use format.

The guide divides central Prague into six areas, each containing listings for Sights & Museums, Eating & Drinking, Shopping, Nightlife and Arts & Leisure, and maps pinpointing their locations. At the front of the book are chapters rounding up these scenes city-wide, and giving a shortlist of our overall picks. We include itineraries for days out, plus essentials such as transport information and hotels.

Our listings give phone numbers as dialled from within the Czech Republic. To call from abroad, preface them with your country's exit code and the country code, 420.

We have noted price categories by using one to four $ signs ($-$$$$), representing budget, moderate, expensive and luxury. Major credit cards are accepted unless otherwise stated. We also indicate when a venue is **NEW**, and give **Event highlights**.

All our listings are double-checked, but places do sometimes close or change their hours or prices, so it's a good idea to call a venue before visiting. While every effort has been made to ensure accuracy, the publishers cannot accept responsibility for any errors that this guide may contain.

Venues are marked on the maps using symbols numbered according to their order within the chapter and colour-coded as follows:

- ❶ Sights & Museums
- ❶ Eating & Drinking
- ❶ Shopping
- ❶ Nightlife
- ❶ Arts & Leisure

Map key	
Major sight or landmark	▮
Railway station	▮
Metro station	Ⓜ
Park	▯
Pedestrian zone	▒
Church	✚
Steps	▬
Area name	JOSEFOV
Tram route	—

Time Out Prague Shortlist 2009

EDITORIAL
Editor Will Tizard
Copy Editor Anna Norman
Researchers Hela Balínova,
Kateřina Kádlecova
Proofreader Jo Willacy
Indexer Rob Norman

DESIGN
Art Director Scott Moore
Art Editor Pinelope Kourmouzoglou
Senior Designer Henry Elphick
Graphic Designers Gemma Doyle,
Kei Ishimaru
Digital Imaging Simon Foster
Advertising Designer Jodi Sher
Picture Editor Jael Marschner
Deputy Picture Editor Katie Morris
Picture Researcher Gemma Walters
Picture Desk Assistant Marzena Zoladz

ADVERTISING
Commercial Director Mark Phillips
International Advertising Manager
Kasimir Berger
International Sales Executive
Charlie Sokol
Advertising Assistant Kate Staddon
Advertising Sales (Prague) ARBOMEDIA

MARKETING
Marketing Manager Yvonne Poon
Senior Publishing Brand Manager
Luthfa Begum
Sales & Marketing Director,
North America Lisa Levinson
Marketing Designers Anthony Huggins,
Nicola Wilson

PRODUCTION
Production Manager Brendan McKeown
Production Controller Caroline Bradford
Production Co-ordinator Julie Pallot

CONTRIBUTORS
This guide was researched and written by Will Tizard.

PHOTOGRAPHY
All photography by Olivia Rutherford, except: page 32 National Theatre; pages 33, 36, 37, 50, 61, 63, 73, 96, 97, 99, 149 Czech Tourism; page 35 courtesy of MOFFOM festival, page 55 courtesy of the Office of the President of the Czech Republic, pages 80, 83, 125, 150, 158, 172 Will Tizard; page 152 Elan Fleisher.

The following images were provided by the featured establishments/artists: pages 13, 26, 28, 31, 76, 33, 151, 161, 163, 174, 178.

Cover photograph: Giovanni Simeone, 4corners images.

MAPS
JS Graphics (john@jsgraphics.co.uk).

About Time Out

Founded in 1968, Time Out has expanded from humble London beginnings into the leading resource for those wanting to know what's happening in the world's greatest cities. As well as our influential what's-on weeklies in London, New York and Chicago, we publish more than a dozen other listings magazines in cities as varied as Beijing and Mumbai. The magazines established Time Out's trademark style: sharp writing, informed reviewing and bang up-to-date inside knowledge of every scene.

Time Out made the natural leap into travel guides in the 1980s with the City Guide series, which now extends to over 50 destinations around the world. Written and researched by expert local writers and generously illustrated with original photography, the full-size guides cover a larger area than our Shortlist guides and include many more venue reviews, along with additional background features and a full set of maps.

Throughout this rapid growth, the company has remained proudly independent, still owned by Tony Elliott four decades after he started Time Out London as a single fold-out sheet of A5 paper. This independence extends to the editorial content of all our publications, this Shortlist included. No establishment has been featured because it has advertised, and no payment has influenced any of our reviews. And, for our critics, there's definitely no such thing as a free lunch: all restaurants and bars are visited and reviewed anonymously, and Time Out always picks up the bill.

For more about the company, see www.timeout.com.

Don't Miss
2009

Sights & Museums

With every architectural period from the last millennium represented in its mosaic, Prague's layers sometimes seem endless. So it's an apt metaphor, in a way, that conservationists have dubbed the Old Town Hall, in Old Town Square, the 'Prague Pompeii' for the fact that so many invaluable remains of its oldest structures – the simple Romanesque ones – are buried beneath this civic edifice and the streets immediately surrounding it. This building is also symbolic of the nation as a whole in that large portions of it were blown up by a foreign occupying power – in this case, the Nazis at the end of World War II. Czechs' national consciousness has much to do with the struggle for sovereignty and identity against the great powers that have always surrounded them. And with a thousand years of such struggle, it's not likely that a new plan to finally rebuild the Old Town Hall, announced in early 2008, will provide much 'closure'. The restoration – which will involve a public contest for designs in 2009 – was moving apace when this guide went to press. But before any work is done, archaeologists plan to thoroughly survey the medieval houses that remain under the building's floors. The city has also pledged to finally get a handle on the spread of billboards and café tables that have been encroaching on Old Town Square for years. However, it might be best to view these pledges with a healthy bit of

Museum of Decorative Arts p11

SHORTLIST

Best revamped
- Jewish Museum (p94)
- National Museum (p124)
- Zoo Praha (p153)

Best Prague experience
- Charles Bridge (p91)
- Old Jewish Cemetery (p95)
- Prague Castle (p54)

Best views
- Astronomical Clock (p91)
- Old Town Bridge Tower (p99)
- Petřín hill (p75)

King of the castles
- St Vitus's Cathedral (p61)
- Vyšehrad (p138)

Best outdoor attractions
- Letenský zámeček (p157)
- Vojanovy sady (p75)

Best architecture
- Church of St Nicholas (p70)
- House of the Black Madonna (p93)
- Municipal House (p97)

Best for kids
- Stromovka (p160)
- Výstaviště (p153)
- Zoo Praha (p153)

Most Kafkaesque
- Church of Our Lady before Týn (p92)
- Museum of Communism (p98)
- Old-New Synagogue (p98)

Best art stops
- Convent of St Agnes of Bohemia (p93)
- Karlín Studios (p151)
- Municipal Library (p97)

Best historic
- National Museum (p124)
- New Town Hall (p126)
- Museum of Communism (p98)
- Old Town Hall (p99)

scepticism: there were seven different competitions in the last century to come up with new looks for the square, none of which resulted in a brick being laid.

But the choice to reshape Old Town Square to remove one of Prague's worst scars is a telling one. Czechs, like many people around the world, generally don't care to dwell on dark episodes from the past. They very rarely bring up in conversation the days of Soviet domination – in fact, it took an American history scholar to launch the Museum of Communism. Yet the past is alive in Prague in a way that's hard to imagine in cities that were flattened during World War II and made anew in the years afterwards. Perhaps reaching back to the 19th century, as so many museums and galleries in Prague do, is a kind of defence. Whatever the reason, collections of things felt worth remembering, whether mammoths at the National

St Vitus's Cathedral

Museum, or the work of painters supported by Rudolph II during the Renaissance, are all around. This city of 1.2 million has more than a dozen significant museums and, for a time, three military ones. Old Town itself has been called an 'open-air museum of architecture', and Old Town Square has four major art collections on or around it that feature Czech work: Kinský Palace, House at the Golden Ring, House at the Stone Bell and the Old Town Hall. One of the most engaging museums, the National Technical Museum – which shows off countless examples of cunning 'Czechnology' in the form of planes, cars and inventions – was, alas, undergoing reconstruction at time of going to press; it's expected to be fully up and running again by 2010. Another great collection of pieces from that heady era is permanently on show, however, at the Museum of Decorative Arts (p98).

Meanwhile, the city's other starring attractions, Prague Castle (p54) and the Old Jewish Cemetery (p95), remain quite static, with the biggest change visible only in the administration of the former. St Vitus's Cathedral, the central point of Prague Castle and the source of the city skyline's most prominent spire, is, of course, church property. But because the state seized control of all churches after the communist coup in 1948, and even went so far as to make clerics state employees, the running of St Vitus is still being sorted out. Court rulings have held that the state must return all control but the prestigious property has long been thought of as a de facto component of the Castle, the ultimate embodiment of state. Thus you shouldn't be too surprised to hear of different St Vitus areas being opened to the public or closed off, or admission fees to the church being waived then reinstated. Such is the shakeout of a thousand-year power struggle between the nation and the bishops. Meanwhile, Prague Castle's displays still consist mainly of dusty mimeographed illustrations, with Russian in prominent use. (In fact, the interiors of Prague Castle are largely absent of wonders: everyone from the late Renaissance Swedes to the Nazis and Soviets have been carting off its most valuable treasures for centuries.) The Old Royal Palace part, though, has been fully redone with exhibitions geared towards international audiences. The displays, which mirror the sprawling nature of the palaces themselves, stretch out over a dozen rooms and feature exciting insights into the lives that have occupied this special space since 3200 BC. Though the roots of the castle itself extend back to a mere 900 AD, the hill now known as Hradčany was clearly of sacred significance to pagan peoples, as shown by the funerary rituals that still have scientists puzzled.

Other key sites in the city have been working to stay fresh. The Museum of Music (p74) on Karmelitská street in the Malá Strana district is worth a visit. Its shows, with colourful, noisy interactive displays, have been a hit with local and visiting crowds since it opened its doors. And one of the most important buildings in the Czech National Revival movement, the National Theatre, is also now getting special treatment. After years of neglect, this house of Czech culture and shrine to Smetana, paid for from the pockets of ordinary citizens, is having its rooftop and accompanying horse chariots redone.

Other attractions, such as the Jewish Museum (p94), Prague's second most visited space, have been running city-wide multi-venue shows in concert with other museums and galleries. And the National Museum (p124) continues to shake off its reputation for dullness with new exhibitions with imaginative themes. The kid-friendly Zoo Praha (p153), is also looking better than ever, with new programmes, a petting zoo and lion feeding times posted on the website.

Yet, despite all these attractions, most people still experience the city mainly by walking its streets, which are conveniently compact (Old Town, with its Astronomical Clock, is just two kilometres across), and, despite record commercial growth, remain little changed from their appearance centuries ago.

Tickets and information

The latest state of the city's main attractions, together with new exhibitions, is reliably posted on the Prague Information Service website (www.pis.cz), while the Prague Tourist Card is a worthwhile investment if you're planning to see much more than Prague Castle – note, though, that it does not cover entry to the Jewish Museum, the National Gallery or all the sites of the National Museum. It does cover four days of visits to dozens of other venues, plus public transport, for the price of 790 Kč, or 530 Kč for students. Pick it up at the Prague Information Service on Old Town Square or at Hlavní Nádraží train station (p180).

Old Jewish Cemetery p11

Café Imperial p17

WHAT'S BEST
Eating & Drinking

Beer and pub culture are on solid ground in the Czech Republic – a country in which nearly every hamlet once had its own brewery, and where some of these breweries are still turning out heady suds 500 years later. Some may dare to say that the self-proclaimed *pivo* capital of the world is basically focused on lager and lacks range, but such heretics notwithstanding, the yellowed walls, thick smoke, marinated herring, pickled cheese and gruff waiters are still to be found all over Prague. What is true, though, is that some of the most uncompromising pubs have been pushed out of the old centre in favour of cleaner, more friendly and far more profitable conceptions

that serve buffalo wings and have sexy waiting staff. And foreign investors have taken over and consolidated many of the traditional breweries, meaning that the smaller independents are increasingly unable to match them on prices and exports and are losing out: a major Czech state subsidy for Plzeňský Prazdroj, maker of Pilsner Urquell – now owned by South Africa's SAB Miller – caused a major stir recently, with critics arguing that the old family-owned brewers were far more in need of support.

Meanwhile, the state-owned Budvar brewery boosts output significantly every year and the Czech beer market overall is growing by four per cent

year-on-year, with output of the majors totalling more than 9.75 million hectolitres annually. One innovative indie, Bernard, is an excellent survivor, and fortunately still on tap at many places such as U Malého Glena (p82). But the soul of the classic pub, as described by Czech literati like Milan Kundera – the places where Vaclav Havel used to take visiting heads of state – somehow remains intact, and it seems a good bet that this national shrine will be with us for a long, long time, whatever's on tap.

The new wave

The religious-like reverence for pubs used to mean that, by and large, no one was interested in having anything more than this in Prague – or that any place that did not serve 19 Kč beer in a chipped mug on a soggy old beermat was a fancy-pants place to be looked on with suspicion and mistrust. But the fact that the city now has that inevitable, long-awaited Michelin star (awarded to the Four Seasons' restaurant, Allegro, in early 2008) and that Gordon Ramsay has set up shop at Maze (p107) – where Czechs make up most of the clientele – show that palates have changed. And not just in the highest echelons of haute cuisine either. This year witnessed the welcome return of local chef/entrepreneur Sofia Aziz's new venture Angel (p100), which mixes South-east Asian flavours with tender continental filets and cool modern design. The nearby Al Dente (p99), with its top-notch Turin trattoria fare, has helped form an Italian alley in Old Town, testament to a growing Czech passion for authentic Mediterranean cuisine to help weather the long Central European winters. Meanwhile, opulent old-Europe dining rooms,

SHORTLIST

Best new
- Al Dente (p99)
- Angel (p100)
- Maze (p107)
- Passion Chocolat (p140)

Best views
- Bellevue (p102)
- Kampa Park (p79)
- Palffy Palác (p79)

Best brunch
- Fraktal (p157)
- Jáma (p129)
- Radost FX Café (p132)

Best hotel dining
- Alcron (p127)
- Allegro (p100)
- Hotel Mandarin Oriental (p167)

Best beer gardens
- Letenský zámeček (p157)
- Park café (p140)

Best dating bars
- Dinitz (p105)
- Monarch (p107)
- Tretter's (p109)

Best pubbing
- U Provaznice (p110)
- U Vejvodů (p110)

Best coffeehouse
- Café Imperial (p102)
- Kavárna Obecní dům (p106)

Most Czech
- U Maltézských rytířů (p80)
- U medvídků (p110)
- U modré kachničky (p110)

Best scene
- Café Montmartre (p103)
- Duende (p105)
- Jáma (p129)

Jáma

such as Palffy Palác (p79) and Francouzská Restaurace (p105), which has scored culinary kudos in the past year, indicate a return to classic culinary mastery of traditional local herbs, spices, farmed meats and game. Café Louvre (p129) is another turn-of-the-century classic that's been tastefully cleaned up, its kitchen expanded and billiard tables dusted off.

All of which give new competition to the stars of the 1990s for cuisine, location and service – Kampa Park (p79) and Celnice (p103). The American influence on Prague continues to nurture a growing demand not just for buffalo wings but for brunches and bagels, with Bohemia Bagel (p102) having redone its hit cafés to offer full menus in some, free Wi-Fi in others, while Sunday midday feasts draw couples and families to Jáma (p129), Fraktal (p157) and Radost FX (p132).

Pubs and bars

Among the classic 'old man' pubs mentioned earlier that have barely budged in the face of more worldly customers are those like U Zlatého tygra (p110), the pub that functioned as the late novelist Bohumil Hrabal's second home, with its underground tank of Pilsner, making for one of the best pours around. Another time capsule is by Prague Castle: U Černého vola pub (p66). A place that more or less acknowledges the 21st century, but also with a fine Pilsner tank and all the trad pub grub on the menu, is buzzing Bredovský dvůr (p127). Kolkovna in Old Town is another modernised, user-friendly version of the ageless Czech pub, but tends to get packed out with tourists because of its location close to Old Town Square.

Bars, which tend to remain in a different league in Prague, are ever on the rise as Czechs' wallets and CVs expand, and the most elegant and expert new additions are nowadays often in hotels, as with Barego (p77).

The Žižkov district remains the capital of more down-to-earth character bars, many around Bořivojova street such as Bukowski's (p149), Hapu (p148) and Akropolis (p148), while Černá kočka Bílý kocour (p148) features appealing grill-bar food. Most bars still have little to eat and pubs tend to shut their kitchens on the dot of 10pm if not earlier, so be forewarned. In Old Town, mixed drinks still score awards at Tretter's (p109) and Čili (p104), with many concentrated around V Kolkovně.

Cafés

With the reopening of the lovingly restored Café Imperial (p102), visitors can now experience again decadent old-world coffeehouse culture in Prague, sipping an espresso amid high ceilings and bespoke ornamental tilework from another era. Prices have risen, of course, and you don't see as many clove-smoking Bohemians with manuscripts under their arms in the city's great cafés (another masterpiece is in the Municipal House, a secession-era showpiece; p97) but there are still some atmospheric holdouts filled with threadbare pre-war sofas and mismatched secondhand tables and chairs, such as Café Montmartre (p103) and, further out, the heady Café Medúza (p139).

Other redolent places such as Dahab (p104), show off the Prague phenomenon of *čajovna* or tearoom, with Persian pillow seating, jangly belly dancing, steamed couscous, mint tea and hookahs, as does Lehká Hlava (p106), with a more innovative vegetarian menu.

Tipping and etiquette

At pubs and beerhalls, tables are often shared with other patrons who, like you, should ask '*Je tu volno?*' ('Is it free?') and may also wish each other '*dobrou chut*' ('Bon appetite!') before tucking in. Prague dines with a relaxed dress code and reservations are necessary at only the new generation of upscale spots in town. Many waiters still record your tab on a slip of paper, which translates at leaving time into a bill. Pay the staff member with the folding wallet in their waistband, not your waiter ('*Zaplatim, prosim*' means 'May I pay, please?'). A small cover charge and extra for milk, bread and the ubiquitous accordion music are still in practice at many pubs, as is tipping by rounding the bill up to the nearest 10 Kč. At nicer places, 10-15 per cent tips are now the rule. While you should have little trouble making a phone reservation in English at modern establishments, at other places it might be easier to book in person.

Palffy Palác

Shopping

While it's an aspect of the city's retail scene that's unlikely to captivate the average foreign visitor, the opening of yet another mega-mall is still an important event in the Prague calendar for many locals. Czechs, it seems, just can't get enough of shopping in these luxury, air-conditioned spaces, with food courts offering more cuisine choices than the entire country did just a few years ago.

But have no fear: the funky little neighbourhood shop is not yet extinct (even if it edges closer to oblivion each year). And there's also almost no risk of encountering universally cheery and helpful service. This is Prague not the US, after all, and some traditions die awfully hard. Thus, while

things have improved greatly, you probably shouldn't expect someone to immediately notice you or inquire what they can do for you unless you're in a crystal shop on Celetná street. Nor are money-back guarantees quite the fashion, yet.

Better news is that Czech small entrepreneurs have long had a knack for building both businesses and customer relations, despite the interruption to normal market activity occasioned by the 1948-89 regime. So the trick is to visit the small shops that still exist, where you're likely to be dealing with the owner (or a family relation), rather than the high street places with obviously bored and miserable staff. And, of course, the city

Globe Bookstore & Coffeehouse p22

remains a wonderful source of the weird, yet still (mostly) affordable trinkets from the past, whether it's antiquarian books or art deco brooches. Head down any narrow side street, even in the old centre of town, and you'll find amazing knick-knacks, 'junque' and artefacts, from gorgeous maps with engraved illustrations to vinyl recordings of forgotten Czech pop stars.

If you're under strict orders to bring home Bohemian crystal or a traditional puppet – and there are good reasons the country is famous for both – then just about any of the dozens of highly visible shops selling these will do (though even here there have been innovations, as Artěl (p111) demonstrates). Another find for design lovers is the Kubista shop (p112), with particularly unique porcelain creations, contained in a building that is itself a shrine to Cubism. As for the more conventional glass shops, there's very little difference

in quality or price, at least in central Prague, and goods can generally be shipped home safely and reliably.

English is spoken widely, if sometimes begrudgingly, at just about all shops in the centre of Prague, and credit cards are in widespread use these days, though – to reiterate – you'll probably find welcoming smiles and offers of 'How may I help you?' fairly rare. Shops also have longer opening hours now than those you'll find outside the touristy areas.

The average Czech salary is still low compared to those of other European countries, and, even with a strong crown, retailers do often price accordingly, meaning bargains. If you do want to try swimming with the locals you'll find them at the malls at Palác Flora and Nový Smíchov. Leather goods and high-quality sports clothing and equipment (Czechs and Slovaks being adept at manufacturing their wilderness gear locally) are a good bet in Prague. Also excellent value is local music, particularly classical recordings on the respected Supraphon label. These sell for about half the price they do in Western Europe and are available at most music shops. (Bontonland on Wenceslas Square has the most comprehensive collection, with listening stations.)

When entering a shop, the salesperson will ask '*Máte přání?*' ('Do you have a wish?'). While ringing up your purchases, they may ask '*Ještě něco?*' ('Anything else?) or '*Všechno?*' ('Is that all?'). Say '*Kolik to stojí?*' to find out what something costs.

Garnets and fashions

Every jeweller worth his weight in carats offers garnet gemstones in Prague, but those businesses with

Boheme p22

distinctive settings are the ones worth noting. Garnets and amber are impossible to miss, featured prominently among the crystal and nesting dolls that line the tourist shops. The fashion dates back at least to the Renaissance days of Emperor Rudolf II, who counted many garnet-encrusted pieces in his collection, as did Russian tsarinas in the 1800s, who used them to decorate their dresses.

Nowadays, garnets come set in gold-plated silver, sterling silver, 14- or 18-carat gold. The Granát facility is the only legal mining operator in the country so always ask for a manufacturer's certificate. True Bohemian garnets will be marked with G, G1 or G2.

But it's the city's Czech fashion that is the real gem of the moment, according to an increasing number of sharp-looking clothes buyers. The work of Hana Stocklassa, showcased at her Boheme shop (p111), and the creations at Pavla & Olga (p112), to be found in a humble boutique on Old Town's western edge, have won over more converts than ever.

For book lovers, the city abounds with *antikvariáts*, fusty places full of old Czech tomes, ornate Bibles, photos, maps, magazines and postcards. Palác Knih Luxor on Wenceslas Square (www.neoluxor.cz) has a great selection of English books and Czech art titles. The *bazars* (second-hand shops) are also fun for a browse. Globe Bookstore (p135) is a good spot in which to refuel after a stocking up on paperbacks. For native crafts with local colour, try Manufaktura (p112); at first sight, it looks touristy, and is in prime tourist locations (including the airport), but it's worth a second look for natural soaps, herbal essences and old-fashioned homewares. Dr Stuart's Botanicus (p112) is another specialist in Czech-made organic

products, from soaps and shampoos to cooking oils and candles. Art is another excellent buy, and it needn't be from a vendor on Charles Bridge. Many galleries scattered around the city offer serious bargains on one-of-a-kind items, as do museum gift shops like Prague Castle (p54) or the National Gallery (p153). And, of course, never underestimate the power of Czech alcohol. A liqueur like Becherovka, bitters like Fernet, plum brandy like Slivovice or a beer like the beloved Pilsner Urquell will keep the Prague memories flowing.

Shopping areas

As you would in most cities, avoid the central shopping areas unless you are rushed or need classic souvenirs. This especially applies to Hradčany and the area around Prague Castle. Staré Město is a little better, especially as you drift towards Nové Město, and many backstreets contain rewarding second-hand junk and bookshops. High fashion and high prices can be found on Pařížská, which you should hit on a sunny day for its tree-lined pavements and inviting outdoor cafés. Mall central, as well as many other chain stores, is along Na příkopě. Wenceslas Square can pretty much be skipped for shopping with nothing too unique – although there are some old standbys if you're looking for crystal. The streets on either side of the square are great for a wander. Beware of some shady characters, however, especially in the evening. Souvenir seekers should stroll any of the streets leading out from Old Town Square, as well as the Malá Strana area near Charles Bridge. Moving further out to Smíchov and Holešovice will pay off for antique junkies, but Prague definitely proves the old maxim that you never can tell where rewarding finds will turn up.

Vagon p25

WHAT'S BEST
Nightlife

Clubbing is an almost inevitable element of a trip to Prague – a city that's become an icon for partying; and it's a worthy pursuit, generally speaking, where many of your best stories of adventure and misadventure will likely be set. Like most cities of the former Eastern Europe, dance clubs (vernacular alert – the word 'nightclub' is understood to mean brothel in Prague) are considered far more than a place to shake your booty. As places once forbidden – or at least as places you visited to hear forbidden music and catch glimpses of decadent Western trends – they have traditionally held a significant role in leading the social revolution. Venues like the Roxy (p114), officially a civic organisation,

still relish their status earned from dragging Prague into the modern world. And this particular club, installed in a former movie house with the seats ripped out, has come a long way since the early days and now satisfies the modern demands of young clubbers with sophisticated sound, lights, bar choices and somewhat improved toilets. But it can be credited with leading the great Prague nightlife tradition of basing a club in a thrilling setting of some neglected or abandoned space, and installing DJs and a hasty bar, with crowds cramming in to dance amid leaky pipes, torn up floors and furniture apparently found in skips.

Clubs continue to pop up in strange and unlikely spaces, as

you'll discover in the pages of the free A5 handouts that lie around most downtown bars, with some in truly amazing venues – if the tram factory's occupied, you may end up in the Parukářka bunker (yes, it's really a Cold War bomb shelter) (p151) or the National Memorial (p147), a hilltop Soviet-era mausoleum. Yet, the latest stars of the scene – places like Retro Music Hall (p143), Duplex (p136) and Misch Masch (p158) – have dispensed with the frisson of raw/barely legal settings entirely. But it's still in an atmosphere of 'anything goes' that the party gets going. Drug laws exist but they're rarely enforced, sexual mores are as loose as ever and anyone who can't cut staying out till sunrise is still considered a sad victim of the system. With drinking age limits equally ignored, there's a sense that much of the in-your-face attitude is generational. And at some places, like the cheesy party palace Karlovy Lázně (p113), where drunk teens seem perpetually headed for trouble, it can take on a dark aspect. Nevertheless, clubs that are so open to overdoing it, combined with the incredibly low price of beer in Prague, make the sport of clubbing extremely popular among the thousands of foreign students doing a semester abroad here. You'll find them fully enjoying the decadence at Cross Club (p157), Nebe (p136) and bars like Marquis de Sade (p107) and Vagon (p115).

As for programming standards, Prague still isn't the most likely city to produce a global DJ star anytime soon (although many do labour hard to keep up with the latest trends – check out www.techno.cz to see who's hottest right now). But the new generation of Czech clubber is fairly well-travelled and with higher standards than

Duplex p25

ever, even if many of Prague's inhabitants still prefer to spend a night out sitting in a pub or wine bar while conversing and smoking. For although Prague nightlife draws many visitors for its decadence, the city still can't be said to be one of Europe's great nightlife capitals – lacking as it does the number and scale of venues that other, larger cities can offer.

Wenceslas Square, while home to Duplex – the club that overlooks it from a dizzying height – has also sprouted neon and hawkers for that other booming end of the nightlife biz: adult clubs. Despite the pleas of many residents tired of witnessing Prague's historic sights being overshadowed by ubiquitous sex clubs and the legions of stag parties they attract, the growth of this prosperous sector is unabated. Hot Pepper's (p136), one of the few such places where lap dancing is as far as the action goes, is now competing with half a dozen adult clubs on

Wenceslas Square alone, many brazenly offering rooms with girls by the half-hour. Prostitution is not legally proscribed in the Czech Republic, but pimping is, which just means that clubs operate openly but categorise the girls as independent contractors – a handy loophole if ever there was one. How many are truly working for themselves and how many may have been trafficked from the east, no one knows, of course. Most also run the standard entrance scam (free first drink or even entry – but another drink required for around ten times the usual cost).

Gay clubs

Many of the best-run clubs – and certainly those with the best soundtracks – are, not surprisingly, gay clubs. These are fairly few in number but the trade-off is that they're concentrated around the old centre and most are quite welcoming to anyone. Valentino (p146) in Vinohrady is a recently opened state-of-the-art venue, with three floors of mad clubbing, including darkrooms, while the American-style Friends (p113) on a quiet street in Staré Město is as amiable as its name, with a grown-up, cosy quality and 200 square metres of up-all-night dancefloor and great sound, providing a break from the city's many gritty grope clubs frequented by German businessmen.

Managing it all

A time-honoured strategy for Prague clubbing is to start pretty much anywhere in the old centre and move on to other venues to check whether you've missed anything, stopping off at any number of dodgy late-night bars and pubs along the way to refuel. U Medvídků (p110) has a bar on one side that's open till 3am, N11 (p114) is open all night and a vast number (too many to mention here) of holes-in-the-wall spots will present themselves as you migrate. Thus, unless a supreme party or DJ is rolling in to town, there's no real need to make a detailed plan in advance. If you did, you'd probably discover that the event's been moved or the club's dark for some reason anyway – that's just how Prague works.

What hot tips and info there are tend to be in free pocket-sized 'zines that come and go like the seasons. *Prague in your Pocket*, a 150 Kč investment available at the Globe Bookstore (p135), is usually plugged in and quite comprehensive. Other useful sources – in English – are the expat websites that you can turn to for amusing forums on dating, laundry or all the other sundry concerns of life in Prague, namely www.expats.cz and prague.tv. *The Prague Post*'s website, www.praguepost.com, has comprehensive food and drink

Valentino

listings and its Night & Day section has pages on music, film and festivals, but there's no systematic clubbing coverage.

As with clubbing anywhere, the good stuff only just starts to get rolling around midnight, which happens to be when the Prague metro shuts down. Don't fret: the city centre is small and by-and-large safe and you may just be able to walk back to your room if it's anywhere near the centre. Otherwise, taxis – at least the reputable ones like AAA (14014) are still cheap and night trams run till 5am on all the main routes from the centre to outlying areas. Hopping aboard one of these in booze-loving Prague is an experience you're not likely to forget in a hurry, though a clothes peg for your nose or being in a high state of intoxication yourself might be the best preparation for a night-tram ride.

Never fear, though: the regular tram and metro services start up again at 5am.

DON'T MISS: 2009

Prague Fringe Festival p32

WHAT'S BEST
Arts & Leisure

In a city that's a living museum of architecture and design, you might expect a thriving arts scene with cross currents flowing in from all over the world. You'd be right to, of course. Events like 2009's Prague Biennale, which has reinvigorated the modern art scene since its launch in 2003, have the city buzzing. Meanwhile, dozens of stages are mounting theatre, dance events and music from every genre there is, from refined classical symphonies to Tuareg music and hip hop shows. And Czech filmmaking is undergoing a rebirth, with the state finally committing to major funding after years of neglect, and with more arthouse cinemas and festivals than ever bringing audiences what the multiplexes won't. Prague's rep as

a literary capital (even if it never did produce the great novelists everyone was predicting after 1989) still stands too, with writers descending on the city annually for inspiration and schmoozing at the Prague Writers Festival in June, and with respected small presses springing up all the time (one beloved expat bar, Jáma (p129), has revived its long-silent literary journal, the *Prague Revue*, in the past year).

So why are so many critics expressing so much frustration and calling for more vision and boldness? To read the reviews in most local papers, you'd think Prague is a provincial backwater, where a handful of schoolmates-turned-Culture Ministry funding officials seem to be forever launching variations on the same old show. Innovative filmmakers like Alice Nellis, whose *Little Girl Blue* has won prizes all over for its atmosphere, writing and handling of a topical subject matter – fittingly, a bored wife of a successful executive and her struggle for meaning and beauty – didn't even enter local festivals like the star-studded Karlovy Vary. And even the former playwright-President, Vaclav Havel, told the National Theatre to take a hike, pulling his return to the stage after 20 years out of the historical Czech shrine and taking it to a small theatre in Vinohrady.

So, what's everybody's beef? Well, as these creatives can tell you, there are still an awful lot of creaking bureaucracies involved in getting art out to the public. The Czech Philharmonic is miserably funded and has to record loads of film soundtracks to keep up with expenses. Czech TV, the state television channel, which has a key role in funding new films, has been fraught with controversy. And the National Gallery has been anything but supportive of the Prague Biennale, choosing to hold its own competing event with a similar name and warning artists away from its upstart competitor.

But the very fact that the cultural establishment has been so out of touch has led to some interesting developments. More and more, artists with original ideas have learned to court sponsors and go their own way rather than try to please fusty old committees. Film festivals like Music on Film/Film on Music grow stronger every year, as do those with special focuses like the One World human rights festival and Febio Fest, with its agenda to support non-commercial movies. Some older cultural institutions, meanwhile, are still going strong (if others have fallen by the wayside),

SHORTLIST

Best travelling shows
- Galerie Rudolfinum (p93)
- Prague Castle Riding School (p60)
- Wallenstein Riding School (p75)

Best on stage
- National Theatre (p137)
- Švandovo divadlo (p86)

Best classical music
- Czech Philharmonic, at Rudolfinum (p116)
- Prague Symphony Orchestra, at Municipal House (p97)

Best rock
- Bordo (p143)
- Archa Theatre (p116)
- Lucerna Music Bar (p136)
- Vagon (p115)

Best jazz
- AghaRTA (p115)
- U Malého Glena (p82)
- U staré paní (p114)

Best modern art
- Galerie Montanelli (p70)
- Kampa Museum (p73)
- Karlín Studios (p151)
- Municipal Library (p97)

Best spectator sport
- Football at AC Sparta Praha (p158)
- Hockey at T-Mobile Arena (p160)

Best active sport
- Boulder Bar (p160)
- Skating in Letná park (p152)
- Tennis at I. ČLTK (p158)

Grandest venues
- Municipal House (p97)
- National Theatre (p137)
- State Opera (p137)

Black Light Theatre
IMAGE

BLACK THEATRE
PANTOMIME
MODERN DANCE

Pařížská 4, Praha 1
GPS: N 50°05'17", E 14°25'12"

Performance daily at 8:00 p.m.

tel.: (+420) 222 314 448, (+420) 222 329 191, fax: (+420) 224 811 167
www.imagetheatre.cz   e-mail: image@imagetheatre.cz

such as the top-rated Prague Spring (www.festival.cz), the best of the local music festivals. At 64 years old in 2009, this month-long fest consists of concerts around town and still draws world-class performers. And the National Theatre (p137) did manage, after all, to pull off one of its biggest recent coups with Milos Forman directing *A Walk Worthwhile*, among other fresh theatre and ballet pieces.

The State Opera (p137), which has been less successful in attracting sponsors, nevertheless has become known of late for its novel staging and fondness for neglected or unexpected work. Meanwhile, one aspect of state support, even if it's clumsy, is the wide accessibility of the arts. Yes, the National Theatre and State Opera may close for long summer breaks just when demand is high, but when they're open, you can get a prime seat for as little as 200 Kč.

One classical music gala on the rise, the Prague Music Festival, mixes popular faves with serious Czech composers, while the Prague Proms has also proven a hit, adding touches like late-night jazz sessions with local stars. Another respected edition, Prague Autumn, www. prazskypodzim.cz, remains a strong presence on the scene.

Visual arts

However fresh the conception of a Prague Biennale or the like, though, there's always someone willing to call it tired old crap and launch a fresher one themselves. Thus you now have more and more events like the 'anti-biennale' Tina B – an acronym for This Is Not Another Biennale (www.tina-b.com). A flurry of artist-run spaces like Futura (p82) are also claiming glory with fascinating, fresh shows. And films like *Pusinky*, a teen road movie with a non A-list director, have recently had critical praise and wide release.

Staging a coup

Early summer now sees exciting shows of contemporary dance, when twin festivals showcase home-grown talent. Czech Dance Platform (www. divadloponec.cz) reprises the best of the previous year every April. In June, Tanec Praha (www.tanecpha. cz) juxtaposes new Czech works with headliner performances by visiting dance troupes.

Autumn brings more great festival events: Four Days in Motion (www.ctyridny.cz) selects a new and unorthodox site every year to stage avant-garde dance and physical theatre pieces. And contemporary dance is on the programme year-round at experimental venues like Roxy (p114) Galerie NoD and Alfred v Dvoře and Divadlo Ponec (www.divadloponec.cz). Keep an eye out too for the local companies, like the excellent cutting-edge theatre-dance project Déja Donné (www.dejadonne.com). And if an established foreign contemporary

Pusinky

dance troupe is touring Europe, a stop at the Archa Theatre (p116) will be on its itinerary. For classical dance fans, the National Theatre ballet company (performing at both the National and Estates theatres) and the State Opera's resident company offer a steady diet, from standards like *Swan Lake* to occasionally inspired originals.

As for theatre, most plays are in Czech, but English-language performances grow in number every year. The Prague Fringe Festival (www.praguefringe.com) in early June is a circus worthy of its namesake in Edinburgh, with dozens of visiting performers filling multiple venues around town.

Performers increasingly visit Prague for 'off-Fringe' nights other times of the year, often held at Palác Akropolis or other welcoming venues. The star of the English-language scene is Švandovo Divadlo (p86), a refurbished theatre in Smíchov that's managed to retain its friendly, funky atmosphere in smart new surroundings. Eight to ten plays are on at any time, about

half of which have English subtitles. The theatre also stages progressive concerts and conversation nights with visiting celebrities and artists of international renown.

During the summer, consider a visit to one of the 'Shakespeare at the Castle' performances (old.hrad. cz). These are in Czech but most audiences should be able to follow a staple like *Romeo and Juliet* in any tongue. And there's nothing like experiencing *Hamlet* staged in a castle as twilight turns to darkness and church bells toll. Or, for family fun, don't forget the mainstays of Czech theatre for export: black light and puppetry, available in many venues throughout the city. You won't be able to miss the signs for these in Old Town in tourist season.

Tickets and information

Many box office clerks have a rudimentary command of English, but you're better off buying tickets through one of the central agencies. These accept credit cards (unlike many venues), you can book via their websites or by telephone in English and there are numerous outlets throughout Prague. Bohemia Ticket International (Malé náměstí 13, Staré Město, 224 227 832/ www.ticketsbti.cz) is the best agency for advance bookings for the National Theatre, Estates Theatre and State Opera. Ticketpro at Old Town Hall (p99) also sells tickets for some events. Ticket touts cluster at many events so you can often get into sold-out (*vyprodáno*) performances, although for a price. Wait until the last bell for the best deal. For the latest art, film, theatre and dance listings, pick up a copy of *The Prague Post* (www.praguepost.com) or drop into your nearest branch of the Prague Information Service or check out its website www.pis.cz.

National Theatre p29

Calendar

Prague Spring p37

There are 12 public holidays in the Czech Republic. Except for Easter Monday, the dates are fixed, with the sliding holiday concept not employed – that is, when they fall on a weekend, the following Monday is a normal business day.

Public holidays are highlighted here in **bold**.

September 2008

8 Mattoni Grand Prix
Staré Město
www.pim.cz
An offshoot of the Prague Marathon (p36), despite the confusing name, with a 5km women's run and a 10km men's race.

12 Sept-1 Oct Prague Autumn
Various venues across Prague
www.prazskypodzim.cz

A festival of world-renowned classical talents, based around the Rudolfinum (p116) in Old Town.

Mid Sept **International Aviation Film Festival**
Various venues across Prague
www.leteckefilmy.cz
A week-long festival of war and action films, with famous pilots and war heroes present.

Late Sept **Burčák arrives**
Various pubs across Prague
Cloudy, half-fermented, early-season wine from Moravia is served from jugs during this month-long festival.

28 Czech Statehood Day

October 2008

Ongoing Prague Autumn
(see Sept 2008)

Mid Oct **Festival of Best Amateur & Professional Puppet Theatre Plays**
Various venues across Prague
www.pis.cz
Innovative puppetry festival.

16-20 Oct **MOFFOM**
Lucerna cinema, p136
www.moffom.org
See box p35.

28 Anniversary of the birth of Czechoslovakia
Various venues across Prague
Fireworks and a public holiday mark independence from the Habsburgs.

November 2008

2 All Souls' Day
Olšany Cemetery, p147
Czech families say prayers for dead loved ones.

Mid Nov **French Film Festival**
French Institute
www.ifp.cz
Indie and pop French movie overload, some with English subtitles.

17 Anniversary of the Velvet Revolution
Wenceslas Square p127, and Národní třída, p120, Nové Město
Flowers are laid out near the equine statue, with a memorial to student protesters.

December 2008

5 St Nicholas's Eve
Staré Město
www.pis.cz
Trios dressed as St Nicholas, an angel and a devil grill children about who's been naughty and who's been nice.

Mid Dec **Christmas Markets**
Wenceslas Square, p127, and Old Town Square, p87
www.pis.cz
Stalls with crafts and Czech Christmas food and drink spread the cheer.

24 Christmas Eve/Midnight mass
St Vitus's Cathedral, p61
old.hrad.cz

The finest Christmas observance in Bohemia fills the (cold) Gothic church; bring your thermal underwear.

25 Christmas Day

26 St Stephen's Day

31 **New Year's Eve**
Wenceslas Square, p127
'Silvestr' sparks off a plethora of fireworks and flying bottles. Bring your helmet along.

January 2009

1 New Year's Day/Prague New Year's Concert
Rudolfinum, p116
www.czechphilmarmonic.cz
Czech Philharmonic's annual concert.

February 2009

Early Feb **Days of European Film**
Various venues across Prague
www.eurofilmfest.cz
Ten days of flicks from across Europe, many with English subtitles.

Mid Feb (7th Sun before Easter) **Masopust**
Various venues in Žižkov
www.palacakropolis.cz
A weekend of street parties, concerts and feasts.

Feb-Mar **Matějská pouť**
Výstaviště, p153
www.pis.cz
St Matthew's Fair marks the arrival of warm weather with cheesy rides for the kids at a run-down funfair.

March 2009

Ongoing Matějská pouť
(see Feb)

20-24 **Easter**

24 Easter Monday
Staré Město
www.pis.cz
Men whack women on the backside with sticks; women douse men with water and give them painted eggs.

Calendar

DON'T MISS: 2009

Tuning in

Prague's most rocking annual event is neither a music festival nor a film festival – it's both. **MOFFOM** (Music on Film/Film on Music; p34) has run for five years so far (since 2004) and the concept seems to be burgeoning every year – as is the festival's audience, through podcasts, ever-increasing hype and massive media coverage, including a *Variety* write-up.

All of which is good news for founder John Caulkins and filmmaker Keith Jones, who, with a small but super-capable staff, run the increasingly complex week of music films, concerts, talks and parties. MOFFOM is based, appropriately enough, at the Lucerna (p136), the most ornate old-fashioned movie palace in Prague. The arcade housing the cinema also features great concert halls equipped with powerhouse sound systems.

Every October, the faux-marble halls of the Lucerna are taken over by film fans, scholars, musicians, indie directors, scouts and agents. Typically, audiences are treated to the kinds of events and screenings that would be impossible to find at any other time of year. Past films have included Pavla Fleischer's no-budget documentary following the Ukrainian lead singer for the band Gogol Bordello on a road trip from hell, British director Don Letts' BBC-produced film *George Clinton: Tales of Dr Funkenstein* and the jazz documentary *Music Inn* – the directorial debut of Ben Barenholtz, an early distributor of US independent talents of the 1970s and '80s.

Amid all the fun, discerning audiences in the hundreds also fill the Wenceslas Square performance and screening spaces for over 60 documentaries and features, plus half as many music videos. The programme is similarly eclectic, featuring anything from Russian cinema to underground rockumentaries, like Michael Apted's *The Long Way Home*, a portrait of rock rebel Boris Grebenshikov of the band Aquarium.

Ten films compete for the grand prize, and their scope tends to cover the most intriguing currents of contemporary world music – everything from Nigerian musical social history to films like *Nomads TX*, which follows two virtuosi of the Basque instrument known as the *txalaparta*.

Time Out Shortlist | Prague 2009 **35**

Mar **Febiofest**
Palace Cinemas, Anděl
www.fest.cz.
The city's biggest film fest offers a huge scope of world cinema.

Mar **One World**
Lucerna cinema, p136, and Světozor cinema, p138
www.jedensvet.cz.
The year's best documentaries and their authors from around the globe appear for screenings and panels.

Mar-Oct **Prague Jazz Festival**
Various venues
www.agharta.cz
Prague's hottest jazz fest brings in the likes of John Scofield. Mainly at Lucerna Music Bar (p136).

April 2009

Ongoing Prague Jazz Festival
(see Mar 2009)

30 **Witches' Night**
Petřín hill, p75
Halloween and Bonfire Night in one.

Christmas Market p34

May 2009

Ongoing Prague Jazz Festival
(see Mar 2009)

1 Labour Day
Letná park, p152

1 May Day
Petřín hill, p75
Czech lovers of all ages kiss in front of the statue of Karel Hynek Mácha.

8 VE Day
Letná park, p152
Czechs now celebrate the Allied victory more openly, with American Jeeps joining the memorials to the Red Army.

May-Sept **Prague Biennale 4**
Karlín Studios, p151
This upstart modern art show, held in a hulking former factory, has knocked the local gallery scene on its ear.

May **Prague International Marathon**
Across Prague
www.pim.cz
Those not up to the full 42km (26mile) race can try the 10km run.

May **Four Days in Motion**
Various venues across Prague
www.ctyridny.cz
Excellent fest of international dance and visual theatre, in unusual venues.

May **Khamoro**
Various venues across Prague
www.khamoro.cz
Concerts, seminars and workshops on traditional Roma culture.

Last weekend May **Mezi ploty**
Around the Psychiatric Hospital, Bohnice
www.meziploty.cz
Events by professional, amateur and mentally or physically disadvantaged artists over two days.

May **Prague Fringe Festival**
Various venues across Prague
www.praguefringe.com
The city's newest theatre festival fills venues like Vyšehrad with cabaret to multimedia.

Masopust p34

Mid May-early June **Prague Spring**
Various venues across Prague
www.festival.cz
The biggest and best Prague music
festival draws international talent.

June 2009

Ongoing Prague Biennale 4 (see
May 2009); Prague Jazz Festival
(see Mar 2009); Prague Spring
(see May 2009)

June **Prague Writers' Festival**
Various venues across Prague
www.pwf.cz
Czech and international literati gather
to read and hobnob.

June **Respect**
Various venues across Prague
www.respectmusic.cz
A celebration of world and ethnic music,
throughout June.

June **Tanec Praha**
Various venues across Prague
www.tanecpha.cz
A top-flight international gala of modern dance with recitals in Prague's
major theatres.

June **United Islands of Prague**
Střelecký ostrov, Žofín
www.unitedislands.cz
Popular weekend of rock, jazz and folk.

July 2009

Ongoing Prague Biennale 4 (see
May 2009); Prague Jazz Festival
(see Mar 2009)

5 Cyril & Methodius Day

6 Jan Hus Day

July **Prague Proms**
Various venues in Staré Město
www.pragueproms.cz
Classical, opera and jazz concerts.

July **Summer Old Music Festival**
Various venues in Staré Město
www.tynska.cuni.cz
Renaissance and baroque music on
period instruments, in historic settings.

August 2009

Ongoing Prague Biennale 4 (see
May 2009); Prague Jazz Festival
(see Mar 2009)

Mid Aug **Letní Letná**
Letná park, p152
www.letniletna.cz
Theatre, music and circus festival
attracting both Czech and European
talents.

Mid Aug **String Quartet Festival**
Bertramka, p86
www.bertramka.com
Prague's best quartets perform in an
idyllic setting.

September 2009

Ongoing Prague Biennale 4 (see
May 2009); Prague Jazz Festival
(see Mar 2009)

Mid Sept **Prague Autumn**
Various venues across Prague
www.prazskypodzim.cz
See Sept 2008.

Sept **St Wenceslas Sacred
Music Festival**
Various venues across Prague
www.sdh.cz
Sacred music festival held at half a
dozen chapels, churches and cathedrals
across Prague.

Sept **Tina B**
Various venues across Prague
www.tina-b.com
An acronym of This Is Not Another
Biennale. This 'anti-biennale' showcases
contemporary art in surprising locations around Prague.

Late Sept **Burčák arrives**
Various pubs across Prague
See Sept 2008.

28 Czech Statehood Day

October 2009

Ongoing Prague Jazz Festival
(see Mar 2009)

Mid Oct **Prague International
Jazz Festival**
Various venues across Prague
www.pragokoncert.com
A mix of local and international jazz
masters perform at some of the city's
top clubs, over several days.

Mid Oct **MOFFOM**
Lucerna cinema, p136
www.moffom.org
See Oct 2008.

**28 Anniversary of the birth
of Czechoslovakia**
Various venues across Prague
See Oct 2008.

November 2009

Nov **FAMU Festival**
Academy of Performing Arts
www.famufest.cz
FAMU students' best work is screened.

**17 Anniversary of the Velvet
Revolution**
Wenceslas Square, p127,
and on Národní třída near No.20
See Nov 2008.

Mid Nov **Alternativa**
Archa Theatre, p116
www.alternativa-festival.cz
Underground film, music and stage
performances.

Mid Nov **French Film Festival**
French Institute
www.ifp.cz
See Nov 2008.

December 2009

5 St Nicholas's Eve
Staré Město
www.pis.cz
See Dec 2008.

Early Dec **International Festival
of Advent & Christmas Music**
Various venues across Prague
www.orfea.cz
Choirs and choruses ring in the season.

24 Christmas Eve/Midnight Mass
St Vitus's Cathedral, p61
old.hrad.cz
See Dec 2008.

25 Christmas Day

26 St Stephen's Day

31 New Year's Eve
Wenceslas Square, p127
See Dec 2008.

Itineraries

50 YEARS
THE BEST AND FIRST MULTIMEDIA
THEATRE IN THE WORLD

Laterna Magika • Národní třída 4 • Praha 1
box office: 224 931 482 • group orders: 222 222 041 • fax: 222 222 039
www.laterna.cz • info@laterna.cz

House of the Black Madonna p43

Century Shuffle

Prague's varied architectural feast is visible in some form in just about every quarter, with the odd tenth-century rotunda popping up in even modern urban grids. But a good sense of the progression (and sometimes regression) of the centuries is afforded by a walk from Prague Castle down to the Vltava river and across into the Staré Město district, the city's oldest and most historically intact quarter – nightclubs and neon-lit crystal shops not withstanding, of course.

While you could (and should) spend at least half a day on the **Prague Castle** (p54) grounds, for this time travel tour, try to confine your visit to a glimpse at the oldest visible ruins in the city, the foundations of the simple **Church of Our Lady**, founded by Prince Bořivoj some time before 885. These are passed by hundreds of Castle visitors a day who likely have no idea of the significance of the pits and walls seen through the glass of the north passage between the Castle's second courtyard and the north-west corner of the grounds. Back in the Third Courtyard, behind the grille on the south side of **St Vitus's Cathedral** (p61), the foundations of the 11th-century **Chapel of St Maurice** are just visible, but are frustratingly limited in their signage and access. Nearby, in a part of the **Old Royal Palace** (p59) that's not accessible, remains of humble single-room houses from the tenth and 11th centuries have been unearthed, as well as nearby Bronze Age graves and dwellings.

St George's Basilica (p60), just to the west, offers a much better sense of the scale and atmosphere of Romanesque Prague, with its intimate spaces between

Rotunda of the Holy Cross

broad, rustic arches. Graves of Přemyslid princes were discovered here from 1959 to 1963, and displays inside the church offer intriguing details.

From here, tear yourself away from the Castle and head east to the **Old Castle Steps**, taking in the fine view of Malá Strana and Staré Město beyond as you descend. From the bottom of the stairs, head a block east to the **Mánesův Bridge**, another Czech nationalist shrine, finished in 1914 and featuring reliefs by two of the country's best sculptors of the period, František Bílek and Jan Štursa (the Charles Bridge, a Gothic wonder by Peter Parler dating back to 1357 and standing just upstream, would make for a better historical progression, of course, but it's generally jammed with tourists and hawkers of pencil portraits). The Mánesův Bridge takes you to one of Staré Město's finest riverside sights and the former home of Parliament, the grand, neo-classical **Rudolfinum** (p116), built from

1875-84 by Josef Zítek and Josef Schulz. The warm-coloured sandstone walls of this concert hall and art gallery are a common feature of many Prague buildings (and one theory behind the origin of the city's nickname 'Golden City').

These last two sights have, of course, skipped you forward several centuries, but have no fear: follow Kaprova south-east three blocks to **Old Town Square** and you'll be immersed in Gothic and Renaissance treasures again. **Old Town Hall**, built out of a private house the civic authorities bought in 1338 before adding the improvement of a wondrous clock tower, provides only a hint of what used to stand here, thanks to the Nazis and their artillery during the Prague Uprising in 1945. But the spindly **Church of Our Lady before Týn** (p92) is a fine Gothic showpiece, particularly its original tympanum, which rise above its Renaissance façade. The **House at the Stone Bell** (p94) just to the north of it across the tiny lane is another excellent, if weathered, original Gothic sandstone structure, with a 14th-century façade harking back to dark days of Old Town Square's once-fetid market.

The next-door **Goltz-Kinský Palace**, finished by Anselmo Lurago in 1755 from a design by the Baroque master Kilian Ignatz Dientsenhofer, shows how harmoniously a different architectural age entirely can be integrated into a space like Old Town Square, which features vastly variegated structures spanning six centuries. Such fanciful chocolate-box palaces and churches are to be found throughout the city, ushered in during the Counter-Reformation in the hope that cherubs and marble would help dispel the troublesome Protestant movements led by the followers of

Laterna Magika

Jan Hus, whose mournful bronze likeness dominates the square.

Now head due east up **Celetná** for a look at where things progressed from the age of rationalism after the heretics finally took control. At the end of this street is a reward that makes it worth enduring all the kitsch shops that line it: the **Municipal House** (p97), a magnificent 1906-12 art nouveau structure that hosts one of Prague's most fabulous concert halls (and murals by the likes of Alfons Mucha, Mikoláš Aleš and Max Švabinský, to name just a few). Pause for a drink in the street-level Vienna-style coffeehouse here and it will be a moment you'll remember for years.

Back down Celetná a block to the west is the entrance to **Ovocný trh**. It's named for a fruit market that once stood here – but it's far more than this. At the far end stands another Baroque classic, the wedding-cake **Estates Theatre** (p116), while at the north end

stands Czech modernism at its finest. Here, in the form of the angular **House of the Black Madonna** (p93), is one of the finest cubist structures anywhere, the 1911-12 former department store by Josef Gočár.

If you continue across Ovocný trh now, past the Estates Theatre, down Rytířská, and then Martinská, turning left on Na Perstyně, you emerge onto the main drag of **Národní**. And here, just where things should have reached their peak of grace, is one of the last great monuments to the fate that ensnared this loveliest of cities in the late 20th century. The fantastically ugly block of 1970s glass that is the **Laterna Magika** (p124), at No. 4, was at least good for one thing. The plotters of the Velvet Revolution secretly met there in 1989 to plan yet again for Czechs to wrest control of their destiny from foreign occupiers.

And as for the crystal shops and corporate offices that followed after that, the less said the better, surely.

Socialist marble relief, Hradčanská metro station

Náhradní
doprava
za metro

Směr ◄ ⬅
Staroměstská

Occupied Prague

Throughout most of its history, the small Czech nation has found itself on the margins of great powers, often serving as a prize to whichever one was prevailing. As with many countries with similar histories, this has consequently shaped the culture and thinking for generations, and visible signs of it are also all around – recalling a past that you could almost forget amid the slick glass towers and chic shops of modern Prague. Throughout the city, squeezed in by designer shoe stores and luxe homewares, there remain dozens of buildings with grimy friezes over the entrance featuring worker heroes, or the remains of old signs in block letters announcing no-nonsense offerings from the past like shoe repairs, or, simply, fruit, veg and ironmonger goods.

This tour of the surviving icons of the bad old days will take a half day,

relying on a mix of walking, trams and the metro – probably the single best surviving Soviet contribution to Czech society in itself.

Start off at the **Hradčanská metro stop**, which was once the last one before Leninova. A circular vestibule stands just below Milady Horakova, a traffic-choked street named for the only woman political prisoner executed during the show trials of the 1950s (the survivor of Nazi concentration camps mounted an eloquent defense, arguing her own case, but had no chance against the state paranoia of the day). In the metro, against the south wall, a classic socialist marble relief remains, featuring a message that translates as 'The entire power of the Czechoslovak Socialist Republic lies in the working people.' (Another Soviet-style metro mural, at the top of the escalator leading out to Nadrážní street at the Anděl station, features in Jan Svěrák's Oscar-winning *Kolja*, about an ageing Czech Romeo forced to adopt a Russian boy.) The Soviets, as part of their post-1968 'Normalisation' programme, began work on Prague's metro in a kind of sister city exchange with the Russian capital, with metro stops in Moscow named after Prague and vice versa. It must be said that the electric system is still fast, eco-friendly, efficient and cheap after all these years.

Descend the Hradčanská metro escalator to take in the large, breezy platforms in the super-sized tunnels that run under the entire city. Most stations are still lined with the retro-cool, outsized and metallic-coloured dimpled tiles that were clearly a hit with the state transit planners of the 1970s. Ride three stops to Můstek station and transfer to the yellow line, taking in the polished sci-fi tunnels connecting the city's lines – they invariably make you think you're on board the Death Star. Ride the yellow line two stops to **Karlovo náměstí**.

Walk west one block, keeping to the north side of traffic-filled Resslova. Here, in a place that hardly invites strolling, is a scene well worth the noise and bustle. In the catacombs under the **Church of Sts Cyril & Methodius** (p121), is a permanent exhibit honouring the Czech resistance fighters who pulled off World War II's highest-level assassination, Operation Anthropoid. Josef Gabčík and Jan Kubiš managed to hide out for weeks after killing Reichsprotektor Reinhard Heydrich, Hitler's heir apparent, in May 1942 but were finally betrayed, and the Gestapo descended on their refuge here. The British-trained Czechs held out and returned fire all night before finally expending their last bullets on themselves. The chilling exhibit gives pause for thought – one

consequence of the assassination was the liquidation of two entire Czech villages.

Now head back to the metro stop and catch tram 22 or 23 north, or take the metro again, alighting at **Můstek**, which places you on **Wenceslas Square** (p127). Look up the great boulevard and try to imagine Soviet tanks firing into the **National Museum** (p124), which sits so majestically at the top. They mistook the building for the Czech Parliament when they rolled into town in 1968, putting a brutal end to the reforms Alexander Dubček had allowed during the Prague Spring. They wouldn't leave for 21 years. Some of their legacy is still visible in the form of signs near the top of the square for Strojimport and Dům Mody (House of Fashion), where more worker heroes overlook the noisiest, most polluted thoroughfare in the city, the communist-designed Magistrale, a dual carriageway that cuts the top off Wenceslas Square. It runs between the top of the boulevard and the National Museum. Plans for a ring road have been discussed for years, but Prague seems no closer to having one than when the monster freeway was built through the town centre.

Note also the smoked meat (*maso uzeniny*) shops that still satisfy old party members (and hordes of other Czechs), before walking north-west up Na můstku and Melantrichova to **Old Town Square**. Here stands the single biggest battle scar of Nazi occupation, the empty space where the rest of **Old Town Hall** (p99) once stood. Blown up by the Nazis after Czech resistance fighters were discovered hiding weapons in its catacombs, the building, which had formed the western end of the square since the early 14th century, lost its neo-Gothic wing and archives, including records from the 1300s, in

ITINERARIES

Church of Sts Cyril & Methodius p45

the Prague Uprising of 5-8 May 1945.
Some 1,691 Czechs and 436 Soviet
soldiers died. Those who would later
fire on the National Museum were
in 1945 still heroes, and memorials
to Red Army fighters still stand
throughout the city. At the base
of the Astronomical Clock is a cup
of soil from the Dukla pass, where
thousands of Ukrainian soldiers
were martyred to the Wermacht.

Now head back up Melantrichova
to the Můstek metro again and take
the green line three stops in the
direction of Depot Hostivár and get
out at **Jiřího z Poděbrad**. From
here, pass the Church of the Sacred
Heart and head up Milešovská two
blocks north towards the bizarre
radio tower you see looming over
the Žižkov district.

The **Žižkov Tower** (p147), which
artist David Černý has covered with
crawling black babies, was the pride
of Soviet engineering in the 1980s,

and used to jam Western radio
signals. Sensitively constructed
on top of a former Jewish cemetery,
part of which still stands, the tower
now sports a bar and observation
tower that must be experienced to
be believed. From inside, you get a
commanding view not only of the
city, but of the **National Memorial**
(p147) fronted by the huge **Jan
Žižka equestrian statue**. This
building once served as resting place
for the country's first working-class
president, Klement Gottwald, and a
host of other high party officials.
These days it's rented out for parties
by the Czech Technical University,
which owns the lease.

Now settle into the glass and
aluminium surrounds of the tower
restaurant and have yourself a meal
of schnitzel and beer, as any good
working-class party member would,
and watch to see if the latest regime
is changing street names again.

Gallery NoD p48

Old Town Ramble

Dlouhá street, whose name translates simply as 'long', indeed lives up to the description in comparison with the other lanes of the Staré Město district – which tend to break off like twigs after short walks, or turn into dead ends or simply change names after a block or two. The once-walled medieval centre is still a jumble of lanes running every which way – and generally good for a surprise or two, whether it's a fabulous designer shop or a timeless pub seemingly passed over by all the millions of developer dosh that's now poured into Prague.

Thus, even with only about 500 metres or thereabouts, **Dlouhá**, which begins at the northernmost corner of Old Town Square and heads north-east, qualifies as a longitudinal champion in Prague – and what's more, it offers a little bit of everything great in this most venerated and unchanged district. It can be casually strolled in 15

minutes but it's best experienced by ducking into its many curious enterprises to check out the enticements, which could make it a good two-hour jaunt, factoring in stopping for refreshment and the average speed of a Czech pub or restaurant server.

Starting in front of the Caffrey's Irish Bar (Staroměstské náměstí 10), which is best kept as a landmark only, head on along the Dlouhá pavement, wandering through the arches and taking in the fin-de-siecle architecture of this elegant street. There's a hunting goods shop on the north side, **Zbraně a Střelivo Brymová** (Staroměstské náměstí 8), which supplies practitioners of the ancient Bohemian avocation of chasing down dinner with a shotgun engraved by your grandfather while wearing a Tyrolean cap. Because of modern airport security, it won't be of interest for much else than caps, but it does reveal much about the Czech love of weaponry.

Continue north and you'll run into Dušní, the next street leading left off Dlouhá. On the south side are two of Prague's most happening fashion boutiques, **Tatiana** (p113) and **Boheme** (p112). They can do far better than green felt caps, with some of the best-selling suits, jackets and separates for stylish women in the city, with both in homely settings that make you feel that old-fashioned sense of being spoilt and waited on as if you were a visiting celeb.

Back on Dlouhá again, continue north to the little square at the next intersection, where you'll find the comforting **Bakeshop Praha** (p100) emitting fresh bread and muffin smells. If you're already in need of fuel, this is a great place for grabbing a latte, a newspaper from the rack and a spot on the streetside bench (or waiting for your partner while she goes wild in the shops).

If you can delay digestive gratification a bit longer, continue up Dlouhá to No. 9, where the district's best flower shop, **Květiny**, stands. With a great range of orchids,

it's worth a stop even if you're not visiting any Czech homes this evening – and if you are, flowers are the customary item to bring along (though you can get away with a bottle of wine these days).

Dahab (p104), a theatrical rendering of tearoom arabesque, is a calming respite from the density of Dlouhá's offerings, with throw pillows, houkas, mint teas and Middle Eastern sweets, while a reliable source of mind-expanding is **Gallery NoD**, which doubles as a bar and café, located on the second floor above the Roxy club (p114). With an avowed role as showplace for the most avant-garde local artists in town, NoD is often confounding but never dull. The building also contains one of the country's five **Fairtrade shops**; with a good stock of top-quality Colombian coffee and chocolates; NaZemi ('On Earth') has begun a trend of consciousness raising among young, retail-mad Czechs.

You'll spot the retail-frenzied breed at **La Casa del Habano** (p112), which is also full of Americans furtively buying boxes of primo Cuban cigars banned in their homeland, though fans of stogies from anywhere will be impressed by the offerings in its humidors and the clubby back corner for lighting up with a good brandy and getting into a chess game. Friends of cigar chompers can score as well, with La Casa's elegant collection of cases, including Porsche Design ones made from oak.

Finally, at the eastern end of Dlouhá, **Antik v Dlouhé** (p111) is a wonderful jumble of granny's brooches, handmade wooden toys (the shop's supplied by a top Czech collector), old books and cards and the odd one-of-a-kind desk lamp you may just have to put into your carry-on.

Antik v Dlouhé

Prague by Area

Strahov Library p65

Hradčany

PRAGUE BY AREA

Other than the Charles Bridge, no single architectural work personifies the city as much as the spire of St Vitus's Cathedral. Rising up above the surrounding Prague Castle atop the hill known as Hradčany, the two have dominated the Prague skyline for ten centuries in some form, though the Castle was only given its current shape in the 18th century under Empress Maria Theresa, and St Vitus's wasn't finally completed until 1929. As the president's office and the seat of the archbishopric, the complex remains the political, spiritual and national heart of the Czech Republic. It's also the top tourist attraction in town, even if church-state struggles have resulted in neglect over the years.

The founders of **Prague Castle**, the Přemyslids, were the greatest of the Bohemian bloodlines, and are somewhat steeped in mystery. They built the earliest part of the Hradčany fortress in the ninth century, gaining a commanding stronghold overlooking miles around. Continuously occupied since then, the Castle has changed shape and form a dozen times, following the fortunes and successors of this family, which also ruled parts of Poland but died out in 1306.

Owing to the high walls that were added later, the best views of Prague are now to be had from the gardens and courtyards around the Castle – unless you're up to a hike up the 96-metre-high Gothic St Vitus tower. It soars above the southern façade, which Charles IV entrusted to Peter Parler, whose work was later spiked by Nicolo

Pacassi in 1770. The church's magnificent flying buttresses and Golden Gothic portals facing the city also shows the 16th-century grace of Bonifác Wohlmut.

Czechs are understandably proud to show off the Castle, by day and by night, and have taken advantage of its grounds reopening to the public after the Velvet Revolution in 1989. The complex continues to undergo makeovers and renovations, with a dozen rooms opened to the public beneath the **Old Royal Palace** two years ago, the first in a series of planned modern developments, which are balanced with archaeological surveys into its still emerging subterranean layers.

The rest of the district comprises the surrounding streets, which stretch north and west from the castle across the hilltop. It's quiet and less touristy than the Castle itself, and the Nový Svět (or 'New World') pocket of streets is particularly enchanting.

The Castle complex is open to the public until midnight and the best chance of avoiding throngs of tourists is to visit during the evening, when the place is at its most romantic. It's dark, but quite safe. The Castle grounds are well worth exploring at any time, however; you'll find a fair number of options for refuelling in the near vicinity and a handful of terrace restaurants visible below. Otherwise, there are richer pickings down the hill in Malá Strana.

Hradčany owes its grand scale and pristine condition to a fire in 1541 that destroyed the medieval district, and to the frenzied period of Counter-Reformation building that followed the Protestant defeat at the Battle of White Mountain in 1620. Little has changed here in the last two centuries.

The area's focal point is **Hradčanské náměstí**, one of the grandest squares in the city, lined with imposing palaces built by the Catholic aristocracy, anxious to be close to the Habsburg court.

St George's Convent, the National Gallery's collection of old masters that resides next to St George's Basilica, was closed for reconstruction at the time that this guide went to press but expected to be back for 2009.

Sights & museums

Černín Palace

Černínský palác
Černínská 5 (224 181 111). Metro Malostranská, then tram 22, 23.
Map p52 A3 ❶

Now serving as the Czech Foreign Ministry, this enormous, imposing structure, with its grey façade articulated by a line of 30 pillars, was commissioned in 1669 by Humprecht Johann Černín, imperial ambassador to Venice; its construction expenses ruined the family. Gestapo interrogations were later conducted here during the Nazi occupation. Its curse surfaced again in 1948, when Foreign Minister Jan Masaryk, the last major political obstacle to Klement Gottwald's communist coup, had a fatal fall from an upstairs window a few days after the takeover.

Funicular

Petřín hill, Karmelitská 1 (no phone). Metro Malostranská. **Map** p53 D5 ❷

Recently restored and gliding again, this feat of engineering is 118 years old in 2008 and still offers a lazy (and fun) way up to the top of the hill from Újezd, running roughly every ten minutes between March and October, from 9am until 11.20pm, and every 15 minutes in winter season, stopping halfway up the hill before continuing to the top. Your tram and metro tickets are all you need.

Karel Hynek Mácha

Petřín hill (no phone). Tram 12, 22, then funicular railway. **Map** p52 C5 ❸

This tragic romantic poet – the unofficial patron saint of lovers – has a

Hradčany

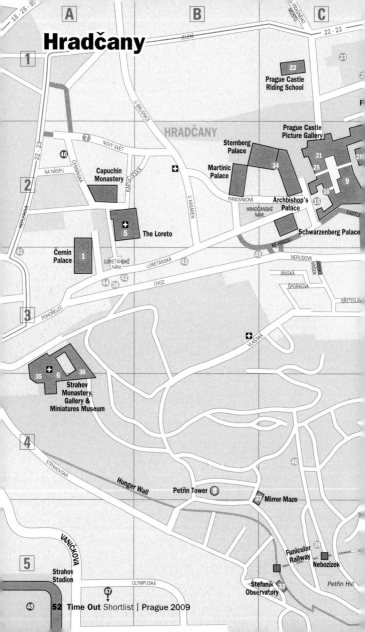

JELENÍ

22 - 23

22

Prague Castle
Riding School

U BRUSNICE

HRADČANY

Prague Castle
Picture Gallery

7

NOVÝ SVĚT

Sternberg
Palace

46

NA NÁSPU

34

CERNÍNSKÁ

KAPUCÍNSKÁ

Martinic
Palace

21

25

28

Capuchin
Monastery

KANOVNICKÁ

16

9

Archbishop's
Palace

15

HRADČANSKÉ
NÁM.

CASTLE

5

The Loreto

Schwarzenberg Palace

41

Černín
Palace

1

LORETÁNSKÉ
NÁM.

LORETÁNSKÁ

43

45

KE HRADU

NERUDOVA

JÁNSKÝ
VRŠEK

JÁNSKÁ

44 38

42

ÚVOZ

ŠPORKOVA

BŘETISLA

POHOŘELEC

VLAŠSKÁ

35 6

36

Strahov
Monastery,
Gallery &
Miniatures Museum

STRAHOVSKÁ

40

Hunger Wall

Petřin Tower 8

37 Mirror Maze

VANIČKOVA

39

Funicular
Railway

Nebozízek

Strahov
Stadion

OLYMPIJSKÁ

Štefánik
Observatory

33

Petřin Hil

47

48

MARIANSKÉ D **HRADBY**

Royal Gardens

The Belvedere 11

E *Chotkovy sady*

F

CHOTKOVA

18 · 20 · 22 · 23 · 57

NA OPYŠI

OLD CASTLE STEPS

KLÁROV

10 Ball Game Court

Stag Moat

13

gue stle

14 Golden Lane 27

12 Toy Museum

4

St George's Convent

24 St George's Basilica

Vitus's hedral

Old Royal Palace

Ledeburg Gardens

Komenský Pedagogical Museum

VALDŠTEJNSKÁ

Malostranská

s on the Ramparts

U ZLATÉ STUDNĚ

VALDŠTEJNSKÉ NÁM.

SNĚMOVNÍ

Wallenstein Palace

TOMÁŠSKÁ

Wallenstein Gardens

LETENSKÁ

ZELENÁ · Ú
NOSTICOVA · GARDEL

MÁNESŮV MOST

THUNOVSKÁ

ZÁMECKÁ

OVA

Church of St Thomas

Vojan's Gardens

Church of St Joseph

Church of St Nicholas

MALOSTRANSKÉ NÁM.

ŠPORKOVA

NERUDOVA

MISEŇSKÁ

CIHELNÁ

Vltava

MALÁ RANA ardens

TRŽIŠTĚ

KARMELITSKÁ

PROKOPSKÁ

LÁZEŇSKÁ

SAUNA

MOSTECKÁ

Church of Our Lady Victorious (Il Bambino di Praga)

Church of Our Lady Beneath the Chain

John Lennon Wall

Buquoy Palace

U LUŽICKÉHO SEMINÁŘE

NA KAMPĚ

HROZNOVÁ

VŠEHRDOVA

ŘÍČNÍ

HELLICHOVA

NEBOVIDSKÁ

PELCLOVA

NOSTICOVA

MAGDALÉNY

CERTOVKA

CHARLES BRIDGE

Kampa Wharf

KAMPA ISLAND

Michna Palace

Museum Kampa

U LANOVÉ DRÁHY

ar Railway

2

ÚJEZD

VÍTĚZNÁ

ŘÍČNÍ

PETŘÍNSKÁ

VSEHRDOVA

MALOSTRANSKÉ NÁBŘ.

0   200 m

0   200 yds

© Copyright Time Out Group 2008

Střelecký ostrov

1

2

3

4

5

Legend

1 Sights & museums
1 Eating & drinking
1 Shopping
1 Nightlife
1 Arts & leisure

statue in the park where every young couple in Prague (or so it seems) turns out on 1 May to smooch. Any lad who hesitates when his girl suggests this is not long for this world – or certainly the relationship.

Lobkowicz Palace

NEW Lobkovický palác
Jiřská 3 (602 595 998/www.lobkowicz events.cz/palace/index.html). Metro Malostranská, then tram 22, 23. **Open** 10.30am-6pm daily. **Admission** 275 Kč; 690 Kč family. **Map** p53 D1 ④
One of several palaces in town owned by the influential Lobkowicz family, who did not fare well under the communists. This one, which was finished in 1658, houses the Historical Museum, comprising a fascinating collection of displays on the roots of the Czech lands' power players. The palace is on Prague Castle grounds but has been returned to its owners.

Loreto

Loretánské náměstí 7 (220 516 740/ www.loreta.cz). Metro Malostranská, then tram 22, 23. **Open** 9am-12.15pm, 1-4.30pm Tue-Sun. **Admission** 110 Kč; 90 Kč reductions. No credit cards.
Map p52 A2 ⑤
The most famous of the world's copies of the church in Loreto, Italy, this full-on Baroque building houses the bearded St Wilgefortis, the skeletons of another two female saints and the highest concentration of cherubs in Prague. The heart is a small chapel, the Santa Casa, spawned from the cult of Mary in Nazareth; it's said that the original was flown to Loreto by angels. Dating from 1626-31 and later completed by the Dientzenhofer team, it claims a brick from its Italian inspiration, as well as a crevice on the wall left by a divine thunderbolt that struck an unfortunate blasphemer. The famous diamond monstrance, designed in 1699 by Fischer von Erlach and sporting 6,222 stones, is in the treasury.

Miniatures Museum

Muzeum miniatur
Strahovské nádvoří 11 (233 352 371). Metro Malostranská, then tram 22, 23.

Open 9am-5pm daily. **Admission** 50 Kč; 30 Kč children. **Map** p52 A4 ⑥
This obsessive collection on the grounds of Strahov Monastery lets you in on monkish work with the aid of magnifying glasses and microscopes. Portraiture on a poppy seed, a caravan of camels painted on a grain of millet, a prayer written out on a human hair and minuscule copies of masterpieces by the likes of Rembrandt and Botticelli are all on display.

Nový Svět

New World
Černínská. Metro Malostranská, then tram 22, 23. **Map** p52 A2 ⑦
The enchanting backstreets north-west of the Castle, starting at Černínská, behind the Loreto, make up the small, storied parcel known as the New World. The quarter was built in the 16th century for Prague Castle retainers. Going down Kapucínská, you pass the Domeček, or 'Little House', at No.10, once home to the notorious Fifth Department – the counter-intelligence unit of the Defence Ministry. Tycho Brahe, the Danish alchemist known for his missing nose and breakthroughs in accurate observations of orbits, lived at No.1, the 'Golden Griffin'.

Petřín Tower

Rozhledna
Petřín hill (257 320 112). Tram 12, 22, then funicular railway. **Open** *Jan-Mar, Nov-Dec* 10am-5pm Sat, Sun. *Apr, Sept* 10am-8pm daily. *May-Aug* 10am-10pm daily. *Oct* 10am-6pm daily. Closed in poor weather. **Admission** 60 Kč; 40 Kč children. **Map** p52 B4 ⑧
With the next-best view to the one afforded by St Vitus's Cathedral tower, this copy of the Eiffel Tower is a thrill to ascend. Built in 1891 for the Jubilee Exhibition, like the neighbouring mock-Gothic castle that houses the amusements below, it still stands strong (and sways on windy days).

Prague Castle

Hradčanské náměstí (224 371 111/ old.hrad.cz). Metro Malostranská, then tram 22, 23. **Open** *Apr-Oct* 9am-5pm.

No warming zone

Václav Klaus

Released in early 2008, the film *Občan Havel* ('*Citizen Havel*') has been the biggest documentary hit in recent Czech history. Made over a period of 13 years, it's an amusing and inspiring look at former president **Václav Havel**'s administration, and highlights the differences between him and **Václav Klaus**, his fearless successor and rival, in power since 2003. Because filmmaker Pavel Koutecky had full and unfettered access to Havel for such a long time, he catches him in intimate occasions, like fussing over the fit of his trousers before state occasions. That's something control freak Klaus would never have allowed on camera. Klaus is highly controversial abroad (many, frankly, think he's a nut) and is nothing if not willing to speak his mind. The tireless Thatcherite and defender of the free market is an economics scholar who has always served as a counterbalance to Havel. While Havel has always sought consensus, Klaus has always taken charge; this has been the case right from the beginning of his post-1989 career, when he demanded the post of Finance Minister and then co-authored the massive privatisation of state assets.

Klaus thoroughly enjoys the limelight – that is, as long as he's allowed to direct it – and feels no compunction about upbraiding the media for not playing along. Havel, meanwhile, has always seemed to bear his publicity with a measure of embarrassment and self-consciousness but would never presume to interfere with a journalist.

Yet Klaus enjoys widespread support among Czechs, many of whom clearly have no problem with his testy schoolmaster persona. However, even supporters get a bit uncomfortable when certain subjects come up. Take global warming, for example. One of Klaus's bugbears is the idea of taking action to reverse the build-up of greenhouse gases in the atmosphere. People who advocate such steps are 'more dangerous' than communists, Klaus has said on speaking tours abroad, and constitute a terrible threat to business. (The white-haired conservative actually got to put his arguments before the US Congress recently, after someone felt an opposing viewpoint to Al Gore's should be heard and no one could think of any other source for it.) As long as Klaus uses his Prague Castle office as a pulpit for such positions, one thing surely won't be heating up soon – the reception the Czech president gets among climate scientists.

Nov-Mar 9am-4pm daily. **Admission** 250-350 Kč; 125-175 Kč reductions; 300-500 Kč family, for two days.
Map p52 C2 ❾

From the time of its founding by the Přemysl prince Bořivoj around AD 870, the citadel on the hill has served as the most impressive manifestation of Prague's rulers – though its role as the seat of their power has been an on-again, off-again affair. The growing spurts of a complex as large as some Czech towns have been ushered in by each successive dynasty, with the Castle morphing completely over the centuries: in 973, St Vitus took form as a rotunda; a fire burnt through in the tenth century; Count Bretislav I rebuilt it in 1041; the Přemyslids moved across the river to Vysehrad; Charles IV ushered in the Golden Age in the 14th century. The final touches, including the present shape of St Vitus's Cathedral, came after 1918 in a furore of nation building. Thus its architectural styles, stretching from Romanesque to modernism, make for a rich tour. The imposing façade enclosing the castle is down to Empress Maria Theresa's desire for coherence but Nicolo Pacassi's work seems to lock away much of its beauty behind flat walls. Václav Havel did his best to enliven the palace, opening it to the public and hiring the costume designer from the film *Amadeus* to remodel the castle guards' uniforms.

There's no charge to enter the grounds or nave, crypt and tower of St Vitus's Cathedral, but you will need a ticket (choose short or long tours) to enter the Old Royal Palace (which features the excellent exhibit on Castle life), St George's Basilica, the Golden Lane and the Powder Tower (except Jan-Apr & Oct-Dec, when the tower is closed and the Golden Lane is free of charge). Entrance to the Toy Museum is extra. It's a stiff walk up to the castle from Malá Strana's Malostranská metro station. The least strenuous approach is to take the No.22 tram up the hill and get off at the Pražský hrad stop. There are a handful of adequate cafés within the castle complex, if you don't mind paying above the odds.

Ball Game Court
Míčovna
U Prašného mostu (224 373 579/ old.hrad.cz). Metro Malostranská, then tram 22, 23. **Open** Events only.
Admission varies. **Map** p53 D1 ❿
On the southern side of the Royal Gardens, overlooking the Stag Moat, lies this Renaissance former hall. Built in 1563-69 by Bonifác Wohlmut, it was originally conceived for Habsburg tennis matches, but hasn't seen sport for centuries. It's now periodically open for exhibitions and, despite awful acoustics, concerts. Look carefully at the elaborate black-and-white sgraffito above the figure of Justice (tenth from the right) and you'll spot some façade work modified under the old regime, which now contains a hammer and sickle.

Belvedere
U Prašného mostu (224 371 111/ old.hrad.cz). Metro Malostranská, then tram 22, 23. **Open** Events only.
Admission Varies. **Map** p53 E1 ⓫
With its signature copper roof resembling an overturned frigate, the Belvedere, also known as the Summer Palace, dominates the eastern end of the Royal Gardens. The stunning Renaissance structure was built by Paola della Stella between 1538 and 1564, forming what's hailed as the best example of Italianate style from the period in Central Europe (except for the roof, a compromise to the climate). Commissioned by Ferdinand I as a gift for his wife, Anne, she never got to enjoy it – she drew her last breath after producing the 15th heir to the throne. Occasional art shows are held here.

Black Tower
Černá věž
Na Opyši (no phone). Metro Malostranská, then tram 22, 23. **Map** p53 E1 ⓬
Setting the stark, medieval tone of the Castle's east end, this tower tops the Old Castle Steps (Staré zámecké schody), which lead up from the park

PRAGUE BY AREA

Funicular, Petřín hill p51

Nebozízek

just east of the Malostranská metro
station. To the left of the entrance gate,
where decorated palace guards stand
all year, is a prime viewing spot over
the red-tiled roofs, spires and domes of
the Lesser Quarter.

Dalibor Tower
Daliborka
*Zlatá ulička (224 371 111/old.hrad.cz).
Metro Malostranská, then tram 22, 23.*
Map p53 D1/E1 ⑬
The former prison rooms, which
housed an inmate who lent his name to
the tower, can't be entered, but standing beneath it you can just imagine
Dalibor, later portrayed in Smetana's
opera, amusing himself by playing the
violin while awaiting his death sen-
tence. Crowds of onlookers turned up at
his execution to weep en masse.

Golden Lane
*Prague Castle, Zlatá ulička (224 371
111/old.hrad.cz). Metro Malostranská,
then tram 22, 23.* **Map** p53 D1 ⑭
Frustratingly closed off from the public access streets for most of the year,
this street is lined with tiny multicoloured cottages that cling to Prague
Castle's northern walls. They were
thrown up by the poor in the 16th century out of whatever waste materials
they could find. Some say its name
alludes to a time when soldiers used
the lane as a public urinal but a more
likely source is the 17th century gold-
smiths who worked here. The house
at No. 22 was owned by Kafka's sister Ottla, and the writer stayed here
for a while in 1917, reputedly drawing the inspiration from the streets for
his novel *The Castle*, a fact that's
shamelessly milked today with souvenirs sold here.

Hradčanské náměstí gates
*First courtyard. Metro Malostranská,
then tram 22, 23.* **Map** p52 C2 ⑮
Linking the Castle's first courtyard
with the outside world is this gateway
that has been dominated since 1768,
by Ignatz Platzer's monumental sculptures of battling Titans. They create
an impressive, if not exactly welcoming, entrance. The changing of the
guard takes place in this courtyard, a
Havel-inspired attempt to add some
ceremonial pzazz to the castle. The
change is carried out on the hour
every day from 5am to 10pm, but the
big crowd-pulling ceremony, complete
with band, takes place at noon.

PRAGUE BY AREA

Matthias Gate
Matyášova brána
*First courtyard (224 371 111/old.hrad.
cz). Metro Malostranská, then tram 22,
23.* **Map** p52 C2 ⑯
Built in 1614 by Rudolf II's rival and
successor, Matthias, to imprint the
Habsburg stamp on Prague Castle,
this elaborate entryway provides
access to the second courtyard. The
admittedly impressive portal, topped
by a double-headed German Imperial
Eagle, remains a painful reminder to
Czechs today – but of course, pleased
Hitler when he came to stay in 1939.

Old Royal Palace
Starý královský palác
*Third Courtyard (224 371 111/old.
hrad.cz). Metro Malostranská, then
tram 22, 23.* **Map** p53 D2 ⑰
Part of the ticketed Castle tour, the
palace offers three areas of royal chambers above ground level, all with badly
photocopied engravings for displays,
most with more Russian text than
English, and, in the cellar, an exquisite,
gorgeously presented new permanent
exhibition focusing on palace life. The
new displays inhabit the 12th-century
Romanesque remains of Prince
Soběslav's residence. A worthwhile
highlight at ground level is the Vladislav
Hall, which was designed by Benedict
Ried at the turn of the 16th century, and
which was where jousters once rode up
the Riders' Staircase and where Václav
Havel was sworn in in 1990. Its exquis-
itely vaulted ceiling represents the last
flowering of Gothic art in Bohemia.

Paradise Gardens
Rajská zahrada
*Below third courtyard (224 371 111/
old.hrad.cz). Metro Malostranská, then
tram 22, 23.* **Open** *Apr, Oct* 10am-6pm
daily. *May, Sept* 10am-7pm daily. *June-
July* 10am-9pm daily. *Aug* 10am-8pm
daily. **Admission** free. No credit cards.
Map p52 C2 ⑱
From the Bull Staircase is the garden
where the Catholic victims of the second and most famous defenestration
by Protestants fell to earth, saved by a
giant dung heap (an obelisk marks the
spot). The gardens, initially laid out in

1562, were redesigned in the 1920s by
Josip Plečnik. You can now make the
descent to Malá Strana via the terraced
slopes of five beautiful Renaissance
gardens, which are open, like most gardens in Prague, from April to October
only. The pride of the restoration is the
lovely Ledebour Gardens (Ledeburská
zahrada), featuring a series of foun-
tains, ornate stone stair switchbacks
and palace yards, and emptying you
out on to the middle of Valdštejnská.
Fit hikers might consider ascending to
the castle this way as well, though
there is an entrance fee of 60 Kč
whichever way you decide to go.

Plečnik Obelisk
*Third Courtyard (224 371 111/old.
hrad.cz). Metro Malostranská, then
tram 22, 23.* **Map** p53 C2 ⑲
After the cathedral, the second most
noticeable monument in the third
courtyard is this fairly incongruous 17-
metre-high (50-foot) granite obelisk, a
memorial to the dead of World War I,
erected by Josip Plečnik in 1928. The
two tapering flagpoles nearby are also
the Slovene's work; he was hired by
President Tomáš Garrigue Masaryk to
create a more uniform look for the seat
of the First Republic.

Powder Tower
Prašná věž
*Third courtyard, (224 371 111/old.hrad.
cz). Metro Malostranská, then tram 22,
23.* **Open** *Apr-Oct* 9am-5pm daily. *Nov-
Mar* 9am-4pm daily. **Admission** 50
Kč; 70 Kč family, or included in Prague
Castle ticket. **Map** p53 C1-2 ⑳
Probably the most atmospheric part of
the ticketed Castle tour, the 15th-century
Mihulka, as it's also known, was where
Rudolf II, King of Bohemia (1576-1612),
employed his many alchemists, who
were engaged in attempts to distil the
Elixir of Life and transmute base met-
als into gold. Today the tower hosts
exhibits (in Czech only) about alchemy
and Renaissance life in the castle.

Prague Castle Picture Gallery
Obrazárna Pražského hradu
*Second courtyard (224 371 111/old.
hrad.cz). Metro Malostranská, then*

St George's Convent p51

with soaring Baroque façade, which hosts the biggest-scale art shows in the Castle complex, often international in scope, with fascinating smaller-scale exhibits on Castle history and local artists. The king's troops indeed learned their horsemanship here but it was converted to an art hall some 50 years ago.

Royal Garden

U Prašného mostu (224 371 111/ old.hrad.cz). Metro Malostranská, then tram 22, 23. **Open** *Apr, Oct* 10am-6pm daily. *May, Sept* 10am-7pm daily. *June-July* 10am-9pm daily. *Aug* 10am-8pm daily. **Admission** free. **Map** p53 C1 ㉓

Cross over the Powder Bridge (U Prašného mostu) from the castle's second courtyard and you'll reach the Royal Garden (Královská zahrada), on the outer side of the Stag Moat (Jelení příkop). Laid out for Emperor Ferdinand I in the 1530s, it once included a maze and a menagerie, but was devastated by Swedish soldiers in the 17th century. In front of the Belvedere palace is the so-called Singing Fountain (Zpívající fontána), created in bronze by Bohemian craftsmen in the 1560s. It used to hum as water splashed into its basin but sings no longer, thanks to overzealous reconstruction.

St George's Basilica

Bazilika sv. Jiří
Jiřské náměstí (224 371 111/ old.hrad.cz). Metro Malostranská, then tram 22, 23. **Open** *Apr-Oct* 9am-5pm daily. *Nov-Mar* 9am-4pm daily. **Admission** 50-350 Kč; 30-175 Kč reductions; 520 Kč family, for two days. **Map** p53 D2 ㉔

This basilica, part of the ticketed Prague Castle tour, was rebuilt by Italian craftsmen in 1142 after a fire, but was actually founded in 905, according to the oldest accounts. It burned again later and has been rebuilt several times, but the 16th-century image of St George slaying a dragon in the south tympanum is a highlight. In the original arcades are remnants of 13th-century frescoes and within are

tram 22, 23. **Open** *Apr-Oct* 9am-6pm daily. *Nov-Mar* 9am-4pm daily; tours Mon-Fri only. **Admission** 150 Kč; 80 Kč reductions; 150 Kč family. No credit cards. **Map** p53 C2 ㉑

On the north side of the courtyard near the Powder Bridge (U Prašného mostu) entrance to Prague Castle is this collection of Renaissance and Baroque works that includes art by Rubens, Tintoretto, Titian and Veronese, as well as lesser-known masters. Though there's no hope of ever piecing together the Emperor's Rudolf II's original collection, which has been scattered to the winds, the Castle has succeeded in recovering a few of the works from the original cache.

Prague Castle Riding School

Jízdárna
NEW *U Prašného mostu (224 371 111/ old.hrad.cz). Metro Malostranská, then tram 22, 23.* **Open** Exhibitions only. **Admission** Varies. **Map** p52 C1 ㉒

On the north side of the Royal Gardens stands this impressive exhibition hall

the bodies of a saint (Ludmila, strangled by assassins hired by Prince Wenceslas's mother Drahomira) and a saint-maker (the notorious Boleslav the Cruel, who martyred his brother Wenceslas by having him stabbed to death). The basilica's restored simplicity and clean lines are a comforting contrast to the dizzying Baroque of most Prague churches.

Spanish Hall

Španělský sál

Second courtyard (224 371 111/old.hrad.cz). Metro Malostranská, then tram 22, 23. **Open** *only during concerts.* **Admission** varies. **Map** p52 C2 ㉕

Most Castle visitors don't get the chance to glimpse the inside of this hall, hidden atop a monumental stairway, just visible from inside the passage between the first and second courtyards. The magnificent gold-and-white Baroque hall is a 17th-century ceremonial chamber redone in the 19th century, when the trompe l'oeil murals were covered with white stucco, and huge mirrors and gilded chandeliers were brought in to transform the space into a glitzy venue for the coronation of Emperor Franz Josef I (who failed to show). In the 1950s, the Politburo met here, protected from assassins by a reinforced steel door.

Summer House

U Prašného mostu (224 371 111/old.hrad.cz). Metro Malostranská, then tram 22, 23. **Map** p52 C1 ㉖

Though not open to the public, the quaint, mustard-coloured Dientzenhofer Summer House, to the right of the Royal Gardens entrance, was the presidential residence from 1948 to 1989. Paranoid old Gustav Husák had enormous slabs of concrete installed as defences against possible missile attacks, an addition so ugly that Václav Havel's wife, Olga, refused to let them move in. It has remained empty ever since.

Toy Museum

Jiřská 4 (224 372 294). Metro Malostranská, then 22, 23 tram. **Open** 9.30am-5.30pm daily. **Admission** 60 Kč; 120 Kč family; under-5s free. **Map** p53 D1 ㉗

Loreto p54

Part of Czech émigré Ivan Steiger's large collection is displayed on the two floors of this museum in the Castle grounds. Brief texts accompany cases of toys, from teddy bears to an elaborate tin train set. Kitsch fans will love the robots and the enormous collection of Barbie dolls clad in vintage costumes that span the decades. Good for a rainy day but probably better for the young at heart than the actual young, most of whom greatly prefer playing with toys than looking at them from a historical perspective.

St Vitus's Cathedral

Prague Castle, third courtyard (233 350 788/old.hrad.cz). Metro Malostranská, then tram 22, 23. **Open** *Apr-Oct* 9am-5pm daily. *Nov-Mar* 9am-4pm daily. **Admission** free. **Map** p52 C2 ㉘

The geometric and formidable aspect of the city's greatest church are deceptive, if effective. For centuries, only St Vitus's Cathedral's western end and bell tower, looking incongruously dominant compared to the nave, stood here. The

Royal rehab

Prague Castle has been opening out, polishing up and dusting off in 2008, in the first major wave of refurbishment in decades. And it's fitting that the crown jewels, a collection of priceless stones kept locked inside St Vitus's Cathedral, are marking the project.

Timed for the 90th anniversary of the founding of the sovereign nation of Czechoslovakia, the Castle set its sights on opening two new palaces and restoring the ancient chambers of its two finest churches for the summer of 2008. The reconstruction of St Vitus is one of the most ambitious tasks being taken on, while the Old Royal Palace will see its interiors, long-neglected showpieces of late Gothic and Renaissance architecture, freshened up and restored.

St George's Basilica is also undergoing a thorough reconstruction, giving a team of excited archaeologists, who have already found important remains of the early Přemyslid dynasty here, another chance to see what's beneath the flagstones and within the thick walls that have been used as tombs for centuries.

The wrought-iron of the Royal Gardens' Belvedere will finally be protected from Prague's cold climate; an insulated terrace should forestall water damage to the Castle's finest late Renaissance gem. Meanwhile, in a vineyard next to St George's Basilica, the Richter Villa will throw wide its doors to the public for the first time, as will the nearby Rožmburk palace.

current form, in a convincing neo-Gothic rush of construction, was only added early in the 20th century in an effort to expand and unify while creating a new Czech icon that had little to do with its past as the shrine of Austrian Habsburg interlopers. It still forms the centrepiece of Prague Castle, but its pinnacles and buttresses are really a patchwork. The cathedral was only completed in 1929, exactly 1,000 years after the murdered St Wenceslas was laid to rest on the site. In pagan times, Svatovit, the Slavic god of fertility, was worshipped here, a clue as to why the cathedral was dedicated to his near namesake St Vitus (svatý Vít in Czech). Charles IV, who won an archbishopric for Prague, hired Frenchman Matthew of Arras to build the Gothic wonder, but it was completed by Swabian Peter Parler, hence the Sondergotik or German late Gothic design. The 19th-century nationalists who completed the work did so according to Parler's original plans, hence the difficulty in telling old from new. Inside, the enormous nave is flooded with multicoloured light from the gallery of stained-glass windows. All 21 of them were sponsored by Bohemian finance institutions including (third on the right) an insurance company whose motto – 'those who sow in sorrow shall reap in joy' – is subtly incorporated into the biblical allegory. The most famous is the third window on the left, in the Archbishop's Chapel, created by Alfons Mucha. It depicts the struggle of Christian Slavonic tribes; appropriately enough, the artwork was paid for by Banka Slavia.

Chapel of St Wenceslas

Svatováclavská kaple
Open 8am-midnight daily.
Admission free. **Map** p53 D2 ㉓
On the right side of the nave is the site of the original tenth-century rotunda where 'Good King' Wenceslas was buried. Built in 1345, the chapel has 1,345 polished amethysts, agates and jaspers incorporated into its design and contains some of the saint's personal paraphernalia, including armour, chain

Petřín Tower p54

shirt and helmet. The chapel itself is gated off, but you can catch a glint of its treasure trove over the railings. On state anniversaries, the skull of the saint is put on display, covered with a cobweb-fine veil. A door in the corner leads to the chamber that contains the crown jewels. A papal bull of 1346 officially protects the jewels, while legend has it that fate prescribes an early death for anyone who uses them improperly. The curse seemed to work on the Nazis' man in Prague, Reichsprotektor Reinhard Heydrich, who tried on the crown and was assassinated shortly afterwards by the resistance. The door to the chamber is locked with seven keys, after the seven seals of Revelations, each looked after by a different Prague state or church official.

Crypt
Open *Apr-Oct* 9am-5pm. *Nov-Mar* 9am-4pm daily. **Admission** 50-350 Kč; 30 175 Kč reductions:; 520 Kč family, for two days. **Map** p52 C2 ⑳

Entering from the centre of the cathedral, you descend into the crypt, which is badly in need of restoration and may disappoint. Herein lie the remains of various Czech monarchs, including Rudolf II. Easily the most eye-catching tomb is Charles IV's modern, streamlined metal affair, designed by Kamil Roškot in the mid 1930s. However, the vault itself, hastily excavated between world wars, has a distinctly cramped, temporary look to it.

Gothic Golden Portal
Zlatá brána
Open 8am-midnight daily.
Admission free. **Map** p52 C2 ㉛
This grandiose southern entrance to St Vitus's Cathedral, visible from the courtyard, and which once overlooked the city, sports a recently restored mosaic of multicoloured Venetian glass depicting the Last Judgement. A Getty-funded project returned the original lustre, taking years of work (outdoor mosaics don't do well this far north in

Europe for climactic reasons). On either side of the central arch are sculptures of Charles IV and his wife, Elizabeth of Pomerania, whose talents allegedly included being able to bend a sword with her bare hands.

Great Tower

Open *Apr-Oct* 9am-5pm. *Nov-Mar* 9am-4pm daily. **Admission** 50-350 Kč; 30-175 Kč reductions; 520 Kč family, for two days. **Map** p52 C2 ③②

Easily the most dominant feature of the cathedral, and accounting for Prague's signature spire, the Gothic and Renaissance tower is topped with a Baroque dome. This houses Sigismund, unquestionably the largest bell in Bohemia, made in the middle of the 16th century and weighing in at a hefty 15,120 kilograms (33,333 pounds). The clapper weighs slightly over 400 kilograms (882 pounds). Getting Sigismund into the tower was no mean feat: according to legend it took a rope woven from the hair of the city's noblest virgins to haul it into position.

Štefánik Observatory

Hvězdárna

Top of Petřín hill (257 320 540/www. observatory.cz). Tram 12, 22, then funicular railway. **Open** *Jan, Feb, Nov-Dec* 6-8pm Tue-Fri; 10am-noon, 2-8pm Sat, Sun. *Mar* 7-9pm Tue-Fri; 10am-noon, 2-6pm, 7-9pm Sat, Sun. *Apr-Aug* 2-7pm, 9-11pm Tue-Fri; 10am-noon, 2-7pm, 9-11pm Sat, Sun. *Sept* 2-6pm, 8-10pm Tue-Fri; 10am-noon, 2-6pm, 8-10pm Sat, Sun. *Oct* 7-9pm Tue-Fri; 10am-noon, 2-6pm, 7-9pm Sat, Sun. **Admission** 40 Kč, 30 Kč reductions; free under-3s. **Map** p52 C5 ③③

If you can ever get the inconvenient hours right, Prague's observatory offers more rewards than the chance to try out its double Zeiss astrograph lens. It's part of a proud tradition of historical astronomical connections. Both the haughty Dane Tycho Brahe and his protégé Johannes Kepler resided in the city. The duo features in the observatory's stellar displays (some of which are in English). Equipped with a 40cm Meade mirror scope since 1999, the

facility offers glimpses of sunspots and solar flares during the day and panoramas of the planets, moon and nebulae on clear nights.

Sternberg Palace

Šternberský palác

Hradčanské náměstí 15 (233 090 570). Metro Malostranská, then tram 22, 23. **Open** 10am-6pm Tue-Sun. **Admission** 130 Kč; free under-10s. No credit cards. **Map** p52 C2 ③④

Enlightened aristocrats trying to rouse Prague from provincial stupor founded the Sternberg Gallery here in the 1790s. The palace, located just outside the gates of Prague Castle, now houses the National Gallery's European old masters. Not a large or well-balanced collection, especially since some of its most famous works were returned to their pre-war owners, but some outstanding paintings remain, including a brilliant Frans Hals portrait and Dürer's *Feast of the Rosary*. All in a setting that looks newly redone, although renovations finished over a year ago. There's now space

Prague Castle p54

for more paintings from the repositories, and improved ceiling frescoes that had long been covered up.

Strahov Library

Strahovské nádvoří 1 (233 107 749/ www.strahovskyklaster.cz). Metro Malostranská, then tram 22, 23. **Open** 9am-noon, 1-5pm daily. **Admission** 80 Kč. No credit cards. **Map** p52 A3/A4
The highlight of the monastery complex is its superb libraries, which appear on posters in universities all over the world. Within the frescoed Theological and Philosophical Halls alone are 130,000 volumes. There are a further 700,000 books in storage and together they form the most important collection in Bohemia. Visitors are only allowed access during guided tours, however. When Joseph II effected a clampdown on religious institutions in 1782, the Premonstratensians managed to outwit him by masquerading as an educational foundation, and their collection was swelled by the libraries. The monks' taste ranged far beyond the

standard ecclesiastical tracts, including such highlights as the oldest extant copy of *The Calendar of Minutae* or *Selected Times for Bloodletting*. Nor did they merely confine themselves to books: the 200-year-old curiosity cabinets house a collection of deep-sea monsters that any landlocked country would be proud to possess. Digital scans of ancient books in danger of disintegrating are to be found online at www.manuscriptorium.com.

Strahov Monastery

Strahovský klášter
Strahovské nádvoří 1 (233 107 705/ www.strahovskyklaster.cz). Metro Malostranská, then tram 22, 23. **Open** 9am-noon, 1-5pm daily. **Admission** 80 Kč. No credit cards. **Map** p52 A3/A4
One of the world's oldest abbeys of Premonstratensian monks, founded in 1143. Since 1990, several have returned to reclaim the buildings nationalised by the communists after 1948. They can sometimes be seen from Úvoz street walking laps around green fields and meditating, and services are once again being held in the Church of Our Lady, based on a 12th-century basilica ground plan. The Strahove gallery contains 1,500 artworks that have also been returned from the state. One interesting access route to the monastery is from the stairs at Pohořelec No.8, the westernmost square in the Hradčany district.

Zrcadlové bludiště

Mirror Maze
Petřín hill (257 315 212). Tram 12, 22, then funicular railway. **Open** *Jan-Mar, Nov, Dec* 10am-5pm Sat, Sun. *Apr, Sept* 10am-7pm daily. *May-Aug* 10am-10pm daily. *Oct* 10am-6pm daily. **Admission** 50 Kč; 40 Kč children. **Map** p52 B4/B5
Housed in a cast-iron mock-Gothic castle, complete with drawbridge and crenellations, is a hall of distorting mirrors that still causes remarkable hilarity among kids and their parents. Alongside is a wax diorama of one of the proudest historical moments for the citizens of Prague: the defence of Charles Bridge during the Swedish attack of 1648 is a fairground-style hall of wacky reflectors.

Malý Buddha

Úvoz 46 (220 513 894). Tram 8, 22.
Open 1pm-midnight Tue-Sun. **$. Asian.**
No credit cards. **Map** p52 A3 ㊳
Although it at first looks like a porcelain
and incense shop, 'Little Buddha' is actually a comforting teahouse with light
vegetarian food. Spring rolls and noodle
dishes go hand in hand with the dozens
of teas brewed by the laid-back owner.
Sit in candlelight and speak in whispers
over your eggrolls. No smoking.

Nebozízek

*Petřín hill, Petřínské sady 411 (257
315 329/www.nebozizek.cz). Metro
Malostranská.* **Open** 11am-11pm
daily. **Czech. Map** p52 C5 ㊴
Conveniently set just next to the top
stop of the funicular railway that runs
up Petřín hill, this admittedly touristy
restaurant can still be worth a visit on a
fine day for its patio view of Old Town
across the river. Prices are elevated with
the view, but it won't break the bank.

Petřínské Terasy

*Seminářská zahrada 13 (257 320
688/www.petrinsketerasy.cz). Metro
Malostranská.* **Open** noon-11pm Mon-
Fri; 11am-11pm Sat, Sun. **$$. Czech.**
Map p52 C4 ㊵
On days with clear visibility and when
you're faint with hunger or thirst from
a hike on the Petřín hill, the Petřín
Terraces can make for a handy, if pricey
option. Exquisite views of Prague Castle
and the city go along with the Krušovice
beer and indifferent service.

Restaurant Hradčany

NEW *Keplerova 6 (224 302 430/
www.hotel-savoy.cz). Tram 22, 23.*
Open 6.30am-10.30am, noon-3pm,
6-11pm daily. **$$$. Continental.**
Map p52 A3 ㉛
The gourmet dining room within the
Savoy promises much to weary travellers who have hiked throughout nearby Prague Castle, having won a spate of
awards in the last year for its cuisine
and service. For hotel guests, a there's a
menu deal of three courses for 38 euros.

U Černého vola

*Loretánské náměstí 1 (220 513 481).
Tram 22.* **Open** 9am-10pm daily.
No credit cards. **Pub. Map** p52 A3 ㊷
Likely the cosiest and least pretentious
pub in the district, the 'Black Ox' is not
quite as ancient as it appears. The
murals make it look like it's been here
forever, but in fact it was built after
World War II. Its superb location, right
above the Castle, made it a prime target
for redevelopment in the post-1989
building frenzy, but the rugged regulars
bought it to ensure that local bearded
artisans would have at least one place
where they could afford to drink. The
Kozel beer is perfection and although
the snacks are pretty basic they do their
job of lining the stomach.

U Císařů

*Loretánská 5 (220 518 484/www.
ucisaru.cz). Metro Malostranská, then
tram 22, 23.* **Open** 11am-midnight
daily. **$$. Czech. Map** p52 B3 ㊸
An upscale version of Czech trad – with
rustic stone-walled interiors and tables
on the square – 'At the Emperor's' is a
short stroll from Prague Castle. It deliv-
ers attentively served platters of pork,
duck, goulash and the trimmings, plus
hearty (and heart-stopping) platters of
smoked meats. The potato-thyme soup
is excellent and the draught beer is as
fine as any around.

U Ševce Matouše

*Loretánské náměstí 4 (220 514 536).
Tram 22.* **Open** 11am-11pm daily.
$. Czech. Map p52 A3 ㊹
The classic steakhouse, Czech style,
with done-to-order tenderloins in tradi-
tional sauces such as green peppercorn
or mushroom. A short walk east of
Prague Castle and in a cosy former
shoemaker's workshop (where it was
once possible to get your boots repaired
while lunching). Reasonable prices
given the prime location.

U Zavěšeného kafe

*Úvoz 6 (257 532 868/www.uzavesenyho
kafe.com). Metro Malostranská.*
Open 11am-midnight daily. **Pub.**
Map p52 B3 ㊺

Toy Museum p61

With a strong local following, the 'Hanging Coffee Cup' is a kind of neighbourhood gathering point. It's an affordable, mellow place with plank flooring, trad grub (like onion soup and duck with sauerkraut) and a long association with local artists and intellectuals. The name comes from an old tradition of paying for a cup of coffee for someone who may arrive later without funds.

Arts & leisure

Gambra
Černínská 5 (220 514 527). Metro Malostranská, then tram 22, 23. **Open** *Mar-Oct* noon-5.30pm Wed-Sun. *Nov-Feb* noon-5.30pm Sat, Sun. **Map** p52 A2 ⁴⁶
A funky gallery specialising in surrealist art, this one happens to be owned by the world-renowned animator Jan Švankmajer, who lives in the attached house. It's a part of the Nový Svět enclave, a collection of brightly coloured cottages restored in the 18th and 19th centuries – all that remains of Hradčany's medieval slums. The rest were destroyed in the great fire of 1541.

Klub 007
Vaníčkova 5, Koleje ČVUT dorm 7 (257 211 439). Metro Dejvická, then bus 143, 149, 217. **Open** 7pm-midnight Mon-Sat. **Map** p52 A5 ⁴⁷
Ugly to look at, tough to find, this student dorm bar is nevertheless host to a regular line-up of impressive rockers from around Europe and the States. Located in the concrete basement of a Czech Technical University dorm (yes, 007), it's the locus of many a loud, late-night ska show. Cheap beer and scary snacks go with the shows and vibe.

Stadium Strahov
Diskařská 100, Břevnov (233 014 111). Metro Karlovo náměstí, then bus 176 or tram 22 to Ujezd, then funicular. **Map** p52 A5 ⁴⁸
Only open for monster concerts, Strahov is a concrete monstrosity built before World War II and without much to offer besides its size to accommodate epic rock shows (capacity 250,000). It's a trek out of the centre, but a bus service is laid on for big gigs. When there's a show here, you'll know about it.

Nerudova street p74

Malá Strana & Smíchov

Malá Strana

Still the city's most enchanting quarter for strolling, with lovely walled gardens waiting to be discovered and alluring riverside green spaces, Prague's left bank is generally on the quiet side – for the hottest clubs and dining, you generally cross the Vltava. Yet, peaceful little Malá Strana has been blooming of late, with more respected galleries, restaurants and even dance club options complementing its array of pretty Baroque palaces, cobbled lanes and stunning churches. Historically, the district was a warren for artists, craftsmen working for the Castle and royal retainers and it continues to retain the

bohemian spirit at modern-day jazz bars, parks and cafés.

Malá Strana (or the Lesser Quarter) lies between the Vltava river and Prague Castle, skirting the hill that makes up Hradčany. Its backstreets reward exploring, with old-world embassies, rustic old pubs (like Baráčnická rychta) and ornate doors and chapels (St Nicholas, Our Lady Victorious and Our Lady Beneath the Chain); former playgrounds of aristocrats, like the Baroque **Wallenstein Gardens** and **Vrbta Gardens**, hold particular appeal. Founded by the Přemyslid Otakar II in 1287 – when he invited merchants from Germany to set up shop on the land beneath the Castle walls – the area was transformed into a sparkling

Baroque district by the wealthy Catholic elite, who won huge parcels of land in the property redistribution that followed the Thirty Years' War.

Kitschy Mostecká street leads from the **Charles Bridge** into the centre of the district, following the **Royal Route** – the path taken by the Bohemian kings to their coronation. **Malostranské náměstí** is a lively square edged by large Baroque palaces and Renaissance gabled townhouses perched on top of Gothic arcades, which inspired the tales of beloved Bohemian writer Jan Neruda, author of *Prague Tales*. The square has been quieter in recent years, but the venerated music club Malostranská beseda, at No. 21, is expected to reopen in 2009, which should liven things up again. Local pubs too are as lively as ever, with **U Malého Glena** and **Popocafepetl** consistently packing 'em in; gourmands, meanwhile, gather at **U Malé Velryby** and increasingly swank restaurants like **Palffy Palác** and **U Patrona**.

The Smíchov district, upstream to the south, is where Prague shows its new face to the world; the place is full of trendy bars and shops and the style chasers that go with them.

Sights & museums

American Embassy

Tržiště 15. Metro Malostranská.
Map p71 A3 ❶
Easily spotted by the queue of frustrated Czech visa applicants outside, the US embassy happens to reside in the 17th-century Schönborn Palace (Schönbornský palác) by one of Prague's many Baroque masters of Italian descent, Giovanni Santini-Aichel (who was actually born in Prague). Though most visitors never get to see them, its chambers have been lovingly restored and are opened to the public for cultural events.

British Embassy

Thunovská 14. Metro Malostranská.
Map p71 A2 ❷
Once the target of communist surveillance teams from Prague Castle just above it, the British Embassy is situated at the end of an alleyway, just north of the main drag of Nerudova. It was known as 'Czechers' amongst the diplomatic set but is now known mostly for its Baroque beauty. Leading up from here are the New Castle Steps (Nové zámecké schody), one of the most peaceful (and least strenuous) routes up to the castle and a star location in the film *Amadeus*.

Chapel to St John of the Laundry

Kaple sv. Jana Na Prádle
South end of Kampa Park. Metro Malostranská. **Map** p71 B5 ❸
Washerwomen once rinsed shirts on the banks of the Čertovka. Today, it's taken up by snoozing office workers and bongo-beating hippies. The river and bridge views are as romantic as they come, while the chestnut trees make shady spots for reading and recharging. In spring, the park is filled with pink blossom. The restaurant Kampa Park (p79) is at the north end of the island, where the Čertovka runs back into the river by Charles Bridge, offering the finest waterfront view of any dining establishment in town.

Church of Our Lady Beneath the Chain

Kostel Panny Marie pod Řetězem
Maltézské náměstí. Metro Malostranská. **Map** p71 B3 ❹
Seemingly a jumble of incongruous parts, this church features Gothic parts built by a military-religious order to guard the Judith Bridge, which spanned the Vltava before the Charles Bridge, close to where the Charles sits today. Its two heavy towers, standing at the entrance, contain some of the most prized apartments in Prague. The Hussite wars barred the construction of the church and it was never finished.

Church of Our Lady Victorious

Kostel Panny Marie Vítězné
*Karmelitská 9 (257 533 646). Tram
12, 22.* **Open** 8.30am-7pm Mon-Sat;
8.30am-8pm Sun. **Admission** free.
Map p71 A4 ⑤

The first Baroque church in Prague
(built 1611 to 1613) belongs to the
Barefooted Carmelites, an order that
cares for the doll-like, miracle-working
400-year-old Bambino di Praga. The
effigy, brought from Spain to Prague in
the 17th century, is said to have protected nuns from the plague. A wardrobe
of over 60 outfits have been changed by
the Order of English Virgins at sunrise
on selected days for around 200 years.

Church of St Joseph

Kostel sv. Josefa
*Josefská and Letenská streets.
Metro Malostranská.* **Map** p71 B3 ⑥

Though seldom visited by anyone but
architecture lovers, this Baroque gem,
set back from the road, features delicate
lines created by Jean-Baptiste Mathey.
Since 1989, it has been returned to the
much-diminished Order of English
Virgins, who were also one-time
owners of the nearby Vojan's Gardens
(Vojanovy sady), one of the most tran-
quil spots in the city.

Church of St Nicholas

Kostel sv. Mikuláše
*Malostranské náměstí (257 534 215).
Metro Malostranská.* **Open** *Nov-Feb*
9am-4pm daily. *Mar-Oct* 9am-5pm
daily. **Admission** 60 Kč; 30 Kč
reductions. **Map** p71 A3 ⑦

The star attraction for fans of Baroque,
this church dome and tower, visible
from the Charles Bridge, form the
signature image of Malá Strana. They
were created to impress, part of the
Catholic Church's campaign to fuel the
Counter-Reformation. The rich façade
by Christoph Dientzenhofer, completed
around 1710, conceals an interior and
dome by his son Kilián Ignaz, dedicated
to high Baroque at its most flamboy-
antly camp – bathroom-suite pinks
and greens, swooping golden cherubs,

swirling gowns and dramatic gestures;
there's even a figure coyly proffering a
pair of handcuffs.

Church of St Thomas

Kostel sv. Tomáše
*Josefská 8 (257 530 556). Metro
Malostranská.* **Open** 11am-1pm
Mon-Sat; 9am-noon, 4.30-5.30pm Sun.
Admission free. **Map** p71 B2 ⑧

On a backstreet east of Malostranské
náměstí, sits the Church of St Thomas.
Its rich Baroque façade, tucked into a
narrow lane, is easy to miss. Based on a
Gothic ground plan, the church was
rebuilt by Kilián Ignaz Dientzenhofer
for the Augustinian monks. St Boniface,
a fully dressed skeleton, occupies a
glass case in the nave. Rubens painted
the altarpiece (now a copy) named the
Martyrdom of St Thomas.

Galerie Montanelli

*Nerudova 13 (257 531 220/
www.galeriemontanelli.com).
Metro Malostranská.* **Open** noon-
6pm Mon-Fri. **Admission** free.
Map p71 A3 ⑨

With a reputation for fostering multiple generations of contemporary
artists, this intelligently run gallery is
a refreshing find on the main pedes-
trian route to the Castle. While it represents some of the established
firmament, like Jiří and Běla Kolář, it
also bolsters the younger generation
with group shows. Opened in 2003, it
co-operates with institutions in Berlin
and Frankfurt to expose these artists
to audiences abroad.

Josef Sudek Atelier

*Újezd 30 (251 510 760/www.sudek-
atelier.cz). Metro Malostranska.*
Open noon-6pm Tue-Sun. **Admission**
10 Kč; 5 Kč students. **Map** p71 B4 ⑩

Still imbued with the creative spirit of
its former resident, master of Czech
photography Josef Sudek, this humble
former studio is accessible through a
residential building courtyard. Select
shows of quality art photography are
held in the intimate exhibition room,
while Sudek memorabilia is on display in a separate small room.

Malá Strana

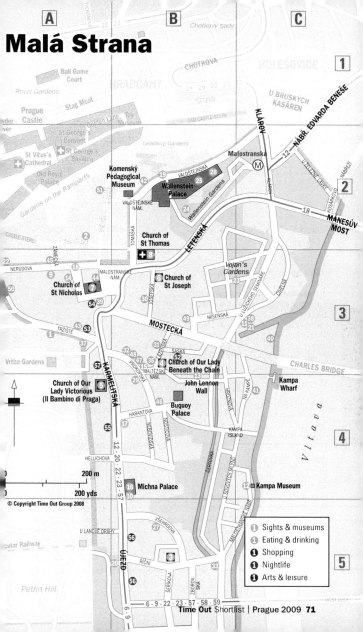

A1 — Ball Game Court
Royal Gardens
Prague Castle
Stag Moat
Golden Lane
Toy Museum
St George's Convent
St Vitus's Cathedral
St George's Basilica
Old Royal Palace
Gardens on the Ramparts
Castle Steps

HRADČANY
CHOTKOVA
Chotkovy sady
HOLEŠOVICE
U BRUSKÝCH KASÁREN
U. BRUSKÝCH
KASÁREN
NÁBŘ. EDVARDA BENEŠE

Ledebug Gardens
OLD CASTLE STEPS

KLÁROV
Malostranská (M)

Komenský Pedagogical Museum
VALDŠTEJNSKÁ
Wallenstein Palace
VALDŠTEJNSKÉ NÁM.
Wallenstein Gardens

MÁNESŮV MOST

NERUDOVA
ZÁMECKÁ
TOMÁŠSKÁ
Church of St Thomas
LETENSKÁ

Church of St Joseph
Vojan's Gardens

Church of St Nicholas
MALOSTRANSKÉ NÁM.
JOSEFSKÁ
MIŠEŇSKÁ
U LUŽICKÉHO SEMINÁŘE
CIHELNÁ

TRŽIŠTĚ
MOSTECKÁ
CHARLES BRIDGE

Vrtba Gardens
SASKÁ
LÁZEŇSKÁ
Church of Our Lady Beneath the Chain
NA KAMPĚ
Kampa Wharf

KARMELITSKÁ
PROKOPSKÁ
MALTÉZSKÉ NÁM.
John Lennon Wall
HROZNOVÁ

Church of Our Lady Victorious (Il Bambino di Praga)
Buquoy Palace
HARANTOVA
NEBOVIDSKÁ
MOSTECKÁ
KAMPA ISLAND

Vltava

HELLICHOVA
12 · 20 · 22 · 23 · 57

SOVOVY MLÝNY

200 m
200 yds
© Copyright Time Out Group 2008

Michna Palace

ÚJEZD
VŠEHRDOVA

Kampa Museum
MALOSTRANSKÉ NÁBŘ.

U LANOVÉ DRÁHY
cular Railway

ŘÍČNÍ
ŠEŘÍKOVÁ
ZBOROV-SKÁ

Petřín Hill
6 · 9 · 22 · 23 · 57 · 58 · 59

A   B   C
1
2
3
4
5

Legend:
- Sights & museums
- Eating & drinking
- Shopping
- Nightlife
- Arts & leisure

CAFÉ 1893 SAVOY

Altprager Café
Seit 1893

Vítězná 5, Praha 5, tel.: +420 257 311 562
www.ambi.cz

Vrtba Gardens p68

Kafka Museum

Hergetova cihelna, Cihelná 2b (257 535 507/www.kafkamuseum.cz). Metro Malostranská. **Open** *Mar-Dec* 10am-6pm daily. *Jan-Feb* 11am-5pm daily. **Admission** *120 Kč.* **Map** p71 C3 ⑪
The city's first museum honouring its most celebrated son hosts haunting long-term exhibits on the author, which have won praise both here and abroad. With a collection that starred at the Jewish Museum in New York before settling here, the Kafka Museum is divided into Existential Space and Imaginary Topography, offering a perceptive look at the man, the city and their unhealthy but eternal effects on each other.

Kampa Museum

U Sovových mlynů 2 (257 286 147/ www.museumkampa.cz). Metro Malostranská. **Open** 10am-6pm daily. **Map** p71 C4 ⑫
One of the most respected and accessible art refuges in this district, the Kampa Museum has an enviable location on the waterfront of the city's loveliest island. Its impresive modern art collection was amassed over decades by Jan Mládek – an international financier

and former Prague student – and his wife, art patron Meda Mládek, both of whom lived in exile before the Velvet Revolution. Sculpture by Otto Gutfreund and work by František Kupka sits alongside refreshing work from abroad. There's a gorgeous terrace café on the Vltava.

Lennon Wall

Maltézské náměstí. Metro Malostranská. **Map** p71 B4 ⑬
At the south end of the square, this graffiti-covered wall was a place of pilgrimage during the 1980s for the city's hippies, who dedicated it to their idol and scrawled messages of love, peace and rock 'n' roll across it. The secret police painted over the graffiti, only to have John's smiling face reappear a few days later. This continued until 1989 when the wall was returned to the Knights of Malta as part of a huge restitution package. The John Lennon Peace Club still encourages modest graffiti.

Lichtenstein Palace

Lichtenštejnský palác
Malostranské náměstí 13 (257 534 205). Metro Malostranská. **Open**

Church of St Nicholas p70

Built in 1640-50, this fine Baroque pile was intended to rival the Wallenstein Palace (p75), itself built to compete with Prague Castle (p57). With these gargantuan ambitions, Francesco Caratti took Versailles as his model in designing the Michna gardens. Today, they contain little but tennis courts.

Museum of Music

Karmelitská 2 (257 327 285/ www.nm.cz). Metro Malostranská. **Open** 10am-6pm Mon, Wed-Sun. **Admission** 100 Kč; 50 Kč reductions. **Map** p71 B4 ⑰
With proud displays of some of the 250,000 artefacts it holds, many having been lovingly restored after the damages of the 2002 Vltava floods, this museum forms a genuine treasury in a music-infused city. It offers the creds of the National Museum plus an impressive palace space in which to encounter an incredible collection of instruments, along with exhibits on the greats, from 1920s jazz star Jaroslav Ježek to the *dudy*, or medieval bagpipes.

Nerudova street

Nerudova. Metro Malostranská. **Map** p71 A3 ⑱
The prime walking lane heading up to Prague Castle is a fine place to begin deciphering the ornate signs that decorate many of the city's houses: the Three Fiddles at No.12, for example, or the Devil at No.4. This practice of distinguishing houses continued up until 1770, when that relentless moderniser Joseph II spoiled all the fun by introducing numbered addresses. The street is crowded with restaurants, cafés and shops aimed at the ceaseless flow of tourists to and from the Castle.

Paradise Gardens

Rajská zahrada
Valdštejnské náměstí. Metro Malostranská. **Open** *Apr-Oct* 10am-6pm daily. **Admission** 60 Kč; 50 Kč reductions. **Map** p71 B2 ⑲
An impressive collection of greenery, terraces and Baroque arches, that make for one of the most unusual ways to access Prague Castle above.

10am-7.30pm daily. *Concerts* 7.30pm. **Tickets** 60-150 Kč. **Map** p71 A3 ⑭
The elegant, well-situated Lichtenstein Palace is the home of the Czech Academy of Music. Regular concerts are given in the Gallery and in the Martinů Hall, although the real star is the summer open-air series of popular operas that take place in the courtyard.

Maltese Square

Maltézské náměstí. Metro Malostranská. **Map** p71 B3 ⑮
The Knights of Malta lived in this quiet square, which is now lined with mellow cafés and pubs, for centuries until the communists dissolved the order. The order regained great swathes of property under the restitution laws, however. Around the corner on Saska ulička are several pretty flower shops and boutiques for clubbing gear.

Michna Palace

Michnův palác
Újezd 40. Metro Malostranská. **Map** p71 B4 ⑯

Some will surely find it easier to start from Prague Castle (descend the Bull stairs from the third courtyard) and descend to Malá Strana.

Petřín hill

Petřínské sady
Karmelitska 1. Metro Malostranská.
Map p71 B5 ㉑
The highest, greenest and most peaceful of Prague's seven hills, this area is the largest expanse of sylvan in central Prague – a favourite spot for tobogganing children in winter and canoodling couples in summer. The hill also features much of the city's Gothic and Romanesque buildings. The southern edge of the hill is traversed by the so-called Hunger Wall (Hladová zeď), an eight-metre-high (23-ft) stone fortification that was commissioned by Charles IV in 1362 to provide work for the city's poor.

Prague Jewellery Collection

Pražský kabinet Šperku
Hergetova Cihelna, Cihelná 2b (221 451 400/www.cihelna.info). Metro Malostranská. **Open** 10am-6pm daily. **Admission** 60 Kč; 50 Kč reductions. **Map** p71 C3 ㉑
Housed in a magnificently reconstructed brickyard on the river, and just a stone's throw from the Charles Bridge, this new museum is the result of a collaboration between the Museum of Decorative Arts and the private COPA company. The collection brings together jewellery and goldsmithing, documenting the evolution of the art from the 17th century to the present, with Tiffany artworks and Fabergé eggs.

Thun-Hohenstein Palace

Thun-Hohenštejnský palác
Nerudova 20. Metro Malostranská.
Map p71 A3 ㉒
Now the Italian embassy, this precious pile, built by Giovanni Santini-Aichel in 1726, is distinguished by the contorted eagles holding up the portal, the heraldic emblem of the Kolowrats for whom the palace was built. The Italians were trumped for a while by the Romanians, who used to inhabit the even more glorious Morzin Palace (Morzinský palác) at No.5, also the work of Santini-Aichel.

Vojanovy sady

U Lužického semináře (no phone). Metro Malostranská. **Open** Oct-Apr 8am-5pm daily. *Mar-Sept* 8am-7pm daily. **Map** p71 B3/C3 ㉓
Not as trafficked nor as carefully groomed and ordered as the district's nearby Wallenstein Gardens (below), this walled sanctuary of greenery and peacocks is a local secret love and great for a relaxing stroll.

Wallenstein Gardens

Letenská, towards Malostranská metro station. Metro Malostranská.
Map p71 B2 ㉔
A door in a wall leads to the best-kept formal gardens in the city. In the early 17th century they belonged, along with the adjoining Wallenstein Palace below), to General Albrecht von Wallenstein, commander of the Catholic armies in the Thirty Years' War and known to be a formidable property speculator. Free concerts are often held here in summer.

Wallenstein Palace

Valdštejnský palác
Valdštejnská 3 (257 071 111/www. senat.cz). Metro Malostranská. **Open** 10am-6pm Tue-Sun. **Admission** 100 Kč; 50 Kč reductions. **Map** p71 B2 ㉕
The palace (which now contains the Czech Parliament) is a suitably enormous, opulent pile designed by the Milanese architect Andrea Spezza in the latter half of the 1620s. It once housed a permanent staff of 700 servants along with 1,000 horses. A little-noticed entrance to the palace gardens, just to the right of the Malostranská metro station exit, provides a wonderful way of cutting through the district and leaving the droves of tourists behind.

Wallenstein Riding School

Valdštejnská jízdárna
Valdštejnská 3 (257 073 136/www.ng prague.cz). Metro Malostranská. **Open**

Rakija'n'roll!

One of the first things you notice at a show by Czech world music band **Gothart** (that is, after the Balkan brass, Yiddish-style clarinet and Mediterranean accordion) is that you're never quite sure what language you're hearing. Isn't that Greek? No, wait, that was a Slovak phrase… but those are Bulgarian chords and rhythms, no? The answer is generally 'yes'. Just as this Prague band has been doing for the last 14 years, in 700 concerts around Europe, Gothart continues to surf cultures, traditions and languages, floating from ancient mountain music to village wedding songs by way of Slavic dances – and maybe a Duke Ellington riff or two.

As crowds at Malá Strana's Baráčnická rychta pub (p77) can attest, it adds up to an infectious, uplifting experience that's hard to sit still for. But crowds don't just hop around at a Gothart show – they'll likely join hands and form a ring, spontaneously performing a traditional Bulgarian folk step.

Oddly enough, the band itself has its roots in medieval ballads. Originally, they played only these on their albums *Por nos de dulta* and *Stella splendens*. But by 1998, Gothart's concert repertoire had shifted to almost exclusively world music, with crowds going wild for their interpretations of Balkan folk songs and dances. The resulting breakthrough release, *Adio querida*, led to starring roles in festivals at home and abroad. In 2001, the band went a step further with the album *Cabaret*, giving full voice to Gothart's special approach to complex Balkan music. The response to what's become known as 'Rakija'n'roll' has been bigger than ever – and their fifth album, released in 2003, took this name.

Since then, Gothart has been too busy playing to packed houses to record much – but their act is best experienced live anyway. And if they're booked at the cavernous, old Baráčnická rychta, it will be a night not to be missed.

■ For info, visit www.gothart.cz.

10am-6pm Tue-Sun. **Admission** 100 Kč; 50 Kč reductions. **Map** p71 B2 ㉖
Part of the Wallenstein Palace complex and operated by the National Gallery, this space holds some of Prague's most popular and well-attended exhibitions. These include everything from artists of the Czech National Revival (symbolist Max Švabinský is beloved) to 20th-century Chinese masters.

Eating & drinking

Bar Bar

Všehrdova 17 (257 312 246/www. bar-bar.cz). Tram 12, 22. **Open** noon-midnight Mon-Thur, Sun; noon-2am Fri, Sat. **$**. **French**. **Map** p71 B5 ㉗
A long-established local hangout on a quiet back street, Bar Bar offers great value and refreshingly light (but not insubstantial) meals. It's usually packed, but the unpretentious cellar bar and restaurant does its best to keep up with the demand for open sandwiches, salads and grill dishes. It's the savoury and sweet crêpes that really stand out, however. English-style pancakes with lemon and sugar are priced at a pittance.

Baráčnická rychta

Tržiště 23 (257 532 461/www. baracnickarychta.cz). Metro Malostranská. **Open** noon-11pm Mon-Sat; 11am-9pm Sun. **$**. **Czech**. **Map** p71 A3 ㉘
One of the last surviving old-style pubs in the district, this well-worn locale in a former 19th-century lecture salon is split into two spaces: one a small beerhall frequented by hardcore *pivo* drinkers, both of the student and middle-aged variety, the other a downstairs music hall that hosts gigs by local rock hopefuls and touring acts from the Balkans.

Barego

NEW *Nebovidská 19 (233 088 777/ www.mandarinoriental.com/prague). Metro Malostranská.* **Open** 10am-3am daily. **Bar**. **Map** p71 B4 ㉙
The epitome of the smart scene for cocktails in Malá Strana, the Mandarin Oriental's gorgeous little design bar is a great place to witness Prague's new chic

ethic. The Monastery Smoky Martini, the house special, goes well with the vibe, as the international elite meet to pull up a red leather seat and trade notes.

Blue Light

Josefská 1 (257 533 126/www.blue lightbar.cz). Metro Malostranská. **Open** 6pm-3am daily. **Bar**. **Map** p71 B3 ㉚
From all appearances, it's nothing but a dark, smoky spot in which to hide out from the tourists, but stick around till midnight and you'll witness a tranformation. The place begins to buzz and then builds to form a major scene, often featuring whatever Hollywood star happens to be in town shooting. The jazz posters and dilapidated walls contribute to the secretive appeal, while the bar stocks a good selection of malt whiskies.

Bohemia Bagel

NEW *Lážeňská 19 (257 218 192/ www.bohemiabagel.cz). Metro Malostranská.* **Open** 7.30am-11pm daily. **Café**. **Map** p71 B3 ㉛
The city's biggest new café chain has expanded its locations and menus, having moved into this spot and several others around town with new offerings and the same old friendly prices and service. Established by the owners of jazz club U Malého Glena, the chain launched the republic's first true bagel source – and it's been packed ever since. Free coffee refills help wash down the goods.

Café El Centro

Maltézské náměsti 9 (257 533 343/ www.elcentro.cz). Metro Malostranská. **Open** noon-midnight daily. **$$**. **Spanish**. **Map** p71 B3 ㉜
An easily overlooked Malá Strana bar just a block off the main square that specialises in mambo soundtracks and tropical cocktails. Efforts to expand into a full restaurant specialising in paella aren't winning over the daiquiri lovers, but the postage-stamp patio at the rear is a boon.

C'est la Vie

Říční 1 (721 158 403/www.cestla vie.cz). Tram 12, 22. **Open** *Apr-Dec*

Barego p77

11.30am-1am daily. *Jan-Mar* 6pm-1am Mon-Fri; 11.30am-1am Sat, Sun. **$$**.
Mediterranean. Map p71 B5 ㉝
Strong on attitude but not necessarily as strong on quality, this upscale spot is at least located in a prime spot on the Vltava. It's clearly geared toward 'Czuppies', but still manages to conjure ambitious meals that do sometimes win praises, such as baked butterfish with mushroom risotto or filet mignon with a good cabernet. Service has improved of late, but is not a strong point either.

Cowboys
Nerudova 40 (296 826 107/www. kampagroup.com). Metro Malostranská. **Open** noon-11pm daily. **$$**.
Steakhouse. Map p71 A3 ㉞
A surprisingly high-quality grill on the main tourist drag leading up to Prague Castle, this western-themed maze of underground caverns leads to an excellent outdoor deck out back. It's a capable steakhouse with hottie servers and occasional live music to go along with the fleet service and tenderness of the T-bones. Prices have inched up since its opening but are still good value, especially for the stunning views of the city.

Cukrkávalimonáda
Lázeňská 7 (257 530 628). Metro Malostranská. **Open** 9am-7pm Mon-Sat; 9.30am-7pm Sun. **Café**. Map p71 B3 ㉟
This hip yet homely café is just a block off the main tourist drag leading from the Charles Bridge. Look out on to a quiet corner of Maltézské náměstí while sipping a Californian chardonnay or tucking into the fresh bakery goods. Expect tall, foamy lattes, a sort of casually alert service, designer benches, hanging greenery and slick magazines for leafing through.

David
Tržiště 21 (257 533 109/www. restaurant-david.cz). Metro Malostranská. **Open** 11.30am-11pm daily. **$$**. **Continental**. Map p71 A3 ㊱
Once known for its quite opulence, David is still a treat to visit, with a clubby feel, but is no longer on the hot list for touring rock stars. Whether that's good or bad news, this discreet, family-run dining room knows how to pamper, with waiters who seem more like butlers efficiently whisking roast boar and port to your table. Definitive Bohemian classics (roast duck with sauerkraut,

rabbit fillet with spinach leaves and herb sauce) are strong. Book ahead.

Gitanes

Tržiště 7 (257 530 163). Metro Malostranská. **Open** noon-midnight daily. $. **Balkan**. Map p71 A3 ㊲
Balkan home cooking can be had at this cosy little resto just off Malá Strana's main square, with dolmas, marinated olives, stuffed peppers, goat's cheese, lamb delights, baclava and hearty red wine. These, plus warm and welcoming service, draw regulars to the three rooms, covered with gingham and doilies. It's like going to your granny's house, only with much cooler music – emanating from speakers hidden in the bird-cages. Don't miss the private table available for curtained-off dalliances.

Hergetova Cihelna

Cihelná 2b (296 826 103/reservations 800 152 692/www.kampagroup.com). Metro Malostranská. **Open** 11.30am-1am daily. $$. **World**. Map p71 C3 ㊳
Impressive value and creative culinary efforts, both signature qualities of owner Nils Jebens, make this a hot venue even in winter. The upstairs bar, which often hosts late DJ parties, shows off an obsession with celeb gatherings that may put off casual diners attracted by the gourmet burgers and pizzas of the main restaurant, but the glare is less intense than at his A-list eaterie Kampa Park (p79) next door. Riverside tables, complete with blankets for when it's chilly, are further draws – and it's more affordable than you'd think.

Jo's Bar

Malostranské náměsti 7 (257 530 162/ www.josbar.cz). Metro Malostranská. **Open** 11am-2am daily. **Bar**. Map p71 A3 ㊴
This street-level bar is an adjunct to the rollicking downstairs Jo's Bar & Garáž (p82). It was once renowned for being every backpacker's first stop in Prague and the original source of nachos in the Czech Republic, but founder Glen Emery has since moved on and Jo's is under new ownership. It's still a good place to meet fellow travellers, but lacks the sense of being in the centre of things nowadays.

Kampa Park

Na Kampě 8B (296 826 112/ www.kampagroup.com). Metro Malostranská. **Open** 11.30am-1am daily; kitchen closes at 11pm. $$. **Seafood**. Map p71 C3 ㊵
Heavy hitter critics from abroad have been dubbing this the city's premier restaurant for over a decade – and it's still hard to fault their reasoning. Executive chef Marek Raditsch has recently rolled out a new menu, featuring squab breast, lamb saddle and a 'sweetly chocolate and bitterly orange tart.' The location's arguably the finest in Prague – in the shadow of Charles Bridge with a beautiful riverside terrace that's open all year (heated for the city's long winters). A slick bar-room scene is to be found inside, which dependably acts as a celeb lightning rod, drawing presidents and Hollywood heart-throbs.

Na Kampě 15

Na Kampě 15 (257 531 430). Metro Malostranská. **Open** 11am-midnight daily. $$. **Pub**. Map p71 C4 ㊶
A rare, if touristy, spot for Bohemian pub grub in all its savoury, greasy glory. In fine weather, grab a spot on the terrace out back or a seat out front and wash down goulash and dumplings or fried mushrooms with well-tapped beer, all for not much more than a real smoke-filled beerhall would charge. Better still, this one's cleaned up for foreigners.

Palffy Palác

Valdštejnská 14 (257 530 522/www. palffy.cz). Metro Malostranská. **Open** 11am-11pm daily. $$$. **Continental**. Map p71 B2 ㊷
With a newly redone menu featuring delectable rack of lamb, duck confits and halibut with mussels and beetroot sauce, it's clear this former Baroque palace still constitutes an only-in-Prague wonder. A supper on the terrace, overhearing strains from the attached classical music academy, is something to savour. It's won over a

U Malé Velryby

U Kocoura

Nerudova 2 (257 530 107). Metro Malostranská. **Open** 11am-midnight daily. **Pub. Map** p71 A3 ⑮
With iconic status in the Prague pubbing world, this smoky, well-worn place was briefly owned by the Friends of Beer (a former political party which has morphed into a civic association). Although its manifesto is a bit vague, the staff's ability to pull a good, cheap pint is beyond question.

U Malé Velryby

NEW *Maltézské náměstí 15 (257 214 703). Metro Malostranská.* **Open** 11am-midnight daily. **$$. Fusion. Map** p71 B4 ⑯
From the king crab pappardelle starter to the spicy meringue roulade dessert, owner Jason Le Gear – veteran chef of several hit Prague restaurants – oversees the most exciting new culinary addition to this district. Hearty ownmade breads and tapas, plus a great wine list, start things off well in the small, open-kitchen dining room. Delicate seafood is a speciality and steaks are light and perfectly cooked.

U Malířů

Maltézské náměstí 11 (257 530 000/ www.umaliru.cz). Tram 12, 22. **Open** 11.30am-11pm daily. **$$$$. French. Map** p71 B3 ⑰
Still one of Prague's most expensive restaurants – which is saying something these days – this quaint 16th-century house with original painted ceilings specialises in authentic, quality French cuisine and a clientele that dines to impress. Pâté with Sauternes wine or sea bass, lobster, lamb and squab are typical offerings. Top-end wine is stocked.

U Maltézských rytířů

Prokopská 10 (257 530 075/www. umaltezskychrytiru.cz). Tram 12, 22. **Open** 1-11pm daily. **$$. Czech. Map** p71 B3 ⑱
This candlelit, Gothic cellar, once an inn for the eponymous Knights of Malta, is justly proud of its venison chateaubriand. Mrs Černiková, whose family runs the place, does a nightly

generation with its atmosphere and service. A worthwhile splashout.

St Nicholas Café

Tržiště 10 (257 530 204). Metro Malostranská. **Open** noon-2am Mon-Thur, Sun; noon-3am Fri, Sat. **Café. Map** p71 A3 ⑬
Under new ownership, this dark and cosy bar in an atmospheric vaulted cellar decked out with steamer trunk tables is a charmer indeed. A mellow but chatty crowd, with lots of foreign students, gathers in the nooks for late evening conversation. Pizzas are a handy option for late-night food – still a rarity in Prague – though they won't win any prizes.

Starbucks

NEW *Malostranské náměstí 28 (no phone/www.starbucks.com). Metro Malostranská.* **Open** 7am-9pm Mon-Fri; 8am-9pm Sat, Sun. **Café. Map** p71 A3 ⑭
The first Czech beachhead of the global chain has proven a hit with tourists and locals seeking a branded coffee experience. Most others are staying well clear. Prime location for convenience, it must be said. See also box p83.

narration on the history of the house, then urges you to eat the admittedly incredible strudel. Booking essential.

U Patrona

Dražického náměstí 4 (257 530 725/ www.upatrona.cz). Metro Malostranská. **Open** 10am-1am daily. **$$**. **Czech**. **Map** p71 B3 49

An oasis of quality in a stretch of town dominated by naff souvenir shops. Fine dining with delicate conceptions of Czech game classics. Just a few tables.

U Sedmi Švábů

Jánský vršek 14 (257 531 455/www. svabove.cz). Metro Malostranská. **Open** 11am-11pm daily; kitchen closes at 10pm. **$$**. **Czech**. **Map** p71 A3 50

A *krčma*, or medieval Czech tavern, the 'Seven Swabians' is a trippy, if borderline tacky, experience with occasional live troubadour music, traditional sweet honey liqueur and salty platters of pork knuckle. Only in Prague.

U Zlaté studně

U Zlaté studně 166 (257 533 322/ www.zlatastudna.cz). Metro Malostranská. **Open** 7am-11pm daily. **$$$**. **Continental**. **Map** p71 A2 51

One of the prettiest dining options on the hill, 'At the Golden Well' is a gorgeous inn. The old-fashioned dining room also makes for a great finish to a Prague Castle visit – you can walk right in from the Castle gardens. There are spectacular views of the Malá Strana district below, plus sharp service and a menu of delicate European cuisine.

Shopping

Květinařství U Červeného Lva

Saská ulička (604 855 286). Metro Malostranská. **Open** 9am-7pm Mon-Sat; 11am-7pm Sun. **Map** p71 B3 52

This crowded little shop is fairly bursting with colour and variety. Dried flowers hang from the ceiling, plants, cut flowers and wreaths cover every available square centimetre.

Phase 2

NEW *Tržiště 8. (257 532 998). Metro Malostranská.* **Open** 10am-6pm Mon-Fri; noon-6pm Sat. **Map** p71 A3 53

British expat Eki Ekanem's enchanting vintage clothes store shows a practiced hand at gold mining. Treasures from First Republic jewellery to fabulous clutches, wraps and dresses fill out the vintage boutique. A good source for a wearable, one-of-a-kind Prague memento.

Nightlife

Jo's Bar & Garáž

Malostranské náměstí 7 (257 530 162). Metro Malostranská. **Open** 9pm-2am daily. **Admission** 50-100 Kč. **Map** p71 A3 54

Multilevel, dark and subterranean, this club makes for a good hideout – bad behaviour is positively encouraged, even if it's no longer the decadent hub of expat life it was back in the mid 1990s. Still, it's a comfortable enough refuge with caverns of bars and dance space, if unpredictable DJ action.

Popocafepetl

Újezd 19 (602 277 226/www. popocafepetl.cz). Metro Malostranská. **Open** 4pm-2am daily. **Admission** free-100 Kč. **Map** p71 A4 55

More and more a venue for great world music, this popular two-level bar and club has rounded out the options, together with the nearby Újezd (below). With blues and Gypsy music theme nights, the smoky little joint is the place for great acts and a host of characters.

Újezd

Újezd 18 (no phone). Metro Malostranská. **Open** *Bar* 2pm-4am daily. *Café* 6pm-4am daily. **Admission** free-100 Kč. **Map** p71 B5 56

Formerly known as Borat (yes, Sacha Cohen once hung out here and was apparently inspired), this three-level club is still the centre of buzz in Prague's left-bank quarter. There aren't many live rock shows these days but the bar is always packed with a youthful crowd of local students anyway, along with artists hanging out beneath the surealist metal decor.

Arts & leisure

U Malého Glena

Karmelitská 23 (257 531 717/www. malyglen.cz). Metro Malostranská. **Open** 10am-2am daily. **Admission** 100-150 Kč. **Map** p71 A3 ⑤⑦

With a newly improved menu but still reasonable prices, the city's most respected jazz club is more appealing than ever. While this is easily the most crammed club in town, patrons forget about the knee-bashing tables the minute the bands start up in the tiny cellar space. There's breathing room in the pub at street level and you can even crash here now as they rent apartments. But it's the jazz and blues that have made 'Little Glenn's' name for over a decade. Get there early for a good seat for the show, which starts around 9.30pm. Sunday jam nights give you the chance to take the stage yourself.

Smíchov

Sights & museums

Futura

Holečkova 49 (251 511 804/www. futuraprojekt.cz). Metro Anděl. **Open** noon-7pm Wed-Sun. **Admission** free. **Map** p84 A2 ⑤③

Curating at this industrial space sets the standard for innovative work this side of the Vltava. The renovated building houses well-designed exhibition halls: white-cubes, cellar spaces, a labyrinthine series of nooks devoted to video works and a Projekt Room presenting experimental shows by up-and-coming artists. Recent ones have been Chinese videographers and 'generational confrontational' avatars Ivan Kafka and Tomáš Svoboda.

Staropramen Brewery

Nádražní 84 (257 191 402/www. staropramen.cz). Metro Anděl.

Admission 100 Kč (tours by appointment only). **Map** p84 B5 ⑤⑨

The biggest and baddest of Prague's breweries hasn't changed much in over a century and still fills tankers and tankards with the city's signature suds (though many insist they prefer Pilsner). The 60-minute tours (English available) are well worth booking and include a good history of Bohemian brewing. There's a restaurant on site too, with nicely done Bohemian classics – well beyond the usual pub grub.

Eating & drinking

El Barrio de Angel

NEW *Lidická 42 (725 535 555/www. elbarrio.cz). Metro Anděl.* **Open** 11am-midnight Mon-Thur; 11am-2am Fri, Sat; noon-midnight Sun. **$$. Argentine**. **Map** p84 B4 ⑥⓪

The district's best steakhouse delivers consistently tender rump roasts and every other kind, nicely charred but melt-in-your-mouth inside. It's also a fun cellar maze of dim dining corners so a good choice for a date. Above-standard service and a nice South American wine list also make for reasons to recommend the Angel.

La Cambusa

Klicperova 2 (257 317 949/www.la cambusa.cz). Metro Anděl. **Open** 7pm-midnight Mon-Sat. **$$. Seafood**. **Map** p84 A5 ⑥①

Prague's original premier seafood establishment, much-loved by ex-President Havel, has probably been surpassed for delicate sauces, decor and service but it's a proud neighbourhood institution that's still pretty darn good.

Jet Set

NEW *Radlická 1c (257 327 251/www. jetset.cz). Metro Anděl.* **Open** 11am-2am daily. **Café**. **Map** p84 A4 ⑥②

Dark, sleek and with a DJ booth as the tell-tale sign, this HQ of hipness for the neighbourhood features a decent, light Mediterranean bar food menu and good coffee. Cocktails are more iffy, as is conversation, unless you're happy to shout it out among your after-party cohorts.

Disdain for the chain

No one disputes that Malá Strana needed another decent café. The area's options for a cosy spot to top up on caffeine are indeed limited. But *Starbucks*?

Praguers have been distinctly cool in their responses to the 2008 opening. The Czech media all reported it as a milestone… but of what, exactly? The news weekly *Reflex* dedicated a feature to weighing up whether the first Starbucks in the Czech Republic signified a gain or a threat to the integrity of this quaint little district.

Starbucks' PR team paints the branch (p80) as proud successor to the coffeehouse that opened on the site in 1874, attracting writers, students and other natives for decades. The company restored the original flooring, researched appropriate paint palettes and adopted 'subdued exterior signage in keeping with the ambience of the square'; it's also sponsoring book releases and readings.

So what's not to like? Well, as one local merchant put it, echoing many in the 'hood, 'Why would I go for latte starting at 80 Kč?'

Another Praguer pointed out that the city has had quality coffee for years and that Czechs are already well versed in the ways of dopio latte, macchiato, mocha and piccolo – and consider the going rate 40-60 Kč.

Perhaps it's also Starbucks' global brand, its dizzying array of choices, the chipper baristas, perky muffins and overstuffed chairs that are so irksome to Malá Strana's hardcore café denizens.

Or maybe it's because locals invest years of patronising their favourite cafés before winning a grudging acknowledgement that the server knows who they are. Then along comes Starbucks, where every schlub who walks in is welcomed warmly.

What kind of sick American imperialism is *that*?

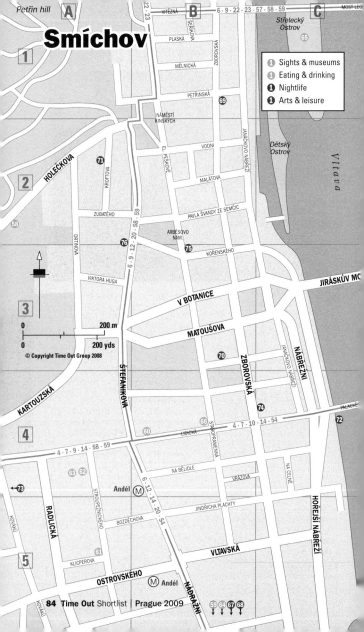

Smíchov

Petřin hill

A

VÍTĚZNÁ B 6 · 9 · 22 · 23 · 57 · 58 · 59 C

MOST LEG

Střelecký Ostrov

65

ŠEŘÍKOVA

PLASKÁ

MĚLNICKÁ

ZBOROVSKÁ

PETŘINSKÁ

69

1

NÁMĚSTÍ KINSKÝCH

EL. PEŠKOVÉ

VODNÍ

JANÁČKOVO NÁBŘEŽÍ

Dětský Ostrov

71

HOLEČKOVA

KROFTOVA

MALÁTOVA

Vltava

2

ZUBATÉHO

PAVLA ŠVANDY ZE SEMČIC

58

DRTINOVA

6 · 9 · 12 · 20 · 58 · 59

76

ARBESOVO NÁM.

75

KOŘENSKÉHO

200 m

VIKTORA HUGA

JIRÁSKŮV MO

3

0

0   200 yds

© Copyright Time Out Group 2008

V BOTANICE

MATOUŠOVA

ŠTEFÁNIKOVA

70

ZBOROVSKÁ

JANÁČKOVO NÁBŘEŽÍ

NÁBŘEŽNÍ

KARTOUZSKÁ

74

PALACKÉ

4

60

66

LIDICKÁ

STROUPRAMENNÁ

4 · 7 · 10 · 14 · 54

72

4 · 7 · 9 · 14 · 58 · 59

63 62

NA BĚLIDLE

VRÁŽOVÁ

NA CELNÉ

73

STROUPEŽNICKÉHO

Andél M

RADLICKÁ

BOZDĚCHOVA

JINDŘICHA PLACHTY

HOŘEJŠÍ NÁBŘEŽÍ

KOVÁKŮ

61

KLICPEROVA

5

OSTROVSKÉHO M Andél

VLTAVSKÁ

KOVÁKŮ

NÁBŘEŽÍ

59 64 67 68
↓ ↓ ↓ ↓

Legend

1 Sights & museums
2 Eating & drinking
3 Nightlife
4 Arts & leisure

Jet Set p82

Nagoya

*Stroupežnického 23 (251 511 724/www.
nagoya.cz). Metro Anděl.* **Open** 6-11pm
Mon-Sat. **$$. Sushi. Map** p84 A4 ㉝
Part of the city's growing Japanese
craze, Nagoya is a worthwhile addition
to the cuisine, though you'll still pay as
much or more for such fare in Prague
than in London or New York.

Potrefená Husa

NEW *Nádražni 84 (257 191 111/
www.ppivovary.cz). Metro Anděl.*
Open 11am-midnight Mon-Thur;
11am-1am Fri, Sat; 11am-11pm Sun.
$. Czech. Map p84 B5 ㉞
This Staropramen-licensed restaurant
chain, the Czech Republic's first, has
built up a rep for renewed classics like
hearty Bohemian soups, smoked meat
dishes and a complement of modern
salads and sides. Young, fast servers
hustle your orders while the fashion-
able hang out at the bar, going in for
newer Staropramen variations like the
foamy Velvet or the ruby-red Granát.

Střelecký ostrov

*Střelecký ostrov 336 (224 934 028/
www.streleckyostrov.cz). Metro Národni
třída, then tram 18.* **Open** 11am-1am
daily. **$. Continental. Map** p84 C1 ㉟
This resto on a lovely Vltava island has
upgraded of late, making its big terrace
even more appealing in mild weather.
When not booked for a private party,
it's a good source for casual fare but
also Czech classics and tender trout, as
well as desserts made table-side.

U Buldoka

*Presslova 1 (257 329 154/www.u
buldoka.cz). Metro Anděl.* **Open** 8pm-
4am daily. **Pub. Map** p84 B4 ㊱
A great survivor from the old days, this
darkwood pub is nevertheless a hot
ticket for the younger generation, with
quick and friendly service and more
adventure on the menu than most pubs.

Nightlife

Big Sister

*Nádražni 46 (257 310 043/www.big
sister.net). Metro Anděl.* **Open** 6pm-
3am daily. **Map** p84 B5 ㊲
The most astounding recent wave in
Prague's booming sex biz, Big Sister
nakedly cashes in on the *Big Brother*

PRAGUE BY AREA

phenomenon by putting live internet cameras inside a brothel. Punters pay only a nominal fee but agree to be on the web in exchange for all the action they can handle. For some reason, this has made global headlines.

Bluesrock Club

Nádražní 39 (774 338 310/ www.bluesrockclub.cz). Metro Anděl. **Open** 5pm-5am daily. **Map** p84 C5 ⑱
Founded by the management of the long-closed Bunkr club, this new magnet for local and touring rock and blues bands is a bunker of a sort. Its underground arched brick chambers are unpretentious, affordable and lively.

Drake's

Zborovská 50 (257 326 828/www.drakes. cz). Metro Anděl. **Open** 24hrs daily. **Map** p84 B1 ⑲
The longest-established gay club this side of the Vltava gets fairly steamy but puts the effort into entertainment with spectacles like 'Slaves in a Cage' and 'Muscle Show'. Not the spot for a casual beer. Free entry for 18 to 25-year olds.

Futurum

Zborovská 7 (257 328 571/www. musicbar.cz). Metro Anděl. **Open** 8pm-3am daily. **Map** p84 B3 ⑳
The district's best sound and lights systems back up progressive programming, excellent local bands and the best non-pop clubbing around, with a proper long bar to boot.

Punto Azul

Kroftova 1 (no phone/www.puntoazul. cz). Metro Anděl. **Open** 6pm-2am Mon-Thur; 7pm-3am Fri, Sat; 7pm-2am Sun. **Map** p84 A2 ㉑
A young local crowd of electronica and techno fans gathers in this trashed, smoky little bar to hear friends spin and to get fairly trashed themselves.

U Bukanýra

Hořejší nábřeží (no phone). Metro Malostranská. **Open** 9pm-6am Fri, Sat. **Map** p84 C4 ㉒
This rollicking houseboat hosts dance parties with locally respected DJs like Braun, and other purveyors

of acid-jazz, lounge and groove, with refreshing river breezes on deck. It's under the Palackého bridge near the Botel Admiral.

Arts & leisure

Bertramka

Mozartova 169 (257 317 465/www. bertramka.com). Metro Anděl. **Open** *Apr-Oct* 9am-6pm daily. *Nov-Mar* 9.30am-4pm daily. **Map** p84 A4 ㉓
The house where Mozart stayed when in Prague is now a museum devoted to him that puts on regular concerts, nearly all featuring his timeless music. It's also host to the new String Quartets festival in late summer, which has won critical praise for its top performers.

Delroy's Gym

Zborovská 4 (257 327 042/www. delroys-gym.cz). Metro Anděl. **Open** 7am-10pm Mon-Fri; 9am-9pm Sat, Sun. **Map** p84 C4 ㉔
Delroy's is spacially challenged but has a strong following nonetheless, specialising in martial arts and boxing but with courses ranging from aerobics to self-defence. The service and quality, along with English-speaking staff, set it apart.

Squash & Fitness Centrum Arbes

Arbesovo náměstí 15 (257 326 041). Metro Anděl. **Open** 7am-11pm daily. **Map** p84 B3 ㉕
A smart fitness club with well-managed courts and a fairly central location.

Švandovo divadlo

Štefánikova 57 (234 651 111/www. svandovodivadlo.cz). Metro Anděl, then tram 6, 9, 12, 20. **Map** p84 A2/A3 ㉖
By far the hippest performance space in the district, this historic theatre stages fresh conceptions of Czech and international plays, from *The Mandrake* to modernised Shakespeare. Václav Havel's *The Beggar's Opera* is in the repertoire too, and a lecture series hosts everyone from Robert Fulghum to Jan Svěrák talking about his latest film. There are English subtitles for Czech performances and a great lobby bar.

Astronomical Clock Tower p99

Staré Město

The heart and soul of Prague lies in the enchantingly blackened and largely car-free district of Old Town, called Staré Město in Czech. The crazy quilt medieval streetplan offers surprise twists and turns for even longtime Praguers, especially with so many new ventures perpetually setting up shop of late. While many locals have called for more restraint on development in Old Town Square and the main walking streets of Celetná and Karlova, the city's primary plaza – overseen by a statue of a gaunt (newly restored) Jan Hus, the great Czech martyr – has fared far better than equivalent public spaces in other European capitals. The district, once a walled city, is filled with Gothic, Baroque and Renaissance architecture and you move through it by discovering passages and courtyards. Because Czechoslovakia fell to the Nazis without resistance, the old centre remained virtually untouched until the 1989 Velvet Revolution, apart from the creeping damage from four decades of communist neglect after 1948. Nowadays, crystal shops aside, compact Staré Město is decidedly on the rise, with a thriving bar scene along Dlouhá and V Kolkovně streets, and a surprising number of clubbing options, often hidden down dark staircases (watch for throngs of Czech youth kitted out head to toe in designer club togs, or young Americans in tattered jeans, as a hint).

Bounded on the north and west by the Vltava river, the one square-kilometre Staré Město district is also a concentrated dose of the new Bohemia. Two of the country's best

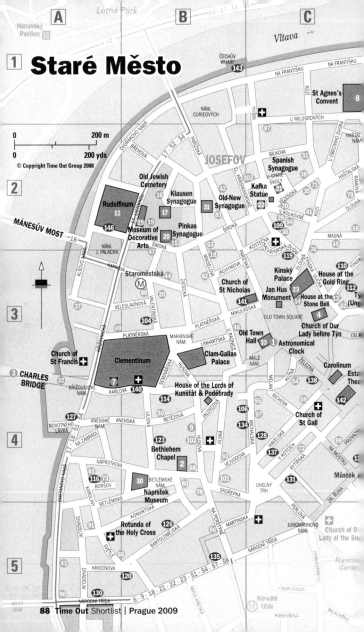

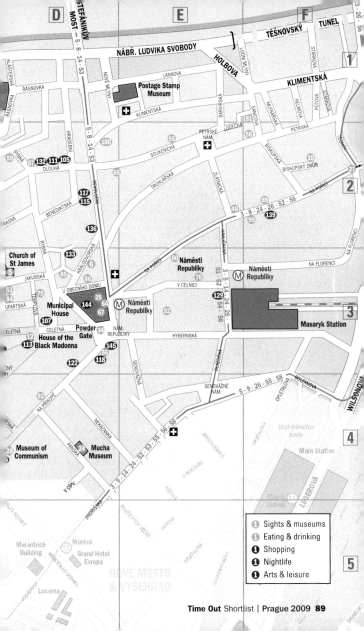

symphony halls, the **Rudolfinum** and **Municipal House**, home to Prague Spring festival, are here. It also hosts some of Prague's best cuisine, with definitive Czech, Italian, French, Asian and seafood options. The gallery scene features more international cross-breeding than ever, as seen at the soon-to-reopen **House at the Golden Ring**, while Czech art not seen since the censored 1970s is resurging at Prague City Gallery's various venues. The district does still draw regular hordes of obnoxious stag parties but they're easy to avoid by moving off onto the more interesting smaller lanes.

Sights & museums

Astronomical Clock

Orloj
Staroměstské náměstí (724 508 584).
Metro Staroměstská. **Open** *Nov-Mar*
11am-5pm Mon; 9am-5pm Tue-Sun. *Apr-Oct* 11am-6pm Mon; 9am-6pm Tue-Sun.
Admission 60 Kč. **Map** p88 C3 ❶
Engineers are still impressed by the ingenious horological parts, some dating back to 1410, that make up the clock face on this icon of the city. The *Orloj* tells time four different ways – including Babylonian, which divides every day into 12 parts – and the innermost ring accurately shows with a sun orb the current zodiac sign. Every hour on the hour, from 8am to 8pm, wooden statuettes of saints appear, with Greed, Vanity, Death and the Turk below. Fortunately it was spared when the Nazis blew up the adjoining Old Town Hall in 1945. See also p99.

Bethlehem Chapel

Betlémská kaple
Betlémské náměstí 4 (224 248 595).
Metro Národní třída or Staroměstská.
Open *Nov-Mar* 10am-5.30pm Tue-Sun.
Apr-Oct 10am-6.30pm Tue-Sun.
Admission 50 Kč. **Map** p88 B4 ❷
The original incarnation of this huge church was erected in 1391, serving as the base for the proto-Protestant Jan

Astronomical Clock

Hus, the Czechs' greatest martyr, who was burnt at the stake for excoriating the papacy in 1415. Having fallen to pieces by the 20th century, it was ironically rebuilt by the communists after World War II; the party saw Hus as a useful working-class revolutionary – but forbade sermons here.

Charles Bridge

Karlův most
East end of Karlova street. **Open** 24hrs
daily. **Admission** free. **Map** p88 A3 ❸
The stone bridge built by Charles IV in consultation with his numerologists, who declared 5.31am, 9 July 1357 an auspicious time to start, is still the city's finest single visual (and the most popular spot for pickpockets and buskers). The statues arrived in the 17th century, when Josef Brokof and Matthias Braun, among other masters, were commissioned to inspire the mass conversions of Bohemian Protestants to the Catholicism of the ruling Habsburgs. Water damage repairs had narrowed

Church of Our Lady before Týn

the walkways at the time of going to press, but the city has pledged to keep the bridge open.

Church of Our Lady before Týn

Kostel Matky Boží pod Týnem
Staroměstské náměstí (222 322 801). Metro Náměsti Republiky or Staroměstská. **Open** *Services* 6pm Wed-Fri; 8am Sat; 9.30am, 9pm Sun. **Admission** free. **Map** p88 C3 ④

A landmark of Staré Město, this improbably spiky church, where the heads of Protestant Czech nobles were buried after they lost the Battle of White Mountain in 1620, dates from the late 14th century. The lovingly lit spires (a must by night) top what became a centre of the reforming Hussites' movement in the 15th century, before being commandeered by the Jesuits in the 17th. The southern aisle houses astronomer Tycho Brahe's tomb.

Church of St James

Kostel sv. Jakuba
Malá Štupartská & Jakubská streets (224 828 816). Metro Náměsti Republiky. **Open** 9.30am-noon, 2-4pm Mon-Sat; 2-3.45pm Sun. **Admission** free. **Map** p89 D3 ⑤

Acoustically speaking, St James is the finest church in the city for organ recitals, the entire structure reverberating magnificently (they are programmed often). With 21 altars, fine frescoes and a dessicated human forearm next to the door, St James stands out. The latter item belonged to a 15th-century jewel thief who tried to steal gems from the statue of the Virgin. The Madonna grabbed him, according to popular accounts, and the limb had to be cut off.

City Bike

Králodvorská 5 (776 180 284/ www.citybike-prague.com). Metro Náměsti Republiky. **Open** 9am-7pm Mon-Fri. **Map** p89 D3 ⑥

Now with new Mongoose Pro mountain bikes on offer, Prague's leading cycle tour company's thrice daily two-hour rides around Old Town are more popular than ever, though the guys at City Bike also run their two-hour rides (helmet and guide included) along the river and citywide. Tours depart at 10.30am, 1.30pm and 4.30pm; call to book.

Clementinum

Klementinum

Mariánské náměstí 4 (221 663 111).
Metro Staroměstská. **Open** *Library*
Jan-Mar 10am-4pm daily. Apr-Oct
10am-8pm daily. Nov, Dec 10am-6pm
daily. **Admission** 190 Kč. **Map**
p88 A4 **⑦**

In the 12th and 13th centuries this
was the Prague headquarters of the
Inquisition. The Jesuits moved in during the 16th century, creating the
Church of St Saviour (Kostel sv.
Salvátora) to reawaken Catholicism
in the Protestant populace. At the centre is the Astronomical Tower, where
Johannes Kepler once stargazed. Czech
students still use the library and the
Chapel of Mirrors is a fabulous Baroque
setting for chamber concerts.

Convent of St Agnes of Bohemia

Klášter sv. Anežky České

U milosrdných 17 (224 810 628/
www.ngprague.cz). Metro Náměstí
Republiky. **Open** 10am-6pm Tue-Sun.
Admission 150 Kč; 200 Kč family.
Map p88 C1 **⑧**

The oldest surviving Gothic building
in Prague, with foundations dating to
1231, houses a collection of Bohemian
and Central European medieval art
from 1200 to 1550. This intimate and
manageable part of the National
Gallery is a fitting home to the 14th-
century Master of Třeboň, who defined
the distorted 'Beautiful Style' that held
sway here till the 16th century. Master
Theodoric's soft style works are treasures, as are his religious sculptures.

Czech Museum of Fine Arts

Husova 19-21 (222 220 218/www.
cmvu.cz). Metro Staroměstská. **Open**
10am-6pm Tue-Sun. **Admission** 50 Kč;
20 Kč reductions. **Map** p88 B4 **⑨**

This mini-museum is home to a vast collection of Czech 20th-century art, which
it's forced to rotate. Fine acquisitions
from the years up to 1968 – including
avant-garde painting from the pre-war
and post-war periods – form a time

capsule. The Soviet invasion froze the
collections until the 1990s, making for
interesting contrasts between current
work and that from older generations.

Galerie Jiří Švestka

Biskupský dvůr 6 (222 311 092/
www.jirisvestka.com). Metro Náměstí
Republiky. **Open** noon-6pm Tue-Fri;
11am-6pm Sat. **Admission** free.
Map p89 F2 **⑩**

Returned emigré Jiří Švestka has been
specialising since 1995 in bold, interna-
tionally recognised Czech artists like
Milena Dopitová and Krištof Kintera
and rising stars like Michal Pechoucek,
plus exhibits of international names
like Leiko Ikemura – all in a spare former photography atelier. There's a
great art bookshop.

Galerie Rudolfinum

Alšovo nábřeží 12 (227 059 309/
www.galerierudolfinum.cz). Metro
Staroměstská. **Open** 10am-6pm Tue-
Sun. **Admission** 100 Kč; 50 Kč
reductions. **Map** p88 A2 **⑪**

Prague's best European kunsthalle
model, this gallery is great for catching
Czech and international contemporary
and modern art, with engaging shows
such as the disturbing photography of
Gregory Crewdson or treatments of
Marilyn Manson by Gottfried
Helnwein. Major shows by middle-gen-
eration local artists like Petr Nikl and
František Skála also trade off with fascinating Chinese art shows, a speciality of the gallery's director. The Rasart
series synergises music, theatre and art.

House of the Black Madonna

Dům U Černé Matky Boží

Ovocný trh 19 (224 211 746). Metro
Náměstí Republiky. **Open** 10am-6pm
Tue-Sun. **Admission** 100 Kč; 150 Kč
family. **Map** p89 D3 **⑫**

This fantastic Cubist building and
gallery strives to present a totally plane-
defying vibe. Worth a visit for the Josef
Gočár-designed building alone, it's about
the finest example of Cubist architecture
in Prague, but with meagre English-language info. Still, one of the most stylish

House at the Golden Ring

cafés in town is attached as is a shop
(Kubista; p112) that recreates pieces
from this seminal design movement.

House at the Golden Ring

Dům U Zlatého prstenu
*Týnská 6 (224 827 022). Metro Náměstí
Republiky.* **Open** 10am-6pm Tue-Sun.
Admission 80 Kč; 160 Kč family.
No credit cards. **Map** p88 C3 ⑬
Reopening in September 2008 after
reconstruction, this beloved, unpredictable former Renaissance manor will
feature a three- to five-year show of Jiří
Příhoda's intriguing architectural art,
plus new statuary and exhibition space.
A broad spectrum of 20th-century Czech
works is shown here, organised intrigu-
ingly by theme rather than by artist or
period, and always well-curated and
fresh. International shows, often exploring digital media, provide balance.

House at the Stone Bell

Dům U Kamenného zvonu
*Staroměstské Náměstí 13 (224 827 526/
www.citygalleryprague.cz). Metro
Staroměstská.* **Open** 10am-6pm Tue-Sun.
Admission varies. **Map** p88 C3 ⑭
Prague City Gallery's Gothic sandstone
building on Old Town Square features
a gorgeous Baroque courtyard and
three floors of exhibition rooms, some
with original vaulting in place. It
favours retrospectives of Czech artists
such as Toyen and Adolf Hoffmeister
and hosts the Zvon biennale of young
Czech and Central European artists.

Jewish Museum

Židovské Muzeum
*U Staré Školy 1 (221 711 511/www.
jewishmuseum.cz). Metro Staroměstská.*
Open *Apr-Oct* 9am-6pm Mon-Fri, Sun.
Nov-Mar 9am-4.30pm Mon-Fri, Sun.
Closed Jewish holidays. **Admission**
300 Kč; 200 Kč reductions; under-6s
free. *Old-New Synagogue* 200 Kč.
No credit cards. **Map** p88 B2 ⑮
The six sites that make up the Jewish
Museum (all listed separately below)
have recently been expanded and
share exhibits with other galleries in
the city. Opening hours are the same
for all of the venues, but vary according to the season, as noted above.
Together they form a bitter tribute to
the third pillar of Czech society that
all but disappeared during the
Holocaust after centuries in Bohemia.
Much of the museum's contents,
now overseen by the thriving Jewish
Community organisation, were seized
from Jews by the Nazis, who had
hoped for a museum dedicated to
an extinct race.

Former Ceremonial Hall

Obřadní síň
*U starého hřbitova 3A, Josefov
(222 317 191).* **Map** p88 B2 ⑯
The Romanesque turrets and arches
of this building at the exit of the cemetery appear as old as the gravestones
but date to just 1906. It hosts fascinating exhibitions on topics like Jewish
customs and traditions focusing on ill-
ness and death.

Klausen Synagogue

Klausova synagoga
*U starého hřbitova 3A, Josefov
(222 310 302).* **Map** p88 B2 ⑰

The great ghetto fire of 1689 destroyed the original Klausen Synagogue along with 318 houses and ten other synagogues. Hastily rebuilt in 1694, its permanent exhibition explores religion in the lives of the ghetto's former inhabitants. It's topped by two tablets of the Decalogue with a golden inscription, visible from the Jewish Cemetery.

Maisel Synagogue
Maiselova synagoga
Maiselova 10, Josefov (224 819 456).
Map p88 B3 ⓭
Mordecai Maisel, mayor of the Jewish ghetto under Rudolf II, was one of the richest men in 16th-century Europe from a lucrative trading monopoly, and paid for the construction of the splendid original synagogue. This burned down in 1689 and then was rebuilt in Baroque style. The building was then rebuilt again in the late 19th century, and now houses exhibitions on the Jewish history of Bohemia and Moravia.

Old Jewish Cemetery
Starý Židovský hřbitov
Široká 3, Josefov (no phone).
Map p88 B2 ⓮
All of Prague's Jews were buried here until the late 1600s, and 12,000 tombstones are crammed into this tiny, tree-shaded patch of ground – a forceful reminder of the cramped ghetto, which remained walled until the late 1700s. Forced to bury the dead on top of one another, an estimated 100,000 bodies lay 12 levels deep. Headstone reliefs indicate the name or occupation of the deceased: scissors, for a tailor, a lion for Rabbi Leow.

Pinkas Synagogue
Pinkasova synagoga
Široká 3, Josefov (222 326 660).
Map p88 B2 ⓴
Founded in 1479, this temple's walls were inscribed in the 1950s with the names of more than 80,000 Czech Holocaust victims. After the Six Day War, the Czechoslovak government blotted them out during 'restoration', but they're all back, a job completed in 1994. Don't miss the exhibition of drawings by children interned in Terezin.

Old Jewish Cemetery

Spanish Synagogue
Španělská synagoga
Vězeňská 1, Josefov (224 819 464).
Map p88 C2 ㉑
Reopened after long neglect in 1998, this temple's domed interior glows with green, red and faux gold leaf, and houses varied and inspired new exhibitions on Jewish history, and a stunning exhibition of synagogue silver. Its predecessor predated the Altneu Synagogue but it was rebuilt in 1868 in the then-fashionable Moorish style.

Kafka statue
NEW *Dušni street. Metro Staroměstská.* **Map** p88 C2 ㉒
Jaroslav Rona's appropriately surreal bronze sculpture of Franz Kafka is, incredibly, the only monument to what most of the world considers Prague's greatest writer. Small plaques have been tacked onto his former residences but it took 80 years after the brooding writer's death for a proper tribute, which indicates how uncomfortable Kafka's literary legacy made the authorities.

Finding Neighbours

Prague's **Jewish Museum** (p94) has more on its plate than just running exhibitions, offering tours and keeping up the five synagogues that make up its collection. Because of its key role in the community that was devastated by the Holocaust, the museum works actively to reawaken people to the part played in Czech society by its Jewish citizens for centuries.

The Education and Cultural Centre of the museum has been running the Lost Neighbours project – a unique education programme for small-town Czech youths – for the past seven years. In towns like Strakonice, in southern Bohemia, the project encourages high-school students to go about their towns like detectives, looking for traces of the Jewish society that was all but wiped out by the Nazis. Although some 80,000 Czech Jews died in the Holocaust, the youths continue to uncover more and more threads as they ask older residents from their towns about what happened.

While the students sometimes encounter hostile reactions from those who would prefer to forget the past, most people are willing to share insights. At a time when neo-Nazi marches have recently been held in both Prague and Pilzen, participants say such outreach is more important than ever.

News of the travelling exhibition relating to the project can be found online at www.zmizeli-sousede.cz/aj.

Kinský Palace

Staroměstské Náměstí 12. (224 810 758/www.ngprague.cz). Metro Staroměstská. **Open** 10am-6pm Tue-Sun. **Admission** 100 Kč; 150 Kč family. **Map** p88 C3 ㉓

The National Gallery's renovated Kinský Palace focuses on calming and redolent Czech landscape painting from the 17th to the 20th centuries, much-influenced by Dutch painters brought in by mad Rudolph II like Roelent Savery and Pieter Stevens. Still lifes and photography from the 19th century to the present – a Czech forte – round out the offerings.

Mucha Museum

Kaunický palác, Panská 7 (221 451 333/www.mucha.cz). Metro Můstek. **Open** 10am-6pm daily. **Admission** 120 Kč. **Map** p89 D4 ㉔

The most famous of all Czech visual artists, Alfons Mucha (1860-1939) created mass-produced decorative panels and posters for Sarah Bernhardt in Paris and did much to spread art nouveau

Kafka statue p95

Municipal House

throughout Europe. His paintings, lithographs, drawings, sketches and notebooks from his Paris days are here, along with photos and an engaging video on his life.

Municipal House

Obecní dům
Náměstí Republiky 5 (222 002 101/ www.obecni-dum.cz). Metro Náměstí Republiky. **Open** 10am-6pm daily. **Admission** 100-150 Kč for exhibitions. **Map** p89 D3 ㉕
This whole building, circa 1910, is a work of art, a shrine to Czech national aspirations, containing murals, mosaics and sculptures by everyone from Mucha to Myslbek. But the exhibition rooms on the top floor of this art nouveau masterpiece are the most accessible – and feature well-curated shows with an emphasis on historically important Central European artists and decorative work.

Municipal Library

Mariánské Náměstí 1 (entrance on Valentinská) (222 310 489/www.city galleryprague.cz). Metro Staroměstská. **Open** 10am-6pm Tue-Sun. **Admission** 120 Kč; 60 Kč reductions. **Map** p88 B3 ㉖

This travertine-covered 1925-28 building is home to a great deal more than books. The second floor halls, run by the Prague City Gallery, showcase large-scale exhibitions of modern art that's had a major impact – as well has much that has not been seen since the cultural chill of the 1970s during the Soviet occupation. Finalists for the Jindřich Chalupecký Award – the most prestigious annual Czech art prize – are also shown here.

Museum of the City of Prague

Muzeum Hlavního města Prahy
Na Poříčí 52 (224 816 773/www. muzeumprahy.cz). **Open** 9am-6pm Tue-Sun. **Admission** 80 Kč; 160 Kč family; under-6s free; 1 Kč first Thur of the month reductions. **Map** p89 F2 ㉗
Antonín Langweil spent 11 years of the early 1800s building an incredibly precise room-sized paper model of Prague. This prize exhibit is the only complete depiction of what the city looked like before the Jewish ghetto was ripped down. Other displays follow the city's development from pre-history through to the 17th century.

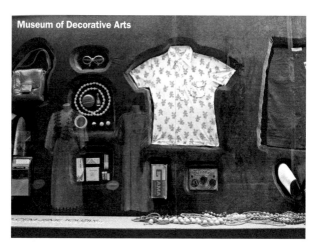

Museum of Decorative Arts

Museum of Communism

*Na Příkopě 10 (224 212 966/www.
muzeumkomunismu.com). Metro
Můstek.* **Open** 9am-9pm daily.
Admission 180 Kč. **Map** p89 D4 ㉙
The first of its kind in the country, the
Museum of Communism puts the communist era in historical perspective
with archive photos, files of hundreds
of relics and exhibits curated by
respected historians. Mock-ups of a
school-room and interrogation room
from the period are eerie indeed, part
of the thematic organisation of communism as dream, reality and nightmare.

Museum of
Decorative Arts

Uměleckoprůmyslové muzeum
*Ulice 17 listopadu 2 (251 093 111/www.
upm.cz). Metro Staroměstská.* **Open**
10am-7pm Tue; 10am-6pm Wed-Sun.
Admission 80-120 Kč. **Map** p88 B2 ㉘
This neo-Renaissance museum, a work
of art in itself, boasts intricately painted plaster mouldings and crystal windows, plus clever exhibits of objects
according to material. Pieces include
exquisite furniture, tapestries, pottery,
clocks, books, a beautifully preserved
collection of clothing and fine displays
of ceramics and glass.

Náprstek Museum

Náprstkovo muzeum
*Betlémské náměstí 1 (224 497 500/
www.aconet.cz/npm). Metro Národní
třída.* **Open** 10am-6pm Tue-Sun.
Admission 80 Kč. **Map** p88 B4 ㉚
The 19th-century nationalist Vojta
Náprstek was fascinated by primitive
cultures and gathered ethnographic
oddities from Czech travellers in this
extension to his house. Native loot
from the Americas, Australasia and the
Pacific Islands are beautifully arranged.

Old-New Synagogue

*Červná 2, Josefov (no phone). Metro
Staroměstská.* **Open** *Apr-Oct* 9.30am-
6pm Mon-Thur, Sun; 9.30am-5pm Fri.
Nov-Mar 9.30am-5pm Mon-Thur, Sun;
9am-2pm Fri. **Admission** 200 Kč;
140 **Kč** reductions; free under-6s.
Map p88 B2 ㉛
Still used for services after 700 years,
this simple, stark brick building is
a fine example of Gothic style, with
interiors that harmonise around the
number 12, after the tribes of Israel –
windows, bunches of grapes and vines
are all in the magic quantity. The tall
seat marked by the gold leaf belonged
to Rabbi Low.

Old Town Hall

Old Town Bridge Tower

Staroměstská mostecká věž
Křížovnické náměstí (224 220 569).
Metro Staroměstká. **Open** *Nov-Feb*
10am-5pm daily. *Mar* 10am-6pm daily.
Apr, Oct 10am-7pm daily. *May-Sept*
10am-10pm daily. **Admission** 60 Kč;
40 Kč reductions. **Map** p88 A4 ⊕
The tower of the 14th-century Gothic
gate to Charles Bridge, with Peter
Parler's frill visible on the east side,
offers a great close-up view of Prague's
domes and spires, the wayward line of
Charles Bridge, the naff Klub Lávka
and the most gigantic addition to
Prague clubbing, Karlovy Lázně, all
below on the river and beyond.

Old Town Hall & Astronomical Clock Tower

Staroměstská radnice
Staroměstské náměstí (724 508 584).
Metro Staroměstská. **Open** *Town Hall*
11am-6pm Mon; 9am-6pm Tue-Sun.
Tower May-Sept 10am-10pm daily.
Oct-Apr 10am-7pm daily. **Admission**
60 Kč. **Map** p88 C3 ⊕
Only half the original Old Town Hall,
built around 1338, remains standing
today. The Nazis blew it up at the
end of World War II but the clock tower
survived and has a viewing platform

definitely worth the climb (see also p91).
Exhibitions such as the World Press
Photo show enliven the town hall itself,
as do tours of its ornate chambers,
which take in the dungeon, former headquarters of the Resistance during the
Prague Uprising in 1945. Enemy supplies and arms were stolen via underground passages. A plaque on the side
of the clock tower thanks the Soviet soldiers who liberated the city afterwards.

Powder Gate

Prašná brána
U Prašné brány (no phone). Metro
Náměstí Republiky. **Open** *Apr-Oct*
10am-6pm daily. **Admission** 50 Kč;
40 Kč under-10s. **Map** p89 D3 ⊕
This 15th-century relic of the fortifica-
tions that used to ring the town moul-
dered until it finally gained a new
purpose, and a name, when it was used
to store gunpowder in 1575. Severely
damaged by the Prussians in 1757, it's
now a neo-Gothic star again.

Eating & drinking

Al Dente

NEW *Věženská 4 (222 313 185/*
www.aldentetrattoria.cz). Metro
Staroměstská. **Open** noon-3.30pm,

PRAGUE BY AREA

6pm-midnight daily. **$$**.
Italian. Map p88 C2 ㉟
Toni Ciullo's colourful, cosy trattoria joins the ranks of three others on this street, which has become Prague's culinary Little Italy. A lovelier spot for tables on the street is scarcely imaginable and the familial staff lay on the love and the carpaccio with equal relish. A nice selection of wines, at fair prices, go along with the perfectly done pastas and aromatic sauces.

Alcohol Bar
Dušní 6 (224 811 744/www.alcohol bar.cz). Metro Staroměstská. **Open** 7pm-3am daily. **Bar**. Map p88 C2 ㊱
A clubby vibe prevails here, with a wall of single malt whiskies, plus rums and tequilas from respected distillers from all over the Caribbean and Mexico. The barmen, endeavouring to pull off a Czech fantasy bar worthy of Manhattan, are true gents, even if it all can feel a bit forced.

Allegro
Veleslavínova 2A (221 427 000/www. fourseasons.com/prague/dining/dining. html). Metro Staroměstská. **Open** *Restaurant* 7am-11pm daily. **$$$$**.
Continental. Map p88 A3 ㊲
Now under new management, the Four Seasons' flagship restaurant, specialising in Tuscan-meets-Czech, hasn't slipped an iota in terms of quality. Piedmont beef sirloin, pan-fried foie gras and truffles or monkfish filled with goat's cheese are still winning over restaurant critics from the ranks of *Zagat*, among others. The terrace looks out on Prague Castle across the Vltava river, a setting more on the level of the cuisine than the conventional, if cosy, restaurant interior. See also box p101.

Amici Miei
Vězeňská 5 (224 816 688/www. amicimiei.cz). Metro Můstek. **Open** 11am-11pm daily. **$$$**. **Italian**.
Map p88 C2 ㊳
Outstanding cuisine in a slightly overlit hall. Veal scallops and simple dishes like tagliatelle with parmesan and

rocket are typical, service is unusually warm and attentive and there's an excellent wine list.

Angel
NEW *V kolkovně 7 (773 222 422/ www.angelrestaurant.cz). Metro Staroměstská.* **Open** 11.30am-midnight Mon-Sat; 11am-4pm Sun. **$$**. **Czech**.
Map p88 C2 ㊴
This fresh new entry into the Old Town dining scene is already a buzz word, thanks to its engaging menu of South-east Asian delights. Javanese slow-cooked lamb shank, prawns in coconut chutney and scallops with laksa and pineapple are all conceived by veteran Prague chef Sofia Smith in a simple, Zen-like space. Book well ahead for the popular – and surprisingly reasonable – brunch menu.

Ariana
Rámová 6 (222 323 438/ariana.dream worx.cz). Metro Náměstí Republiky. **Open** 11am-11pm daily. **$**. **Afghan**.
Map p88 C2 ㊵
A cosy little Afghan eaterie with excellent tender spiced lamb and sumptuous vegetarian chalous. Staff are friendly and straightbacked chairs, rugs and brass lamps make up the decor. Locals, who are getting increasingly adventurous, will be sitting around you.

Bakeshop Praha
Kozí 1 (222 316 823). Metro Staroměstská. **Open** 7am-7pm daily.
Bakery. Map p88 C2 ㊶
San Franciscan Anne Feeley launched this expat mainstay seven years ago and hasn't looked back. Zesty quiches, traditional nut breads, muffins and peanut-butter cookies have every Westerner in town tucking in. Take-away cakes make many a party and great coffees join the arsenal.

Barock
Pařížská 24, Josefov (222 329 221). Metro Staroměstská. **Open** 10am-1am daily. **Café**. Map p88 B2 ㊷
A gleaming zinc bar, floor-to-ceiling windows and a credible sushi platter with suitably aesthetic nigiri are some

Going global

Maze

The commotion has been almost at the same volume as on Gordon Ramsay's cooking shows. Every Czech lifestyle magazine (and there are dozens now, each out to lead the way in luxe living and rake in the presumably attendant advertising revenues) has been lining up for a taste at **Maze** (p107), the new Ramsay venture at Prague's Hilton Old Town.

One magazine, in a transparent bid to be different, pronounced it nothing special, and went on to ridicule the lighting. No one's paid the curmudgeon any mind, though, and tables are now booked a month ahead at the Secession-style room, diffused as it is with indirect, gauzy light and fitted with black-upholstered mini-booths.

One Czech journalist on a recent visit confessed she was amazed to hear her fellow diners speaking mainly Czech. The notion that Maze is for rich foreigners has clearly been put asunder.

But will it be a lasting hit among locals or is it just a flash in the pan? Being seen here is a requirement for anyone claiming to

be a gourmand, as is dinner at the other starring hotel dining room, the Four Seasons' **Allegro** (p100), which recently scored the Czech Republic's first Michelin star.

But will Ramsay pull off another coup in the land where schnitzel and goulash reign supreme? Can a precious starter of poached lobster salad with apple and fennel really cut it in potato soup country? And what will first-time locals make of braised ox tongue?

It's been an axiom of new restaurants in Prague for years that, yes, you can get away with fusion food, and even spicy exotic fare from farflung corners of the globe, as long as you remember to keep garlicky potato pancakes and pork with *zeli*, the Czech version of sauerkraut, somewhere on the menu. Places like Maze and Allegro, however, seem to be betting that those days are over and that Prague has now entered into the international cuisine realm wholeheartedly. Only time will tell, but the indications are promising. And the proof's in the sticky toffee pudding with rum custard.

PRAGUE BY AREA

of the highlights at Barock. The reasonably priced breakfast menu and powerhouse lattes are further draws. Posing actively encouraged.

Bellevue
Smetanovo nábřeží 18 (222 221 443/ www.pfd.cz). Metro Národní třída. **Open** noon-3pm, 5.30-11pm daily. **$$$$**. **Fine dining**. **Map** p88 A5 ㊸
Thought of as the city's finest haute cuisine source in the mid 1990s, this elegant little room with a fine view of the Castle has since been outgunned but puts up an able effort nevertheless. Despite occasional service issues, staff lay on a fine veal loin in black truffle sauce, New Zealand lamb and Czech venison in juniper sauce. The menu's fairly constant year in, year out, but the mastery shows. Bellevue's Sunday brunch is another institution. The space is formal and traditional. Booking is essential.

La Bodeguita del Medio
NEW *Kaprova 5 (224 813 922/www. labdelm.cz). Metro Staroměstská.* **Open** 11am-2am daily. **Bar**. **Map** p88 B3 ㊹
Pretty much permanently packed with revellers since its opening in Prague in 2002, the Czech branch of the 60-year-old Havana institution that claims credit for inventing the mojito (and hooking Hemingway on it) is a jumping joint. Live salsa bands, Cuban and creole seafood and oceans of good rum.

Bohemia Bagel
Masná 2 (224 812 603/www.bohemia bagel.cz). Metro Staroměstská. **Open** 7am-midnight Mon-Fri; 8am-midnight Sat, Sun. **Café**. **Map** p88 C2 ㊺
One of the republic's first true bagel cafés has expanded its offerings to go well beyond the free coffee refills, fresh muffins, breakfast bagels and bagel sandwiches. Grill foods, soups, breakfast fry-ups, burgers and made-to-order salads now go along with the Jewish wonder bread. For purists, there are still poppyseed, cinnamon raison, tomato basil and chocolate chip bagels. There's also internet access and a play corner for the kiddies. What's not to like?

Brasiliero
U Radnice 8 (224 234 474/www. ambi.cz). Metro Staroměstská. **Open** 11am-midnight daily. **$$**. **Steakhouse**. **Map** p88 B3 ㊻
The local Ambiente group's a hit in the city, thanks to branches like Brasiliero, which specialises in hearty Brazilian butchery, with enough chops and fillets to stop any healthy heart. The inevitable sushi bar has been added of late, part of a citywide craze.

Le Café Colonial
Široká 6, Josefov (224 818 322/ www.lecafecolonial.cz). Metro Staroměstská. **Open** 10am-midnight daily. **$$**. **French**. **Map** p89 B3 ㊼
Airy, with teak accents, miniature quiches, delicate pork and delightful salads. More formal dining is found on the other side where there's a veranda and designer furniture in Matisse-inspired tones. Resolutely French.

Café Imperial
NEW *Na Poříčí 15 (246 011 600/ www.hotel-imperial.cz). Metro Náměstí Republiky.* **Open** 7am-11pm daily. **Café**. **Map** p89 F2 ㊽
A lot like stepping into a Stanley Kubrick film, this incredibly ornate art nouveau shrine, with walls and ceiling covered with sculpted porcelain, has been restored to the opulence it had when it opened in 1914. Now attached to the nearly as posh Hotel Imperial, this old-world dining room offers elegant renditions of trad schnitzels and rump steak but seems more suited to lighter fare, conversation and crisp white wine.

Café Indigo
Platnéřská 11 (no phone). Metro Staroměstská. **Open** 9am-midnight Mon-Fri; 11am-midnight Sat, Sun. **Café**. **Map** p88 A3 ㊾
A post-industrial, comfortable art café with a menu limited to light snacks and sweets but with cheap wine for students from nearby Charles University and an upbeat and easygoing vibe. There's a small children's corner in the back.

La Bodeguita del Medio

Café Montmartre

Řetězová 7 (222 221 244). Metro Staroměstská. **Open** 9am-11pm Mon-Fri; noon-11pm Sat, Sun. **Café**.
Map p88 B4

Czech literati like Gustav Meyrink and Franz Werfel all enjoyed tipples here before it became a Jazz Age hotspot. Creative miscreants still gather around the threadbare sofas and battered tables for late-night talk.

La Casa Blů

Kozí 15 (224 818 270/www.lacasablu. cz). Metro Staroměstská. **Open** 9am-11pm Mon-Fri; 11am-11pm Sat; 2-11pm Sun. **$**. **Mexican**. Map p88 C2 ⑤

Friendly, highly informal and well worn in, this Latino-owned bar and eatery features rugs draped over hardback chairs, street signs and tequila specials with an authentic Mexican menu. Try the buzzer even if the door is locked – people routinely wheedle their way in past closing time.

Celnice

V Celnici 4 (224 212 240/www.celnice. com). Metro Náměstí Republiky. **Open** 11am-midnight Mon-Thur, Sun; 11am-1.30am Fri, Sat. **$$$**. **Czech**.
Map p89 E3 ⑤

One of several Pilsner-licensed restaurants to be found in the city, Celnice is a mix of classic Czech, with updated fare like *kyselo*, or sauerkraut soup, pickled Prague ham and pastas and a sleek, modern sushi bar with DJ dance fare emanating from the basement on weekend nights.

Chateau

Jakubská 2 (222 316 328/www. chateaurouge.cz). Metro Náměstí Republiky. **Open** 4pm-4am daily.
Bar. Map p89 D3 ⑤

With some 13 years on the scene, this dim, packed and rollicking bar is still appealingly risqué and a major pick-up zone, helped perhaps by the suspiciously sweet smell of the smoke inside. New energy has gone into booking, with live acts like the Mobydicks and the Rocket Dogs and wacky contests sponsored by the *Reflex* magazine Cannabis Cup filling out the programme. Note that the name and hours change regularly.

PRAGUE BY AREA

Chateau p103

Čili

Kožná 8 (777 945 848). Metro Můstek.
Open 11am-midnight daily. **Bar.**
Map p88 C4 54

A decisive hit on the competitive Prague bar scene, probably for its hidden location on a narrow backstreet off Old Town Square and its outsize mojitos, G&Ts and comfortably broken in, living-room vibe. The overstuffed leather armchairs are the prize real estate.

Country Life

Melantrichova 15 (224 213 366).
Metro Národní třída. **Open** 9am-7pm Mon-Thur; 8.30am-5pm Fri; 11am-6pm Sun. **$. Vegetarian.**
Map p88 C4 55

A Czech neo-hippie fave cafeteria with dirt-cheap vegetarian dishes that are made with organically grown ingredients. Country Life specialises in massive DIY salads, fresh carrot juice, delectable lentil soup and crunchy wholegrain breads, but it's best to avoid the lunchtime crush.

Credo

Petrská 11 (222 324 634/www.
credo-restaurace.cz). Metro Náměstí
Republiky. **Open** 10.30am-midnight
Mon-Sat. **Café. Map** p89 F2 56

Small, informal and a bit off the beaten path, Credo makes for a surprisingly good lunch option, and is just two blocks east of Old Town. Well chosen California and Chilean wine go with gorgonzola-stuffed baked fig and rocket starters, caper and walnut salad and main courses such as creamy risotto or fillet of sole with Spanish rice.

Dahab

Dlouhá 33 (224 827 375/www.dahab.
cz). Metro Náměstí Republiky. **Open**
noon-1am daily. **$. Middle Eastern.**
Map p89 D2 57

Much like a Hollywood movie set of a harem worthy of Valentino, this calming spot is a definitive, candlelit Prague tearoom, with cushion seating, pistachio cookies, couscous, Turkish coffees and occasional belly dancing. Grilled food is available in the far less groovy Dlouhá street end.

DeBrug

Masná 5 (724 122 994). Metro
Náměstí Republiky. **Open** 11am-1am
daily. **$$. Belgian. Map** p88 C2 59

The Prague passion for Belgian mussels, frites and beer continues to blossom. First it was Stella Artois in Czech beer heaven (once unimaginable); now the Belgian bistro trend is spreading throughout the city. This elegant bar/restaurant, with fleet-footed service, illustrates why.

La Degustation

Haštalská 18 (222 311 234/www.la degustation.cz). **Open** 5pm-midnight Mon-Sat. **$$$$**. **Fine dining**. Map p89 D3 ⑤⑨

The seven courses, alternating with seven to ten amuse bouche (is there not a limit to how amused a mouth can be at one time?) will take up most of an afternoon or evening, offering the 'flavours and tastes of molecular cuisine' – or so promises the Mount Everest of Prague haute cuisine. That it generally pulls this off is no mean feat – and probably makes the pretense forgivable. Choose from three fixed-price meals – Bohemian Bourgeoise, Earth and Sea, or Traditional Bohemian – featuring Wagju beef, organic Argentine ribs, sweetbreads, tongue, truffles and Valrhona Jivara chocolate.

Dinitz

Na Poříčí 12 (222 314 071/www.dinitz. cz). **Open** 8am-3am Mon-Fri; 9am-3am Sat, Sun. **Café**. Map p89 E3 ⑥⓪

This stylish retro café in the former YMCA Palace (no joke) is surprisingly well appointed, with soaring ceilings and menus to match the classy old-school decor. It draws a mixed crowd of arty types and the well-to-do, with light savoury delights plus a short list of well-shaken cocktails, and jazz and blues acts in the corner.

Duende

Karoliny Světlé 30 (775 186 077/ www.barduende.cz). Metro Národní třída. **Open** 1pm-midnight Mon-Fri; 3pm-midnight Sat; 4pm-midnight Sun. **Café**. Map p88 A4 ⑥①

One of the smokiest bars in a city with a very lightly enforced smoking ban, but nevertheless a soulful, hearty hangout for interesting miscreants. New Bohemian in a nutshell, with fringed lampshades, boozy regulars and low-budget Prague intellectuals

from the publishing and film scenes. Stay late and try the potato soup.

Ebel Coffee House

Týn 2 (224 895 788/www.ebelcoffee.cz). Metro Náměstí Republiky. **Open** 9am-10pm daily. **Café**. Map p88 C3 ⑥②

One of the original purveyors of serious coffees (more than 30 prime arabica varieties), courtesy of journalist and designer Malgorzata Ebel, plus passable quiches, bagels and brownies, served in a lovely, if touristy, cobbled courtyard.

Franz Kafka Café

Široká 12, Josefov (222 318 945). Metro Staroměstská. **Open** 10am-8pm daily. **Café**. Map p88 B2 ⑥③

This dark-wood, old-world coffeehouse features intimate booths, old engravings of the Jewish Quarter and, naturally, lots of Kafka portraits. Tables on the street are convenient when touring Josefov.

Francouzská Restaurace

NEW *Náměstí Republiky 5 (222 002 770/www.francouzskarestaurace.cz). Metro Náměstí Republiky.* **Open** 11am-11pm daily. **$$**. **Continental**. Map p89 E3 ⑥④

With the city's finest art nouveau pile as a backdrop, this absurdly ornate dining room, recently featured in Jiri Menzel's feature *I Served the King of England*, also happens to be a consistent award-winner for cuisine. Try a classic roast duck or let the chefs go wild with a prawn saffron risotto. There's a lovely Sunday jazz brunch too.

Himalaya

Soukenická 2 (233 353 594/www. himilayarestaurant.cz). Metro Náměstí Republiky. **Open** 11am-11pm Mon-Fri; noon-11pm Sat, Sun. **$**. **Indian**. Map p89 D2/E2 ⑥⑤

Easily the most affordable and credible Indian option for a relaxed dinner in the Old Town area, this cosy little split-level spot is good for the soul of many an expat who feels starved of spice. Samosas, vindaloo, rogan and korma feature on the well-thumbed menu.

PRAGUE BY AREA

Kabul

Karoliny Světle 14 (224 235 452/ www.aa.cz/kabulrestaurant). Metro Národní třída. **Open** 10am-11pm daily. **$. Afghan. Map** p88 A5 🟡

Hasib Saleh's cosy little eaterie, done up in Persian rugs and hanging lanterns, is a local fave, serving up fine specialities like ashak pastry pockets and bamya okra fingers, all with fresh flatbreads.

Kavárna Obecní dům

Náměstí Republiky 5 (222 002 763/ www.vysehrad2000.cz). Metro Náměstí Republiky. **Open** 7.30am-11pm daily. **Café. Map** p89 D3 🟡

This gorgeous humming space, with a grand piano tinkling away, is the Vienna-style coffeehouse component to the multifaceted, magnificently restored Municipal House. Replete with secessionist brass chandeliers, balconies and always a few grand dames (and more than a few tourists), there's no more memorable venue for an espresso.

Klub Architektů

Betlémské náměstí 5A (224 401 214/ www.klubarchitektu.com). Metro Národní třída. **Open** 11.30am-midnight daily. **$. Continental. Map** p88 B4 🟡

This dim designer cellar of an architecture and design gallery is great value with credible, creative Euro cuisine and a fine, quiet summer patio next door to the Bethlehem Chapel. The place is often booked by groups, so make your reservation early.

Kogo Pizzeria & Caffeteria

Havelská 27 (224 214 543/www. kogo.cz). Metro Můstek. **Open** 8am-11pm Mon-Fri; 9am-11pm Sat, Sun. **$$. Italian. Map** p88 C4 🟡

Scampi, bruschetta, bean soup and focaccia done quickly, stylishly and surprisingly affordably, all served up on white linen tables by foxy waitresses, while avoiding stuffiness. Nicely topped pizzas and tiramisu are further draws.

Kolkovna

V kolkovně 8 (224 819 701/www. kolkovna.cz). Metro Staroměstská. **Open** 11am-midnight daily. **$. Czech. Map** p88 C2 🟡

Business is so brisk here that it can feel like the customers are cattle, but the staff does its best to hustle and keep up. Crowds of post-1989 generation locals pack the pretty re-creation of old Prague, which is licensed by the brewery Pilsner Urquell. The art nouveau interior and trad pub grub like potato pancakes and beer-basted goulash attract bright and beautiful patrons.

Kozička

Kozí 1 (224 818 308/www.kozicka.cz). Metro Náměstí Republiky. **Open** noon-4am Mon-Fri; 6pm-4am Sat; 6pm-3am Sun. **Bar. Map** p88 C2 🟡

A popular, unpretentious local scene can be found in the subterranean labyrinth found down the stairs from the street. The place has homely nooks and crannies throughout, mighty steaks are served until 11pm and Krušovice is available on tap. Service isn't always spotless.

KU Bar Café

Rytířská 13 (221 181 081/www. kubar.cz). Metro Můstek. **Open** 5pm-3am Mon-Fri; 5pm-4am Sat, Sun. **Bar. Map** p88 C4 🟡

Natalie Portman shook it up here all night in 2006, but anyone more interested in good DJ tracks, drink-mixing and atmosphere will find this place heavy on pretense, if possibly fun for one (pricey) shot.

Lehká Hlava

Boršov 2 (222 220 665/www.lehka hlava.cz). Metro Můstek. **Open** 11.30am-11.30pm Mon-Fri; noon-11.30pm Sat, Sun. **$$. Vegetarian. Map** p88 A4 🟡

Now with brunch offerings, this appealingly spaced out holistic eaterie offers affordable meals in a setting that could be a modern art gallery. In fact, it's a soothing New Age veggie venue with a good track record (and you can buy the art on the walls). New brunch offerings beef up the other options: wholewheat ragoût, goat's cheese dishes and an amazing range of teas and juices. The entrance is in the courtyard.

Mama Lucy

Dlouhá 1 (222 327 207). Metro Staroměstská. **Open** 11am-midnight daily. **$$. Mexican. Map** p88 C2 ⑦⓸

There's never much of a wait here and it's handily located, just a block off Old Town Square. But this definitive Czech-Mex establishment does fajitas, burritos, enchiladas and quesadillas that are passable, if hardly inspired. All served with a smile but at rates that reflect its location.

Marquis de Sade

Templová 8 (no phone). Metro Náměstí Republiky. **Open** 4pm-3am daily. **Bar. Map** p89 D3 ⑦⑤

JB Shoemaker – the legendary former owner – has now gone, but little else has changed at this infamous expat drinking hole (except for the beer prices), where bad behaviour is ever-encouraged and way too much absinthe is sampled nightly.

Maze

NEW *V Celnici 7 (221 822 100/ www.gordonramsay.com/mazeprague). Metro Náměstí Republiky.* **Open** 11am-11pm daily. **$$. Fusion. Map** p89 E3 ⑦⑥

The city's first beachhead by the annointed Gordon Ramsay has lived up to its fanfare just fine thus far. It offers stunning little degustations of lamb loin and garlic purée or glazed pork belly with tempura of black pudding, served up in a newly made-over Secessionist dining room conceived by David Collines in black, white and cream; and yet, a casual atmosphere prevails. Enjoy the same delights you'd find at the original London Maze but at surprisingly reasonable Prague prices with inspired lunch tasting menus. See also box p101.

Metamorphis

Malá Štupartská 5 (221 771 068/ www.metamorphis.cz). Metro Náměstí Republiky. **Open** 9am-1am daily. **$$. Pasta. Map** p88 C3 ⑦⑦

Sedate and capable, this family-run pasta-café and pension has just one disadvantage: it's directly on a main tourist route to Old Town Square, and is thus often crowded. The cellar restaurant within is enhanced by live jazz at night.

Monarch

Na Perštýně 15 (224 239 602/www. monarch.cz). Metro Národní třída. **Open** noon-midnight Mon-Sat. **Wine bar. Map** p88 B4 ⑦⑧

A great wine shop and bar with more than 25 varieties of cheese and a good selection of regional sausages. The place for South American or California imports, plus the best local vintages.

Orange Moon

Rámová 5 (222 325 119/www. orangemoon.cz). Metro Náměstí Republiky. **Open** 11.30am-11.30pm daily. **$. South-east Asian/ Indian. Map** p88 C2 ⑦⑨

Thai, Burmese and Indian food served in a warm, unpretentious, well-lit cellar space. Eager servers bring over the curries and Czech beer, a divine combination as it turns out. The entrance is easy to miss, so just follow the voices of customers regaling.

Papas

Betlemské náměstí 8 (222 222 229/ www.papasbar.cz). Metro Vltavská. **Open** 11am-midnight daily. **Café. Map** p88 B4 ⑧⓪

A lively cocktail specialist with deep maroon red interiors, Papas is no shrinking violet, and a fave of expat students and 'Czuppies' alike. Caipirinha's are mixed with gusto by the energetic staff and the bar food is colourful and varied enough to do well for lunch.

Perpetuum

Lodecká 4 (224 810 401/www. cervenatabulka.cz). Metro Náměstí Republiky. **Open** 11.30am-11pm daily. **$$. Continental. Map** p89 F1 ⑧①

Cosy, if a challenge to find, with off-beat playschool decor and poultry comfort food on offer, as well as the likes of lava-grilled lamb, baked duck-leg with bacon dumplings, apple and sauerkraut, cheerily served up alongside rabbit skewer with cream and lime sauce.

Papas p107

Pivnice u Pivrnce

*Maiselova 3, Josefov (222 329 404).
Metro Náměstí Republiky.* **Open**
11am-midnight daily. **S. Czech**.
Map p88 B3 ③②

Easily spotted by the blissfully tasteless
cartoons by one of the regulars, Pivnice
u Pivrnce offers old-fashioned Czech
cooking and above-average presenta-
tion. Svíčková (beef in lemon cream
sauce) and duck with sauerkraut are
key features on the menu. The Radegast
beer is well tapped and nicely priced.

Pravda

*Pařížská 17, Josefov (222 326 203/
www.pravdarestaurant.cz). Metro
Staroměstská.* **Open** noon-midnight
daily. **$$$. World**. **Map** p88 B2 ③③

Owner Tommy Sjoo, who helped
bring fine dining to post-1989 Prague,
runs this airy, elegant spot. Chicken
in Senegal peanut sauce vies against
Vietnamese nem spring rolls and
borscht, all done credibly. Service is
cool and graceful.

La Provence

*Štupartská 9 (296 826 155/ reservations
800 152 672/www.kampagroup.com).*

Metro Náměstí Republiky. **Open**
noon-11pm daily. **$$$. French**.
Map p89 D3 ③④

Run capably by Nils Jebens, the Czech
Republic's answer to Terence Conran,
this French eaterie does fine foie gras,
tiger prawns, roast duck and monkfish
in a setting that's rustic, classy and comfortable – something most unusual for
a location close to Old Town Square.

Red Hot & Blues

*Jakubská 12 (222 323 364). Metro
Náměstí Republiky.* **Open** 9am-11pm
daily. **S. Mexican**. **Map** p89 D3 ③⑤

An early expat institution, this genial
spot still features a regular blues play-
er on a stool, along with fresh house
salsa for the Mexican food, Cajun
chicken recipes and American-style
brunch served on a patio that's conveniently heated for winter.

Sarah Bernhardt

NEW *U Obecního domu 1 (222 195
195). Metro Náměstí Republiky.* **Open**
7am-11pm daily. **$$$. Continental**.
Map p89 D3 ③⑥

The favourite model for Alfons Mucha
has lent more than her name to this

fabulously gilded lobby restaurant of the Hotel Pařiž. The award-winning chef has revived the place of late, and a series of tasting menus overseen by celeb guest chefs, as well as a vinotheque, complete with takeout foie gras, have built up further buzz. Worth a splashout even if staying at the storied hotel is not within the budget.

La Scene
U Milosrdnych 6 (222 312 677). Metro Staroměstská. **Open** noon-midnight Mon-Fri; 6pm-midnight Sat. **Wine bar**. Map p88 B2/C2 ⑥⑦
A quiet, sleek lounge wine bar with pan-fried foie gras and rhubarb purée and some of the best lamb in town, served with gingerbread crust. The modern interior complements the 13th-century convent and hall of the National Gallery.

Siam-I-San
Valentinská 11 (224 814 099). Metro Staroměstská. **Open** 10am-midnight daily. **Thai/Japanese**. Map p88 B3 ⑧⑧
An improbable mix of designer glass shop and fashionable Thai food restaurant, Siam-I-San has attracted the local glitterati for years. It also still offers an impressive selection of fiery South-east Asian appetisers, which attract well-heeled expats.

Siam Orchid
Na Poříčí 21 (222 319 410/www.siamorchid.cz). Metro Náměstí Republiky. **Open** 10am-10pm daily. **$$**. **Thai**. Map p89 F2 ⑥⑨
This easy-to-miss family joint up some stairs leading off of a shopping passage has the most authentic, unpretentious Thai in town: chicken satay and delish mains of fried tofu with mung beans, plus fiery chicken and cod curries, are some of the highlights. To quell your thirst, there's Thai beer.

Slavia
Smetanovo nábřeží 2 (224 218 493/www.cafeslavia.cz). Metro Národní třída. **Open** 8am-11pm daily. **Café**. Map p88 A5 ⑨⓪

The mother of all Prague cafés, where Karel Tiege and a struggling Václav Havel once tippled and plotted the overthrow of communism, the Slavia would hardly be recognised by its former customers today. Still, it has stunning Castle views and a decent salmon toast – plus the misfortune of being favoured by some very accomplished pickpockets.

Století
Karoliny Světlé 21 (222 220 008/www.stoleti.cz). Metro Národní třída. **Open** noon-midnight daily. **$**. **Continental**. Map p88 A5 ⑨①
A longtime local secret and a surprisingly affordable option for its location, this veteran offers imaginative fare. Blue cheese, pear and almond salad named after Valentino, or a spinach soufflé or tender steak go with the old world decor and swift service.

SushiPoint
Na Příkopě 19 (608 643 923/www.sushipoint.cz). Metro Můstek. **Open** 11am-11pm daily. **Japanese**. Map p89 D4 ⑨②
Part of the major Prague sushi wave that it helped start, SushiPoint is still the favoured place to be seen tossing back raw tuna and pickled ginger. It's also the spot to spy the new generation of young Czech consumers fresh from the nearby shopping malls.

Le Terroir
Vejvodova 1 (602 889 118). Metro Můstek. **Open** 11am-11pm daily. **Wine bar**. Map p88 B4 ⑨③
A place ideally suited to riding the new Czech wave of wine appreciation. There are just a few warm starters on the menu, but it does feature a killer foie gras terrine. It's all served in an ancient cellar space that's grand for sipping when the sun goes down.

Tretter's
V kolkovně 3 (224 811 165/www.tretters.cz). Metro Staroměstská. **Open** 7pm-3am Mon-Sat; 11am-2am Sun. **Bar**. Map p88 C2 ⑨④
The beautiful, competent staff and incredible selection of cocktails are

Mike Tretter's points of pride, and there's often a singer or someone else lounging on top of the bar. The drinks creations are inspired and the bar staff win regional mixology awards yearly.

U Govindy Vegetarian Club
Soukenická 27 (224 816 631). *Metro Náměstí Republiky.* **Open** 11am-5pm Mon-Fri. **$**. **Vegetarian**. **Map** p89 E2 **95**
Cheap but not so cheerful, this Krishna restaurant offers a basic self-service vegetarian Indian meal for a mere 85 Kč. Still, it's a clean spot for sharing a table while seated on floor cushions (there are real tables and chairs too).

U medvídků
Na Perštýně 7 (224 211 916/www. umedvidku.cz). *Metro Národní třída.* **Open** 11.30am-11pm daily. **$$**. **Czech**. **Map** p88 B5 **96**
Five centuries of cred as a beerhall makes the 'Little Bears' a mecca for Budvar drinkers. Now new micro-brews have been added to the mix, expanding the options. Elevated pub grub includes the likes of pork in plum sauce and fillets in dark beer reduction.

U modré kachničky
Michalská 16 (224 213 418/ www.umodrekachnicky.cz). *Metro Staroměstská.* **Open** 11.30am-11.30pm daily. **$$**. **Czech**. **Map** p88 C4 **97**
One of the most successful little dining rooms to appear in Prague since the Velvet Revolution. U modré kachničky is located in a granny's house setting on a narrow side street, and serves slightly modernised classics, such as roast duck with pears and boar steak with mushrooms.

U Provaznice
Provaznická 3, Nové Město (224 232 528). *Metro Můstek.* **Open** 11am-midnight daily. **Pub**. **Map** p88 C4 **98**
Incredibly enough, this classic pub, with all the Bohemian trad fare (duck, smoked meat and dumplings) is friendly, buzzy, reasonably priced and within spitting distance from the Můstek metro and tourist throngs.

U Rozvařilů
Na Poříčí 26 (224 219 357). *Metro Náměstí Republiky.* **Open** 11am-11pm Mon-Fri; 11am-8pm Sat, Sun. **$**. **Czech**. **Map** p89 F2 **99**
A chrome-covered, mirrored version of that old pre-revolutionary classic, the workers' cafeteria. Servers in worn white aprons, harassed-looking customers in white socks and sandals and soups, guláš, dumplings and chlebíčky (open-faced mayonnaise and meat sandwiches) are all features.

U Sádlů
Klimentská 2 (224 813 874/www. usadlu.cz). *Metro Náměstí Republiky/ tram 5, 14, 26.* **Open** 11am-1am Mon-Sat; noon-midnight Sun. **$**. **Czech**. **Map** p89 D2 **100**
OK, it's medieval kitsch – but efficient, tasty, fun and affordable medieval kitsch. Enjoy a mead accompanied with pepper steak or boar. Nice armour is on display in the bar area.

U Vejvodů
Jilská 4 (224 219 999/www.restaurace uvejvodu.cz). *Metro Můstek.* **Open** 10am-4am Mon-Sat; 11am-3am Sun. **$$**. **Czech**. **Map** p88 B4 **101**
Popular with German tour bus loads, but still an iconic, vast beerhall with quick service and old-style wood interiors, accented by the obligatory huge copper beer vat lids.

U Zlatého tygra
Husova 17 (222 221 111/www. uzlatehotygra.cz). *Metro Staroměstská.* **Open** 11am-11pm daily. **Pub**. **Map** p88 B4 **102**
The former haunt of beloved Czech novelist Bohumil Hrabal, who died in 1997, is still filled with his cranky contemporaries but it does serve some of the finest Pilsner Urquell in Old Town if you're willing to suffer their stares.

La Veranda
Elišky Krásnohorské 2 (224 814 733/www.laveranda.cz). *Metro Staroměstská/tram 17, 18.* **Open** noon-midnight Mon-Sat; noon-10pm Sun. **$$$**. **Fusion**. **Map** p88 B2/B3 **103**

Considered the pinnacle by local foodies and critics, this *très moderne* gustatory sanctuary for the newly rich lays on garlic foam fish ragoût soup alongside classic Czech dishes such as roast duck with thyme. It's hardly subtle and all a bit OTT, but is a pampering experience all the same.

Shopping

Alma Mahler

NEW *Valentinská 1 (222 325 865/www.almamahler.cz). Metro Staroměstská.* **Open** 10am-7pm Mon-Fri. **Map** p88 B3 **104**

Whether it's pre-war jewellery, gorgeous old table lamps or antique toys, this treasure trove of junk is varied, characterful and wallet friendly. The kindly staff of this family-run business, established shortly after the Velvet Revolution, are, alas, not for sale. Comfortably musty.

Antik v Dlouhé

Dlouhá 37 (224 826 347). Metro Staroměstská. **Open** 10am-7pm Mon-Fri; noon-6pm Sat, Sun. **Map** p89 D2 **105**

A gold mine of Bohemian goodies from yesteryear, ranging from handmade toys to lovely art deco table lamps. Tin advertising signs and lovely pins, brooches and rings, some quite affordable and all thoroughly unique, are stocked. The friendly staff speak English too.

Art Deco

Michalská 21 (224 223 076). Metro Staroměstská or Národní třída. **Open** 2-7pm Mon-Fri. **Map** p88 B4 **106**

The place to begin a campaign to return to the age of style, when men wore hats. Vintage clothing and lots of jewellery are stocked, as well as an eclectic mix of other random goodies. Prices are retro as well.

Artěl

NEW *Celetná 29 (entrance on Rybná) (224 815 085/www.artelglass.com). Metro Náměsti Republiky.* **Open** 10am-8pm daily. **Map** p89 D3 **107**

Alma Mahler

Something different in the classic art of Czech crystal – that's been designer Karen Feldman's conception since opening this speciality business in the 1990s, now with a downtown retail location. A variety of designs are etched into glassware by local artisans, which have proven to be hot sellers.

Big Ben Bookshop

Malá Štupartská 5 (224 826 565/ www.bigbenbookshop.com). Metro Náměsti Republiky. **Open** 9am-6.30pm Mon-Fri; 10am-5pm Sat; noon-5pm Sun. **Map** p89 D3 **108**

The best collection of books on Prague and Bohemia in English (and those by their native sons and daughters), Big Ben also has an excellent children's section and tons of English-language newspapers and magazines. Its friendly staff know their stock. Fiction, non-fiction, bestsellers and old faves.

Boheme

NEW *Dušní 8 (224 813 840/ www.boheme.cz). Metro Náměsti Republiky.* **Open** 11am-7pm Mon-Fri; 11am-5pm Sat. **Map** p88 C2 **109**

PRAGUE BY AREA

Jan and Hana Stocklassa founded the label behind this shop back in 1991 and the latter's designs for comfortable, wearable but distinctive knits and leather work have been a hit ever since. With an understated sense of style that welcomes not just young things, and which is not afraid to embrace monochrome classic tones, it's not hard to see why.

Bric a Brac
Týnská 7 (222 326 484). Metro Staroměstská or Náměstí Republiky. **Open** 11am-7pm daily. **Map** p89 D3 **110**
This shop is tiny, but so crammed full of treasures that you could lose yourself, or at least an hour. Street signs, jewellery and old cameras are only a few of the finds.

La Casa del Habano
Dlouhá 35 (222 312 305/www.lacasa delhabano.cz). Metro Staroměstská. **Open** 9am-9pm daily. **Map** p89 D2 **111**
A franchise of the Cancun-based chain of luxe cigar emporiums-cum-bars, this darkwood, clubby room is bound to attract the Czech nouveaux riches with its 40-year-old single malts, humidors and impressive selection of Cuban stogies.

Dr Stuart's Botanicus
Týnský Dvůr 3 (224 895 446/ www.botanicus.cz). Metro Náměstí Republiky. **Open** 10am-6.30pm daily. **Map** p88 C3 **112**
A grand option for an unusual locally made gift, Botanicus stocks handmade soaps, lotions and bathing salts and gels, plus herbal oils, teas, honey and other food stuffs. All products are 100% Czech, made with ingredients grown outside of Prague.

Kubista
Dům u Černý Matky Boží, Celetná 34 (224 236 378/www.kubista.cz). Metro Náměsti Republiky. **Open** 10am-6pm Tue-Sun. **Map** p89 D3 **113**
Fans of Cubism, or anyone looking for something original, may be seduced by unique porcelain, lovingly wrought

recreations and art books from this shop of the excellent museum at the House of the Black Madonna.

Manufaktura
Karlova 26 (221 110 079). Metro Staroměstská. **Open** 10am-6pm daily. **Map** p88 B4 **114**
A treasure trove of Czech-made goods, especially blue print items – items made by a fabric dyeing technique used in Bohemia in the late 18th century. The placemats, tablecloths and handkerchiefs make great gifts.

Modes Robes
Benediktská 5 (224 826 016/ www.cabbage.cz/modes-robes). Metro Náměsti Republiky. **Open** 10am-7pm Mon-Fri. **Map** p89 D2 **115**
Czech fashions, all designed by local artists, in a decade-old collective that creates clothing, accessories and art with a wide range of dresses for every body and every age.

Pavla & Olga
Karoliny Světle 30 (no phone). Metro Národní třída. **Open** 10am-7pm daily. **Map** p88 A4 **116**
This boutique, run by two hip Czech sisters, is made up of just one small room, yet it manages to get itself featured in all the glossy magazines with its creations for local celebrities. These incorporate fresh, sophisticated designs and quality materials – alas, nothing for guys, though.

Pohodlí
Benediktská 7 (224 827 026/ www.etno.cz). Metro Náměsti Republiky. **Open** 11am-7pm Mon-Fri; 10am-4pm Sat. **Map** p89 D2 **117**
'We are the world, and we have the music from all corners to prove it' seems to be the motto here. Indian and African music is stocked, plus some local Czech and Moravian folk and world as well.

Slovanský Dům
Na Příkopě 22, (221 451 100/ www.slovanskydum.cz). Metro Můstek. **Open** 10am-8pm daily. **Map** p89 D3 **118**

Prague's slickest downtown mall is to be found on Na Příkopě, and contains the city's most popular multiplex cinema, a decent Italian café, plus a nice sushi restaurant. Jewellery and fashion shops fills out the rest. And once you're all shopped out, revive your weary muscles with a Thai massage.

Tatiana

Dušní 1 (224 813 723/www.tatiana. cz). Metro Staroměstská. **Open** 10am-7pm Mon-Fri; 11am-4pm Sat. **Map** p88 C3 ⓫⓳

Very wearable, if not exactly affordable, designer fashion that mixes elegance and practicality. Clothes are perfectly cut and beautifully styled, with small details that make each piece striking yet functional. And prices aren't as sky-high as you might expect.

Toalette

Karoliny Světlé 9 (777 128 729). Metro Národní třída. **Open** 10am-7pm Mon-Fri. **Map** p88 A5 ⓫⓴

Monika Burdová's secondhand-clothes-shop-cum-boutique is a great find on one of Old Town's most appealing little lanes. Quirky streetwear meets affordable fashion by local artists.

Trafika Můstek

Václavské náměstí (no phone). Metro Můstek. **Open** 8am-10pm daily. **Map** p88 C4 ⓫㉑

If it's an English-language periodical you're looking for, this kiosk at the bottom of Wenceslas Square should be your first port-of-call. If it doesn't have what you're looking for, you probably won't find it in the city.

Nightlife

Banco Casino

Na Příkopě 27 (221 967 380/www. bancocasino.cz). Metro Náměstí Republiky. **Open** 24 hrs daily. **Map** p89 D3 ⓫㉒

Classy enough to serve as a set in Prague-shot Bond flick *Casino Royale*, the Banco is a reputable, plush establishment with private salons and high-tech slots for those not into green felt.

Blues Sklep

Liliová 10 (774 277 060/www.blues sklep.cz). Metro Můstek. **Open** 7pm-1am daily. **Map** p88 B4 ⓫㉓

Find the entrance in a passage off a quiet street and descend into an arched cellar bar that books capable young jazz and blues acts in a relaxed space. The sofa's tempting but this cool venue can also get a bit dank so wooden chairs may win out.

Cabaret Captain Nemo

Ovocný trh 13 (224 211 868/www. escort.cz). Metro Můstek. **Open** 8pm-5am daily. **Map** p89 D3 ⓫㉔

This busy strip club adds water to the usual array of nude dancers and private rooms, apparently to some effect. In Prague's sea of such clubs, at least this one is imaginative.

Casino Palais Savarin

Na Příkopě 10 (224 221 636/www. czechcasinos.cz). Metro Náměstí Republiky. **Open** 1pm-4am daily. **Map** p89 D4 ⓫㉕

Old-school Mitteleuropa gambling with hushed, well-groomed croupiers, and with an old, grand palace stairway to sweep you in. The vibe is professional and assured, so wear a jacket and expect complementary drinks.

Friends

Bartolomějská 11 (226 211 920/ www.friends-prague.cz). Metro Národní třída. **Open** 4pm-3am daily. **Map** p88 B5 ⓫㉖

A welcoming, sociable gay bar with a sizeable dancefloor and amusingly kitsch tunes rolling out over a good sound system all night long. A grown-up break from the more predatory bars featuring rent boys and German businessmen.

Karlovy Lázně

NEW *Smetanovo nábřeží 19 (222 220 502/www.karlovylazne.cz). Metro Národní třída.* **Open** 11am-5am daily. **Map** p88 A4 ⓫㉗

This former public spa building is Prague's only megaclub (which is something to be thankful for). With five floors, each billed as separate clubs with different programmes, it can be a laugh to shake it in a dry swimming pool. But it's ruled by teens – kids of 16 and up are welcome, despite the full bar. This, in turn, attracts those eager to pick up smashed 16-year-olds. Well, at least it's handy, just off the Charles Bridge.

Meloun

Michalská 12 (224 230 126). Metro Můstek. **Open** *8pm-5am daily.* **Map** p88 C4

A slice of small-town Czech Republic in the centre of Prague, this collection of cellar rooms blasts loud local rock through the cigarette haze to young patrons too blitzed to notice. The terrace restaurant provides a welcome break at least.

Millennium Casino

V Celnici 10 (221 033 401/www. millenniumcasino.cz). Metro Náměstí Republiky. **Open** *3pm-4am daily.* **Map** p89 E3 ⊕

Roulette, poker and blackjack in a classy setting with professional, unintimidating croupiers. Millennium offers a good, clean bet in a city where many casinos can be dodgy.

N11

Národní třída 11, Nové Město (222 075 705/www.n11.cz). Metro Národní třída. **Open** *8pm-4am Tue-Thur; 7pm-5am Fri, Sat. Call for Sun opening hrs.* **Map** p88 A5 ⊕

A crisp sound system makes this small, clean club a good bet for taking in pop rock. Sunday blues acts like Stan the Man keep the crowd on its feet, with decent bar food on tap.

Petrovič

Rytířská 8 (224 210 635). Metro Můstek. **Open** *6pm-midnight daily.* **Map** p88 C4 ⊕

Not just a handy downtown Russian restaurant with authentic cuisine and staff, but also a rising venue for jazz and rock acts with an appreciative local audience that enjoys lurking in the deep club cellar.

Roxy

Dlouhá 33 (224 826 296/www.roxy.cz). Metro Náměstí Republiky. **Open** *7pm-2am Mon-Thur; 7pm-4am Fri, Sat.* **Map** p89 D2 ⊕

The centre of progressive programming in Prague, the good old Roxy is nevertheless dominated by digital dance tracks, but this crumbling former movie house is also a hot live venue for folk like Roisin Murphy or local and Euro tribal and electronica acts. The (free) Monday night events are a good bet, when local talent takes over.

Tropison cocktail bar

Náměstí Republiky 8 (224 801 276/ www.tropison.com). Metro Náměstí Republiky. **Open** *8pm-5am Mon-Fri; 7pm-5am Sat; 6pm-5am Sun.* **Map** p89 D3 ⊕

Come here for the stunning terrace views atop what was once a communist department store, and the silly Latin dance parties, rather than for the service or uninspiring menus.

U staré paní

Michalská 9 (224 228 090/ www.ustarepani.cz). Metro Můstek/

Roxy

Národní třída. **Open** 7pm-2am daily. **Map** p88 B4 **134**

A comfortable, dark, jazz cellar with cheap wine and grub, the Old Lady features hot Czech jazz players with late, unscheduled jams sometimes rounding out Fridays and Saturdays.

Vagon

Národní třída 25 (221 085 599/ www.vagon.cz). Metro Národní třída. **Open** 6pm-5am Mon-Sat; 6pm-1am Sun. **Map** p88 B5 **135**

A venerated, smoky little cellar with a long history that attracts students, young DJs and bands covering rock and reggae. The entrance is in the shopping passage.

Velmý Jemný Klub Limonádový Joe

Revoluční 1 (221 803 304/www. velmijemnyklub.cz). Metro Náměstí Republiky. **Open** 10am-3am daily. **Map** p89 D2 **136**

Limonádový Joe was a beloved Czech singing cowboy from the movies and this eclectic, highly local club situated next to the Kotva department store has a bit of a western theme, but mostly it's known for a retractable roof, late hours, cheap drinks and amusing local rock bands.

Vertigo

Havelská 4 (774 744 256/www.vertigo-club.cz). Metro Můstek. **Open** 9pm-4am daily. **Map** p88 C4 **137**

Three levels of capable café and clubbing space, with decent DJs, decor, lights and sound. The atmosphere, like at many Prague clubs, can range from hot and buzzy to sleepy and far from lively.

Arts & leisure

AghaRTA

NEW Železná 16 (222 211 275/ www.agharta.cz). Metro Můstek/ Staroměstská. **Open** Club 6pm-1am daily. Concerts 9pm. Jazz shop 5pm-midnight Mon-Fri; 7pm-midnight Sat, Sun. **Admission** 200 Kč. **Map** p88 C4 **138**

This club, having moved from its former location off Wenceslas Square, is one of the best for modern jazz. An even mix of Czechs and foreigners mingles in the relatively small but comfortable space. The CD shop sells local record-ings for 150-400 Kč. Look for releases on the club's own ARTA label.

Archa Theatre
Divadlo Archa
Na Poříčí 26 (221 716 333/www.archatheatre.cz). Metro Náměstí Republiky or Florenc. **Open** *Box office* 10am-6pm Mon-Fri & 2 hrs before show time. **Tickets** 100-300 Kč. **Map** p89 F2 ⓮

Prague's hippest and most daring theatre brings international avant-garde luminaries of dance, theatre and music to its versatile and well-equipped space. The cream of Czech avant-garde – Filip Topol, Petr Nikl and Agon orchestr – also perform here, as well as international acts like the Tiger Lillies and Einstürzende Neubauten.

Chapel of Mirrors
Zrcadlová kaple
Klementinum, Mariánské náměstí (221 663 111/212). Metro Staroměstská. **Open** *Box office* 2hrs before the concert. Concerts usually start 5pm & 8pm. **Map** p88 B4 ⓰

Mozart used to perform in this pink marble chapel in the vast Clementinum complex and his artistic chamber music descendants carry on today, often during afternoons.

Church of St Nicholas
Chrám sv. Mikuláše
Staroměstské náměstí (224 190 994). Metro Staroměstská. **Open** Concerts usually start at 5pm or 8pm. **Map** p88 B3/C3 ⓱

This gorgeous Baroque church right on Old Town Square features ornate touches to take in while listening to one of the concerts regularly booked here – most quite affordable. Instrumental concerts and string recitals are just as grand as the setting.

Estates Theatre
Stavovské divadlo
Ovocný trh 1 (224 901 448/www.nd.cz). Metro Můstek/Staroměstská. **Open** *Box office* 10am-6pm daily. **Map** p88 C4 ⓲

The theatre in which Mozart premièred *Don Giovanni* and *La Clemenza di Tito* was built by Count Nostitz in 1784. It has since become the German opera house, with Carl Maria von Weber as director. Some of the dance perfor-mances sometimes use taped music (!).

Jazz Boat
Čechův most (603 551 680/www.jazzboat.cz). Metro Staroměstská. **Open** 8.30pm-11pm daily. **Map** p88 B1 ⓳

Find the EVD pier No. 5 just down-stream from the Čechův bridge and board the *Kotva* for the most tuneful cruise in town, where top jazz players serenade your dinner of schnitzel and beer (not included in the 590 Kč entry).

Municipal House
Obecni dům
Náměstí Republiky 5 (222 002 336/101/www.obecni-dum.cz). Metro Náměstí Republiky. **Open** *Box office* 10am-7pm daily. **Map** p89 D3 ⓴

The highest form of Czech art nouveau, built around the Smetana Hall, home to the Prague Symphony Orchestra. The Prague Spring Festival kicks off here every year, in a setting of ceiling mosaics of old Czech myths.

Palace Cinemas Slovanský dům
Na Příkopě 22 (257 181 212/www.palacecinemas.cz). Metro Náměstí Republiky. **Map** p89 D3 ⓵

Prague's most central multiplex shows recent Czech films with English subti-tles and international ones in their orig-inal language. It also boasts a high-tech digital projector that can simulcast live concerts or show digital films. There's a 30% ticket discount on Wednesdays.

Rudolfinum
Alšovo nábřeží 12 (227 059 352/www.rudolfinum.cz). Metro Staroměstská. **Open** *Box office* mid Aug-mid July 10am-6pm Mon-Fri. **Map** p88 A2 ⓶

A gorgeous neoclassical cream and blue concert venue with two halls: the Dvořák for orchestral works, the Suk for chamber and vocal music. An evening here cuts to the heart of old Europe.

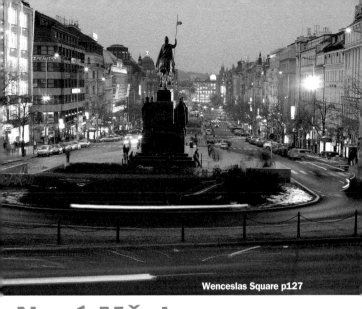

Wenceslas Square p127

Nové Město & Vyšehrad

Nové Město

Providing the cash-infused, modern and rapidly developing counterbalance to Staré Město (the Old Town), this area immediately to the south is laid out on a grid and is enjoying a boom time. It's not as welcoming as the old quarter, but its pragmatism still only goes so far – this being Prague afterall. 'New Town' has grown from a collection of horse markets six centuries ago to the bustling boulevards surrounding **Wenceslas Square** today. The massive rectangular 'square' has been the focus of justifiable criticism against city authorities for having put making a fast buck ahead of

aesthetics – prominent neon signs advertising adult clubs are now more prevalent in the square than ever. But the city fathers have at least committed to cleaning and greening up the square and reintroducing the tram that once rattled its length.

The area also offers a growing collection of worthy dining and gallery options with the buzz now around places like **Bredovský dvůr**, **Modry zub**, **Brasserie M** and, a bit further out, wacky clubbing and social scenes at places like **Be Kara OK!** and **Karavanseráj**. Nightlife is strong here too, with **Radost FX Café**, **Nebe** and the **Lucerna Music Bar** leading the way.

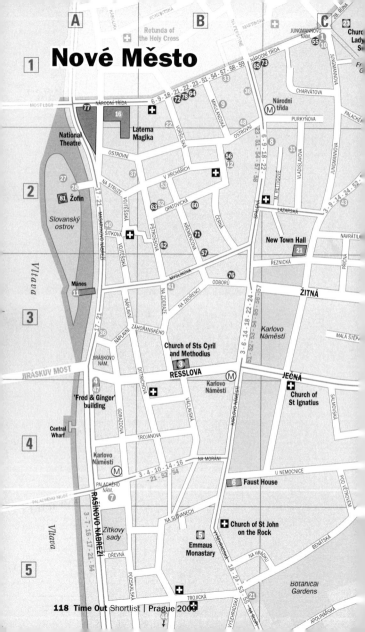

Nové Město

A · B · C

1

Rotunda of the Holy Cross

Jungmannovo nám.
Church of Our Lady of the Snows

National Theatre
Laterna Magika

Národní třída

Národní třída

2

Žofin
Slovanský ostrov

New Town Hall

Vltava

Mánes

3

Karlovo Náměstí

ŽITNÁ

Karlovo Náměstí

Church of Sts Cyril and Methodius
RESSLOVA

Karlovo Náměstí

JEČNÁ
Church of St Ignatius

JIRÁSKŮV MOST

'Fred & Ginger' building

Central Wharf

4

Karlovo Náměstí

Faust House

Church of St John on the Rock

Vltava

Žitkovy sady

Emmaus Monastery

Botanical Gardens

5

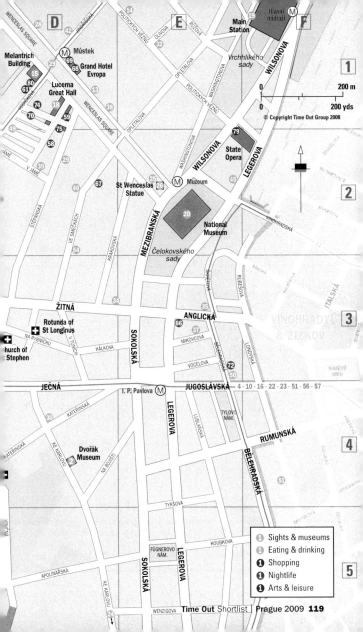

Lucerna Pasáž p124

Aside from being the hub of Prague's burgeoning consumer culture, central Nové Město is where modern art competes for billing with traditional and local streams. Progressive galleries like the newly opened **Leica Gallery** and the **Prague House of Photography** show off this Czech forte, while **Gallery Art Factory** takes art to the street.

And, despite a permanent traffic jam, the streets around here feature a wealth of architectural wonders, many right on Wenceslas Square.

The area is bounded roughly to the north by Národní, which forms the border with Staré Město, and to the east by Legerova, which forms the border with Vinohrady. The arterial Wilsonova, with its heavy traffic, forms an unsightly gash down the middle and along the eastern edge of the district. On the western edge of Nové Město lies the Vltava river, whose embankment makes for lovely walks as afternoon light illuminates ornate façades.

Sights & museums

Adria Palace
Jungmannovo náměstí 28. Metro Můstek. **Map** p118 C1 ❶
A living monument to the heady pre-war movement known as Rondocubism, this arcade and collection of galleries and offices features a fine terrace from which to sip and take in the rest of the architecture all around the busy commercial stretch of Národní street below. Constructed from 1923 to 1925, it's only now that it's really beginning to be revived.

Antonín Dvořák Museum
Muzeum Antonina Dvořáka
Villa Amerika, Ke Karlovu 20 (224 918 013/www.nm.cz/ceske-muzeum-hudby/antonin-dvorak.php). Metro IP Pavlova. **Open** *Apr-Sept* 10am-1.30pm, 2-5.30pm Tue-Sun. *Oct-Mar* 9.30am-1.30pm, 2-5pm Tue-Sun. **Admission** 50 Kč. **Map** p119 D4 ❷
A fair bit off the beaten path, but a calming place for classical music lovers to breathe in the atmosphere that surrounded one of the great Czech composers as he worked and sought inspiration. Catching a chamber recital

of Dvořák's music in this villa by Kilian Ignaz Dientzenhofer is a special thrill.

Church of Sts Cyril & Methodius

Kostel sv. Cyrila a Metoděje
Resslova 9 (224 920 686). Metro Karlovo náměstí. **Open** *Mar-Oct* 10am-5pm Tue-Sun. *Nov-Feb* 10am-4pm Tue-Sun. **Admission** 60 Kč. **Map** p118 B3 ❸

The scene of a pivotal event in the Czech resistance movement during World War II, this Baroque 1730s church is scarred by shelling. That happened when two Czech paratroopers, trained in England, Josef Gabčik and Jan Kubiš, were discovered hiding here by the Nazis. Dropped into Bohemia in late 1941 to assassinate Reinhard Heydrich, Reichsprotektor of Bohemia and Moravia, they succeeded but met their end when the SS and Gestapo bombarded the church all night until the assassins took their own lives.

Dancing Building

Tančicí dům
Masarykovo nábřeží & Resslova streets. Metro Karlovo náměstí. **Map** p118 A4 ❹

Still one of the most controversial contributions to Prague's famous architecture, this collaboration between Croatian architect Vlado Milunic and the US-based Frank Gehry, completed in 1996, is no shrinking violet. Its whimsical glass tower is also known locally as 'Fred and Ginger' for the pinch in the middle of the tower that makes it resemble the famous hoofers in action.

Emmaus Monastery

Emauzy
Vyšehradská 49 (221 979 211/ www.emauzy.cz). Metro Karlovo náměsti. **Open** 9am-4pm Mon-Fri. **Map** p118 B5 ❺

One of the few places where the devastation of World War II is visible in Prague (most of it was in its human toll), this 14th-century church lost its roof to an Allied bombing crew that was off course and mistook the city for Dresden. Its two modern replacement spires look incongruous but are said to be reaching up in an appeal for mercy.

Faust House

Faustův dům
Karlovo náměsti 40. Metro Karlovo náměsti. **Map** p118 B4 ❻

PRAGUE BY AREA

ZANECHTE ZDE SVOU STOPU!
LEAVE HERE YOUR TRACE!

National Museum p124

Slovanský Island p127

The locus of a persistent legend despite the total lack of any real evidence , this highly ornate 17th-century villa is where Edward Kelly, the earless English alchemist, once lived. The story is that a poor student was lured into a pact with the Prince of Darkness, accepting incredible riches in exchange for his soul, which Satan then snatched through a hole in the roof.

František Palacký statue

Palackého náměstí. Metro Karlovo náměstí. **Map** p118 A4 [7]
This huge bronze tribute to the 19th-century historian who took 46 years to write the first history of the Czech people in Czech was created by Stanislav Sucharda. The solemn Palacký sits on a giant pedestal, oblivious to the beauties and demons flying around him.

Galerie České pojišťovny

Spálená 14 (224 054 368/www. galeriecpoj.cz). Metro Národní Třída. **Open** 10am-6pm daily. **Admission** 10Kč. **Map** p118 C2 [8]
One of the newer galleries in the district departs from the sometimes obscure tradition of rare art galleries. Follow one of three passages (from Spálená, Purkyňova or Vladislavova streets) through a courtyard to this exhibition space in an art nouveau building designed by Osvald Polívka. Contemporary Czech photography and painting by artists of the middle generation, such as Tomáš Císařovský, Jaroslav Rona and Richard Konvička are exhibited here.

Galerie Gambit

Mikulandská 6 (602 277 210/ www.gambit.cz). Metro Národní třída. **Open** noon-6pm Tue-Fri. **Admission** free. **Map** p118 B1 [9]
This pocket-sized art gallery concentrates on small exhibitions of new works by leading Czech postmodernists – the likes of Michael Rittstein, Petr Nikl and Barbora Lungová – while also presenting fresh young artists, contemporary design and themes such as Eros in art.

Galerie Kritiků

Jungmannova 31 (224 494 205/ www.galeriekritiku.cz). Metro Národní Třída. **Open** 11am-6pm Tue-Sun. **Admission** 40 Kč; 20 Kč reductions. **Map** p118 C1 [10]
This elegant space in the Adria Palace, with its grand pyramid skylight, has proved itself to be a class act. It is particularly strong on group shows. Its offerings of international art often come from Japan.

Galerie Mánes

Masarykovo nábřeži 250 (224 930 754/ www.nadace-cfu.cz). Metro Karlovo náměstí. **Open** 10am-6pm Tue-Sun. **Admission** varies; free children. **Map** p118 A3 [11]
A fine functionalist art work in its own right, this building straddling a lock of the Vltava river is the largest of the Czech Fund for Art Foundation's network of galleries. The beautiful, if run-down, piece of 1930s culture by Otakar Novotný hosts anything from international travelling shows to exhibitions of contemporary Czech artists and sometimes filmmakers.

Galerie Velryba

Opatovická 24 (224 931 444/www. kavarnavelryba.cz). Metro Národní třída. **Open** noon-10pm Mon-Sat. **Admission** free. **Map** p118 B2 [12]
If you can find this space, down the back stairs of a popular local student/art bar – the trendy Velryba café – you win bragging rights. The gallery nurtures students in the photography department of the Czech film academy FAMU and, increasingly, photography departments of other schools.

Gallery Art Factory

Václavské náměstí 15 (224 217 585/ www.galleryartfactory.cz). Metro Můstek. **Open** 10am-6pm Mon-Fri. **Admission** varies. **Map** p119 D1 [13]
A welcome break from the commercialism of Wenceslas Square, this innovative space is lodged in the interior of the former printing house of the main communist-era newspaper. The painted concrete floors and old industrial hardware

serve as a backdrop to shows by Slovak artists, and the gallery also organises the annual Sculpture Grande outdoor exhibition of large-scale sculptures up and down the square and on Na Příkopě.

Gestapo Headquarters

Politických vězňů 20 (224 262 874). Metro Můstek. **Open** 8am-1pm daily. **Map** p119 E1 🄪
Many a Czech was tortured here during the German occupation. Tours of the grim SS interrogation chambers can be booked a week in advance. The street on which it lies translates as 'Political prisoners', and still has bad karma (a block north lies the home of the Communist Party of Bohemia and Moravia).

Langhans Galerie

Vodičkova 37 (222 929 333/www. langhansgalerie.cz). Metro Můstek. **Open** noon-6pm Tue-Sun. **Admission** 60 Kč; 30 Kč reductions. **Map** p119 D1 🄯
Once home to the Jan Langhans Atelier, where anyone who was anyone in interwar Prague had their portrait made. Now the emphasis is on historical shows, mixed in with work by established and emerging photographers. The recurring theme of memory here has made for some rather haunting exhibitions.

Laterna Magika

Národní třída 4 (224 931 482/ www.laterna.cz). Metro Národní třída. **Open** Box office 10am-10pm Mon-Sat. **Map** p118 A1/A2 🄰
The 'Magic Lantern', a frosted-glass monstrosity, was built between 1977 and 1981 as a communist showpiece; the interior of the 'non-verbal' theatre, filled with imported marble and leather, is now well-worn and patched. The black light shows that plays here aren't worth the admission, perhaps in keeping with an unintentionally ironic socialist relic, but the building holds historical interest.

Leica Gallery

NEW *Školská 40 (no phone/www.lgp. cz). Metro Můstek.* **Open** 10am-6pm Tue-Sun. **Map** p119 D2 🄱
This respected and innovative photography gallery, run by the same folks

who put a travelling show into a train car last year, is back in a new location. The venerated Leica lost its lease at Prague Castle and has now set up shop across the river, with a new line-up of Czech and international stars.

Lucerna Pasáž

NEW *Vodičkova 36 (www.lucerna.cz). Metro Můstek.* **Map** p119 D1 🄲
Built from 1907 to 1921, this art nouveau arcade is a remarkable island of character on Wenceslas Square. Within its halls, which contain shops, concert halls, theatres and obscure offices, are faux-marble pillars, arches and grand stairs. Hanging prominently in the largest section is satirist/artist David Černý's take on St Wenceslas, here with his horse inverted and dangling from a rope.

Main Station

Hlavní nádraží
Wilsonova 8 (972 241 883). Metro Hlavní nádraží. **Map** p119 F1 🄳
Undergoing a confusing remake to convert the city's main rail hub into a German-style slick retail centre, the station – also known as Wilsonovo nádraží, or Wilson Station – also hosts scores of seedy types. Its lower levels still feature tons of typical 1970s communist architecture. A glimpse of its art nouveau former self is visible in the Fanta Kavárna, the upstairs café overlooking the main passenger corridor to the platforms.

National Museum

Národní muzeum
Václavské náměstí 68 (224 497 111/ www.nm.cz). Metro Muzeum. **Open** May-Sept 10am-6pm daily. Oct-Apr 9am-5pm daily. **Admission** 120 Kč; 150 Kč family; free under-6s. **Map** p119 E2 🄴
The iconic neo-Renaissance museum at the top of Wenceslas Square has done more than just take Soviet bullets in 1968; its displays have finally been modernised, with interactive exhibitions on new media now running alongside the older cases of fossils, geodes and stuffed animals. There's still a

Stuffed on the square

Wenceslas Square's infamous sausage stands were recently in danger of becoming extinct, following controversial proposals by the city authorities to ban them as part of a general drive to clean up the boulevard.

Prague hasn't taken much pride in its grandest square since 1989, when hundreds of thousands of Czechs turned out here to demand freedom. Back then, it was lined with state enterprises with Orwellian names, and Tuzex foreign goods shops. But things went downhill in the 1990s. The state enterprises withered and sleazy entrepreneurs now run gambling rooms, cheesy discos and sex clubs, whose neon signs light up the square.

But city officials and local businesses, finally having had enough, recently solicited ideas for improving and reclaiming the street, and chose a design calling for more greenery, which would push brothels onto sidestreets and restore the former tram line.

All of which is grand, of course, except for the fact that the plan will cost millions – and for the small matter of the accompanying sausage stand ban, which caused something of a local uproar. For there's no better, cheaper source of fuel when you're sloshed at 2am – especially on a freezing February night. Over 50,000 signatures were gathered in defense of the besieged *klobosa* mongers, and city officials eventually gave in on the ban, but demanded that the 24 stands counted on the square in late 2007 be reduced to 20. But the people rallied again: what meaning has freedom if you can't get a greasy, gristly sausage, complete with hot mustard and spongy rye bread when you want one? They finally settled for no longer allowing the stands to sell hard liquor all night, limiting their licenses to beer (an unheard of encroachment in Prague). City authorities insist that the stands attract the homeless. Odd how much the homeless resemble German teens and Brit stag party members, mixed in with the bleary local clubbing crowd who are still grateful for any kind of hot food after 10pm.

Isn't democracy grand, though?

PRAGUE BY AREA

Alcron

lack of labels in English but an audio guide is available for an extra 200 Kč.

New Town Hall
Novoměstská radnice
*Karlovo náměstí 23 (224 948 229/
www.novomestskaradnice.cz). Metro
Karlovo náměstí.* **Map** p118 C2
Dating back to the 14th century, this tower established the uniquely Czech form of civil protest known as defenestration when local burghers tossed occupying Habsburg officials to their deaths from a high window in 1419. The Town Hall's current incarnation was built during the 19th and early 20th centuries.

Nová síň
*Voršilská 3 (224 930 255/www.
novasin.cz). Metro Národní třída.* **Open** 11am-6pm Tue-Sun. **Admission** 20 Kč. **Map** p118 B1
The 1934 product of the Union of Creative Artists is still a central plank of the Prague art scene. It's a skylit white cube in which many artists rent space and curate their own shows. It's also home to a culture club in which anything from Italian food events to vintage Czech rock'n'roll can take over by night.

Our Lady of the Snows
Kostel Panny Marie Sněžné
Jungmanovo náměstí. Metro Můstek.
Map p118 C1
The towering black-and-gold Baroque altarpiece is awe-inspiring. Also worth seeking out is the church's side chapel (accessible via a door on the right in the rear), where you can gawp at the trio of gruesome crucifixes. Outside is the world's only Cubist lamp post.

Police Museum
Muzeum policie ČR
*Ke Karlovu 1 (974 824 855/www.
mvcr.cz/ministerstvo/muzeum.html).
Metro IP Pavlova.* **Open** 10am-5pm
Tue-Sun. **Admission** 30 Kč; 50 Kč family. **Map** p119 D5
Sadly, Brek – the stuffed wonder dog responsible for thwarting the defection of several hundred dissidents – has been given a decent burial, but there are still plenty of gruesome exhibits to delight the morbid, like killer lighters and pens.

Real Tour
*Václavské náměstí (602 459 481/
www.walkingtoursprague.com).
Metro Muzeum.* **Open** Tours 12.30pm
Mon, Wed, Fri, Sat. **Map** p119 E2

One of the more popular walking tour options in the city, Real Tour conducts three-hour strolls leading to Prague Castle. They depart from the equestrian statue of St Wenceslas (below) daily, led by the clever and entertaining Paul and Michal, who charge 300 Kč a head for their historical/pop culture schtick. Pub breaks fill out the sights.

St Wenceslas statue

Top of Václavske náměstí. Metro Muzeum. **Map** p119 E2 ㉖

The Czech patron saint, sitting astride his mount, is still the most popular meeting spot in Prague (as in 'meet me at the horse'), surrounded by Saints Agnes, Adelbert, Procopius and Ludmila, Wenceslas's grandmother. A few steps below is a headstone with the images of Jan Palach and Jan Zajic, who burned themselves alive here to protest the Soviet-led occupation of 1968.

Slovanský Island

Masarykovo nábřeží. Metro Národní třída. **Map** p118 A2 ㉗

In the days before slacking became an art form, Berlioz was appalled at the 'idlers, wasters and ne'er-do-wells' who congregated on this little Vltava River landfall. It's still hard to resist the outdoor café or the rowing-boats available for hire.

Wenceslas Square

Václavské náměstí. Metro Mústek. **Map** p119 D1 ㉘

The modern hub of Nové Město (and indeed the entire city), this broad, one-kilometre boulevard has been the backdrop to every major event of the city's recent history, from the founding of the Czechoslovak Republic in 1918 to the 1989 Velvet Revolution.

Eating & drinking

Alcron

Štěpánská 40 (222 820 038/www.alcron.cz). Metro Mústek. **Open** 5.30-10.30pm Mon-Sat. **$$$$**. **Seafood**. **Map** p119 D2 ㉙

Rated the No. 2 restaurant in the country by local critics, this historic art deco hotel dining room, with just seven tables, is a serious seafood star. Chef Jiří Štift is master of the pike-perch and the savoury sauce. It's ensconsed in the SAS Radisson, formerly known as the Alcron, and only those with membership cards can reserve lunch from noon to 3pm.

Banditos

Melounova 2 (224 941 096/www.banditosrestaurant.cz). Metro IP Pavlova. **Open** 9am-12.30am Mon-Sun. **$$**. **Mexican**. **Map** p119 D4 ㉚

A favourite expat haunt, this little bar doubles as a Tex-Mex joint serving decent southwest American favourites, from enchiladas to layers of nachos and jalapeños and good burgers to boot. Its friendly atmosphere is a big part of the draw. Recommended dishes include spicy chicken sandwich, Caesar salad and cheeseburgers.

Brasserie M

NEW *Vladislavova 17 (224 054 070/www.brasseriem.cz). Metro Národní třída.* **Open** 8.30am-11pm Mon-Fri; noon-midnight Sat. **$$$**. **Continental**. **Map** p118 C2 ㉛

This big room has won praises and crowds in the past year for its delectable French grill fare, including tender steaks in tangy sauces and an impressive but reasonably priced wine list. Sunday brunches are the toast of expat families.

Bredovský dvůr

NEW *Politických vězňů 13 (224 215 428). Metro Mústek.* **Open** 11am-midnight Mon-Sat; 11am-11pm Sun. **$$**. **Czech**. **Map** p119 E1 ㉜

This resolutely Czech dining room is an open secret among the office workers around Wenceslas Square; it comes complete with gruff waiters and one of the best Pilsner pours in town, thanks to the beer tank, which preserves body and flavour. The place for pork knuckle, sauerkraut and dumplings. It may explain why office productivity in this district drops to near zero after lunch.

PRAGUE BY AREA

Café Louvre

Café Louvre

NEW *Národní 22 (224 930 949/ www.cafelouvre.cz). Metro Národní třída.* **Open** 8am-11.30pm Mon-Fri; 9am-11.30pm Sat, Sun. **Café**. **Map** p118 B1 ③③

Founded in 1902 and once patronised by Albert Einstein and Franz Kafka, Prague's most elegant old-school café is still thriving. Vested waiters serve espresso on silver trays, while lovers, business folk and school mates meet up at little tables. Rabbit in wine sauce and the like go well beyond the usual café fare, while the non-smoking room and billiards tables, plus Wi-Fi on the back patio, only add to the appeal.

Cicala

Žitná 43 (222 210 375/www.trattoria. cicala.cz/cz). Metro IP Pavlova. **Open** 11.30am-10.30pm Mon-Sat. **$**. **Italian**. **Map** p119 D3 ③④

Cicala's owner brings in fresh Italian wonders weekly, whether it's calamari or figs, presented like a work of art. This easily missed subterranean two-room eaterie on an otherwise unappealing street is worth seeking out, as it's a bastion of Prague's Italian community.

Il Conte Deminka

Skřetova 1 (224 224 915/www. deminka.com). Metro IP Pavlova. **Open** 11am-11pm Mon-Fri; noon-11pm Sat, Sun. **$**. **Italian**. **Map** p119 E3 ③⑤

This storied café, dating back to 1886, has morphed through several forms (at least two since 1989) but seems to have settled on a classically renovated space for gourmet Italian cuisine. Not to be confused with the next-door classic Czech place that also uses the hallowed Deminka moniker.

Don Pedro

Masarykovo nábřeží 2 (224 923 505/ www.donpedro.cz). Metro Karlovo Námĕsti. **Open** 5-11pm Mon-Thur; 11.30am-11pm Fri-Sun. **$$**. **Colombian**. **Map** p118 A3 ③⑥

A true rarity in Prague, this homely, bright Colombian eaterie serves up authentic zesty empanadas, spicy beef and potato soup and gorgeously grilled meats. Oxtail *cola guisada* with yuca root is a fave, and well worth the South American-speed service.

Dynamo

Pštrossova 29 (224 932 020/www. dynamorestaurace.cz). Metro Národní třída. **Open** 11.30am-midnight daily. **$$$**. **Continental**. **Map** p118 A2 ③⑦

Known throughout the district for its excellent lunch specials, which range from venison to diet-friendly but tasty specials, Dynamo is a sleek designer diner. Staff have managed to establish a strong point in the hotbed of great restos and bars south of the National Theatre. The modern art above diners' heads is for sale. Don't miss the wall of single-malt Scotches.

Hot

Václavské námĕstí 45 (222 247 240/ www.hotrestaurant.cz). Metro Muzeum. **Open** 9am-midnight daily. **$$**. **Steakhouse**. **Map** p119 D1 ③⑧

This sleek, modernist steakhouse and pasta specialist (with Wi-Fi) in the lobby of the sleek, modernist Hotel Jalta occupies prime real estate on Wenceslas Square, thus its tables fill up fast.

Jáma

V Jámĕ 7 (224 222 383/www.jama pub.cz). Metro Můstek. **Open** 11am-midnight Mon, Sun; 11am-1am Tue-Sat. **$**. **Czech-Mex**. **Map** p121 D2 ③⑨

The refurbishment of this bar was a major point of discussion among its army of regulars, but they finally conceded as the old one was falling apart. American-owned Jáma is a friendly and attentive home away from home that specialises in Mexican and Czech food, all improved under a new chef. Patio space out back, rock'n'roll vibe and top-value lunch specials. See also box p133.

Karavanseráj

NEW *Masarykovo nábřeží 22 (224 930 390/www.karavanseraj.cz). Metro Karlovo námĕsti.* **Open** 9am-11pm Mon-Thur; 9am-midnight Fri; noon-midnight Sat; noon-10pm Sun. **$**. **Lebanese**. **Map** p118 A2 ④⓪

Karavanseráj is one of those only-in-Prague conceptions: an affordable

PRAGUE BY AREA

Lebanese restaurant, complete with belly dancing, that doubles as a lecture and social club for budget travellers. Don't be troubled if someone starts projecting their slides of the Grand Canyon during your dinner.

Lemon Leaf

Myslíkova 14 (224 919 056/www.lemon. cz). Metro Karlovo náměstí. **Open** 11am-11pm Mon-Thur; 11am-12.30am Fri; 12.30pm-12.30am Sat; 12.30-11pm Sun. **$$$. Thai. Map** p118 B3 ④

Probably the most comfortable of the city's new wave of Thai and South-east Asian eateries, Lemon Leaf delivers a homely vibe with a warm yellow and dark wood setting. Bargain midday specials keep the place close to capacity. No compromises for spice-phobic Czechs have been made with the *tom ka kai* or prawn curries.

Modrý Zub

NEW *Jindřišská 5 (222 212 622/ www.modryzub.cz). Metro Můstek.* **Open** 11am-11pm daily. **$. Thai. Map** p119 D1 ④

A reasonably priced, quick and healthy non-Czech lunch option: spicy Thai noodles, a modern, casual streetside setting and takeaway service at the back. They even brought the first wire-handled cardboard Asian takeaway boxes to the Czech Republic.

Novoměstský Pivovar

Vodičkova 20 (222 232 448/www.n pivovar.cz). Metro Můstek. **Open** 10am-11.30pm Mon-Fri; 11.30am-11.30pm Sat; noon-10pm Sun. **$$. Czech. Map** p118 C2 ④

One of a surprisingly small number of brew pubs in Prague, Novoměstský is a vast underground warren with great beer and pub grub. Unfortunately, however, it also has the bus-loads of tourists, slack service and occasionally dodgy maths that often go with them.

Oliva

Plavecká 4 (222 520 288/www.oliva restaurant.cz). Metro Karlovo náměstí. **Open** 11.30am-3pm, 6pm-midnight Mon-Sat. **$$$. Mediterranean. Map** p118 B5 ④

The Czech couple behind this buzz-worthy little spot learned the trade abroad and have brought the goods home: duck and orange salads, delicate veal steaks, pungent sauces and grilled red snapper with spicy aubergine. Out of the centre but worth seeking out.

Opera Garden

*Zahrada v opeře
Legerova 75 (224 239 685/www. zahradavopere.cz). Metro Muzeum.* **Open** 11.30am-1am daily. **$$. Fusion. Map** p119 E2 ④

As much a visual experience as a feast for the taste buds, airy Opera Garden still stands up as a top dining option for quality and value in the Wenceslas Square area. The entrance is still hidden behind security barricades that date from the days of 9/11 (the building is shared with Radio Free Europe) but there's more incentive than ever to venture inside.

Pack

Ve Smečkách 21 (222 210 280/www. thepack.cz). Metro Muzeum. **Open** 11am-1am daily. **Sports pub. Map** p119 D2 ④

Perhaps named after the mobs of yobs who were anticipated as customers, the Prague version of Hooters offers buffalo wings and hangover breakfasts served by girls in tight sweaters.

La Perle de Prague

Rašinovo nábřeží 80 (221 984 160/ www.laperle.cz). Metro Karlovo náměstí. **Open** 7-10.30pm Mon, Sun; noon-2pm, 7-10.30pm Tue-Sat. **$$$. French. Map** p118 A4 ④

One of the most expensive options in the district, La Perle attacts the local business elites but does indeed impress. Its penthouse location atop Frank Gehry's Dancing Building (p121) is half the appeal (though windows are small). The other half is the top-drawer French cuisine and thoroughly refreshed menus, plus the equally top-drawer wine list.

Pivovarský Dům

Lipová 15 (296 216 666/www. npivovar.cz). Metro Můstek.

Radost FX Café p132

Open 11am-11.30pm daily. **$$.**
Czech. Map p118 C4 48

With a minimum of seven classic and speciality beers on tap, genial service and all the classic pub grub from pork knuckle to dumplings stuffed with smoked ham, this microbrewery has been a hit since 2000. This modernisation of the cheap-and-not-so-friendly pub was the first of many now blooming in Prague.

Pizza Coloseum

*Vodičkova 32 (224 214 914/www.
pizzacoloseum.cz). Metro Můstek.*
Open 11am-11.30pm daily. **$. Italian**.
Map p119 D1/D2 49

This handy cellar just off Wenceslas Square, is right up there near the top of Prague's dozens of pizzerias. Excellent bruschetta, flame-baked pizza and big, saucy pastas complement well-stocked wine racks (half-caraffes are standard) and a familiar range of steak and fish.

Radost FX Café

*Bělehradská 120 (224 254 776/www.
radostfx.cz). Metro IP Pavlova.* **Open**
Restaurant 11.30am-3am daily. *Club*
10pm-4am Thur-Sat. **$. Vegetarian**.
Map p119 E3 50

The city's original hot button night-club-cum-vegetarian resto is still delivering the goods in both departments. Its regular makeovers keep things fresh (if the constant staff turnover makes for suspense when ordering). Radost still has the latest opening hours around, plus all-night pastas, couscous and big salads. The ornamental tables do bash your knees but it's as popular as ever – especially the groovy, gold-gilt backroom lounge.

Samurai

NEW *Londýnská 120 (222 515 330/
www.sushi-restaurace-samurai.cz).
Metro IP Pavlova.* **Open** 11am-11.30pm
Mon-Sat; 6-11.30pm Sun. **$$. Sushi**.
Map p119 F4 51

Taking the Prague sushi craze one step further, Samurai whips out the butcher knives for its attention-getting Teppanyaki grill. They've laid in the tatami mats and sliding paper-walled panels too. It's not just decor, of course: the seafood and sashimi are excellent.

Tulip Café

*Opatovická 3 (224 930 019). Metro
Národní třída.* **Open** 11am-2am Mon-Thur, Sun; 11am-7am Fri, Sat. **$.**
Diner. Map p118 B2 52

Constant changes in management have taken their toll as people wait ages for their food and aren't always rewarded for their patience. Nevertheless, the back patio is heavenly on a warm night – just not, perhaps, if you're starving. Be forewarned: the place is also student heaven.

Universal

*V Jirchářích (224 934 416/www.
universalrestaurant.cz). Metro Národní
třída.* **Open** 11.30am-midnight
Mon-Sat; 11am-midnight Sun. **$.**
Continental. Map p118 B2 53

Old French advertisements, servers who know their stuff and daily specials (cod in white sauce, flank steak and rolled veggie lasagne) come with delectable sides of fresh spinach or roasted gratin potatoes.

Zlatá Hvězda

*Ve Smečkách 12 (296 222 292/
www.sportbar.cz). Metro Muzeum.*
Open 11am-midnight Mon, Tue;
11am-2am Wed-Sun. **Sports bar**.
Map p119 D2 54

An oldie but sometimes a goodie. Scuffed interior, poor service and very mediocre pizzas have done nothing to chase off the sports fans who gather here to watch all the games on the battered big-screens.

Shopping

Antikvariát Galerie Můstek

*Národní 40 (224 949 587). Metro
Národní třída.* **Open** 10am-7pm
Mon-Fri; noon-4pm Sat; 2-6pm Sun.
Map p118 C1 55

A discriminating *antikvariát* with fine antiquarian books and a reliable stock of major works on Czech art.

Jáma tales

When American Max Munson realised it was finally time to retire his bar after 14 years – just the bashed-up bar itself, not **Jáma** (p129), the beloved pub that contains it – he was hardly expecting the hue and cry of hundreds of patrons. But, after so much faithful service in the line of duty to so many drinkers, this scratched, cigarette-burned, creaky wooden construction designed by amateurs had become something of an icon. Impassioned debate ensued: customers weighed in on what properties the new Jáma bar must have. Granted, the old one was not ideally suited to cocktail making and had a bias toward beer taps. But how could the new bar address the changing tastes of customers without losing its essential character? And, just as importantly, where was the old one going? Every regular, it seems, wanted a piece of it as a cherished keepsake, presumably for their trophy room.

So when, for the first time in its history, Jáma closed for a weekend to install its new centrepiece, the suspense was palpable throughout the Nové Město district and beyond. But patrons need not have worried. Having launched four other businesses since his arrival in 1994, Munson and partners have shown repeatedly that they understand the unique demands of Prague's drinkers. Klub X only lasted a while, owing to landlord troubles, but the Pack bar did well (it has since been sold) and a wine-importing business proved a hit too – in fact, Munson is now a columnist on viniculture for *The Prague Post*.

And the end result for the bar? Decidedly a success. Jáma's heart still feels laid-back but eminently capable, sturdy but whimsical, efficient but functional but as approachable as ever. And it's now a great cocktails well too.

National Theatre p137

Antikvariát Kant

Opatovická 26 (224 934 219/
www.antik-kant.cz). Metro Národní
třída. **Open** 10am-6pm Mon-Fri.
Map p118 B2 🟢

A collector's dream, this old bookstore
is an eclectic mix of prints and dust-
encrusted tomes. There's quite a large,
although strange, section of English
books and an extensive and very
organised postcard collection. The
prints on the walls are varied and the
cheap books in the entranceway are
worth more than a passing glance.

Bazar Antik Zajímavosti

Křemencova 4 (no phone). Metro
Národní třída . **Open** 9am-6pm
Mon-Fri. **Map** p118 B2/B3 🟢

Find your way to this jumble of well
chosen junk to check out the offerings.
The place is heavy on glass, and
tea-cup fans will think they've found
nirvana, but other shoppers can
appreciate the linens and the small
collection of paintings, plus the
unique lamps.

Beruška

Vodičkova 30 (224 162 129). Metro
Můstek. **Open** 10am-6.30pm Mon-Fri;
11am-4pm Sat. **Map** p119 D2 🟢

A wardrobe-sized shop filled with toys
for both younger and older children
but with a handy locale in the Lucerna
passage on Wenceslas Square. Stuffed
animals, cleverly designed wooden
toys and puzzles and board games
are all sold here.

Cellarius

Lucerna Passage, Štěpánská 61
(224 210 979/www.cellarius.cz).
Metro Můstek. **Open** 9.30am-8pm
Mon-Sat; 2-8pm Sun. **Map** p119 D1 🟢

A huge selection of wines is crammed
into the small space that is Cellarius.
It's maze-like, so be sure to look
both to the left and the right so that
you don't miss anything. The owner
stocks wine from local vineyards as
well as some well-selected imports,
including French, Bulgarian and
Chilean varieties. Tasting is encouraged in the adjacent wine bar.

Fashion Galerie No.14

Opatovická 14 (777 768 406). Metro Národní třída. **Open** 11am-6pm Mon-Sat. **Map** p118 B2 ⑥⓪

Not for the budget conscious, but definitely for the fashion plate. Each item here is an original and the quality and designs are beautiful. Mainly dresses, but there are some casual items too.

Foto Škoda

Palác Langhans, Vodičkova 37 (222 929 029/www.fotoskoda.cz). Metro Můstek. **Open** 8.30am-8.30pm Mon-Fri; 9am-6pm Sat. **Map** p119 D1 ⑥①

Sales, repairs, developing, supplies: this photography shop has everything you could possibly want. It's excellent for the professional, but amateurs will be able to find what they need as well, especially the novel add-ons for digital cameras.

Globe Bookstore & Coffeehouse

Pštrossova 6 (224 934 203/www.globebookstore.cz). Metro Národní třída. **Open** 9.30am-midnight daily. **Map** p118 B2 ⑥②

The original version of this bookstore was a magnet for literary types from Richard Ford to the beat poets, but that was long ago. Now the Globe is a handy spot for picking up paperbacks and getting online with a light menu of soups, salads and such. No beef there – just don't go expecting to feel like Hemingway.

Hamparadi Antik Bazar

Pštrossova 22 (no phone/hamparadi.prodejce.cz). Metro Národní třída. **Open** 2.30-6.30pm daily. **Map** p118 B2 ⑥③

Quirky treasures are scattered among the typical bazaar offerings of porcelain and glass. Be sure to browse carefully as it's easy to overlook something fun. Toys and old advertisements add to the nostalgic motif.

Le Patio

Národní 22 (224 934 402). Metro Národní třída. **Open** 10am-7pm Mon-Sat; 11am-7pm Sun. **Map** p118 B1 ⑥④

Le Patio brings the world to Prague with an eclectic mixture of imported home furnishings.

Tesco

Národní třída 26 (222 003 111). Metro Můstek or Národní třída. **Open** *Department store* 8am-9pm Mon-Sat; 9am-8pm Sun. *Supermarket* 7am-9pm Mon-Sat; 9am-8pm Sun. **Map** p118 B1 ⑥⑤

Always packed, the big international supermarket chain covers all your expat needs: from wasabi paste to taco shells downstairs, plus pharmacy supplies, souvenirs, clothes, electronics and blank DVDs upstairs.

Nightlife

For **Radost FX Café**, see p132.

Be Kara OK!

NEW *Legerova 78 (222 240 035/ www.karaokebox.cz). Metro IP Pavlova.* **Open** 6pm-2am Mon-Thur; 6pm-5am Fri, Sat. **Map** p119 E3 ⑥⑥

Billing itself as the first karaoke box club in the Czech Republic, the collection of padded cellar rooms (with attached sushi bar, natch) has proven a sensation for song-loving Czechs. With fully equipped and miked box rooms available for 400-1,500 Kč per hour, it's indeed finally okay to wail drunkenly in semi-public. Just swipe the bar-coded songlist containing 9,000 tunes in five languages to throw the track you want onto the plasma screen, and sing your heart out.

Darling Club Cabaret

Ve Smečkách 32 (732 250 555/ www.kabaret.cz). Metro Muzeum. **Open** 8pm-5am Wed; noon-5am Thur-Tue. **Map** p119 D2 ⑥⑦

Still the king of the hill when it comes to Prague's strip and sex clubs – and that's one big hill these days – Darling Club Cabaret brings in high-rollers from all over. The place boasts of more than 100 girls per night at times, all out of a Las Vegas fantasy. A limo service will pick up customers gratis.

Duplex

Václavske náměsti 21 (732 221 111/www.duplex.cz). Metro Můstek. **Open** 10pm-5am Wed-Sat. **Map** p119 D1 **63**

Under new management, this dance club atop a Wenceslas Square tower draws a casually stylish mix of aficionados with its crisp sound-system, multi-level steel and glass space and top local DJs like Chris Sadler and Milhaus.

Hot Pepper's

Václavske náměsti 21 (724 134 011/www.hotpeppersprague.cz). Metro Můstek. **Open** 8.30pm-5am daily. **Map** p119 D1 **69**

This hit strip and lap-dance club (nothing more at this one) on Wenceslas Square has taken on the older rivals with racks of costumes, props and theme nights, including the enthusiastic Army of Pepper's. There's a decent menu available too, although the free entry policy is soon eclipsed by the high drink and food prices.

Lucerna Music Bar

Vodičkova 36 (224 217 108/www.musicbar.cz). Metro Můstek. **Open** 8pm-2am daily. *Concerts* 9pm. **Map** p119 D1 **70**

Incredible rock, jazz and blues talents roll through this neglected old cellar concert space, from Fernando Saunders to Atomic Hooligan. Lucerna has in fact always hosted the greats, including the likes of Satchmo and Josephine Baker in times past. Beware of the packed-out so-called '80s Night' on Fridays.

Nebe

Křemencova 10 (777 800 411/www.nebepraha.cz). Metro Národni třida. **Open** 6pm-4am daily. **Map** p118 B2 **71**

A cellar bar-club where English voices can be heard nightly, along with breakbeats. Well-worn and a magnet for US college students taking a semester in Prague, Nebe does at least know how to rock.

Rock Café

Národni třida 20 (224 933 947/www.rockcafe.cz). Metro Národni třida.

Open 10am-3am Mon-Fri; 5pm-3am Sat; 5pm-1am Sun. *Concerts* 9pm. **Map** p118 B1 **72**

With one of the more consistent programmes for live (if very diverse) rock, this big underground venue must be credited for its energy. The Legendary Pink Dots are regulars, while other acts come in from the far out fringe (vis Tracy Gang Pussy, billed as 'fucking punkrockers made in Paris!').

Arts & leisure

Evald

Národni třida 28 (221 105 225/evald.cinemart.cz). Metro Národni třida. **Map** p118 B1/C1 **73**

This tiny screening room is one of the city's more respected downtown art-house cinemas, and has exclusive bookings on some European art, independent American and Czech films. They're often screened with English subtitles. Booking is recommended for new films.

Kino Lucerna

Vodičkova 36 (www.lucerna.cz). Metro Můstek. **Map** p119 D1 **74**

Still holding on to quickly fading glory, this art nouveau masterpiece is a reminder of cinema-going's glory days. The elevated lobby bar has large windows that let you scan the 1920s-era shopping arcade, and somebody still occasionally tickles the ivories.

Lucerna Great Hall

Vodičkova 36 (224 212 003/www.lucpra.com). Metro Můstek. **Open** *Concerts* start 7-8pm. **Map** p119 D1/D2 **75**

Run independently from the Lucerna Music Bar (above), this vast, pillared underground performance hall hosts winter balls in the chilly months but also big-time acts from the likes of Morcheeba and Maceo Parker. There are no regular box office hours so book through an agent like Ticketpro (p186).

MAT Studio

Karlovo náměsti 19 (224 915 765/www.mat.cz). Metro Karlovo náměsti. **Map** p118 B3 **76**

PRAGUE BY AREA

Definitely the smallest cinema in town. The intimate screening room shows a fair mix of off-beat films, Czech classics with English subtitles and rare selections from the Czech TV vaults.

National Theatre

Národní divadlo
Národní 2 (info 224 901 448/ box office 224 901 377/www.nd.cz). Metro Národní třída. **Open** *Box office Sept-June 10am-6pm daily.* **Map** p118 A1 ⑰
Undergoing a badly needed restoration (which has not affected programming as yet), this symbol of Czech nationalism concentrates on Czech opera, the core of the repertoire being Smetana and Dvořák, together with some Janáček. Non-Czech operas and impressive ballets are also performed.

Reduta

Národní třída 20 (224 933 487/ www.redutajazzclub.cz). Metro Národní třída. **Open** *Box office*

3-7.30pm Mon-Fri. *Club* 9pm-midnight daily. *Concerts* 9pm. **Map** p118 B1 ⑱
Yep, this is where Bill Clinton blew his sax. Virtually unchanged since the Velvet Revolution, this old chestnut of a club steadfastly hangs on to its cramped, awkward seating and expensive beer. But some of the best musicians in town often sit in with the evening's band.

State Opera

Státní Opera
Wilsonova 4 (224 227 266/www.opera. cz). Metro Muzeum. **Open** *Box office 10am-5.30pm Mon-Fri; 10am-noon, 1-5.30pm Sat, Sun.* **Map** p119 E2/F2 ⑲
Once the German Theatre, opened in 1887, and where Mahler conducted, the State Opera is still an architectural wonder, with soaring balconies and a magnificent dome. It's also the second house of the National Theatre with consistently bold contemporary opera alongside the Italian, German, French and Russian repertoires.

Vyšehrad p138

Světozor

Vodičkova 39 (224 946 824/www. kinosvetozor.cz). Metro Můstek. **Map** p119 D1 ⑩

Part of the repertory house association Osa 9, this veteran movie house has proven its credentials by hosting film fests as well as a great repertoire of indies, usually with original soundtracks and most often with English subtitles (worth checking in advance though – look for '*angl. titulky*').

Žofín

Slovanský ostrov (224 934 400/ www.zofin.cz). Metro Národní třída. **Map** p118 A2 ㉛

A newly restored cultural centre on an island in the Vltava River, this large yellow building dating from the 1880s hosted tea dances and concerts until just before World War II. Today, you're more likely to find lectures and concerts being held here, alongside one of the sweetest riverside beer gardens in Prague.

Vyšehrad

Sights & museums

Vyšehrad

Soběslavova 1 (www.praha-vysehrad.cz). Metro Vyšehrad. **Map** below A2 ㉜

These tenth-century hilltop castle ruins feature a cemetery that holds a dozen of the greats of Czech culture and the neo-Gothic Saints Peter and Paul, whose spires dominate this side of the river's skyline.

Eating & drinking

Rio's

Štulcova 2 (224 922 156/www.rio restaurant.cz). Metro Vyšehrad. **Open** 10am-midnight daily. **Map** below A2 ㉝

The cuisine and service are unexceptional here – the main draw is the view from Prague's oldest hilltop castle ruins, located a 12-minute metro ride south of the centre.

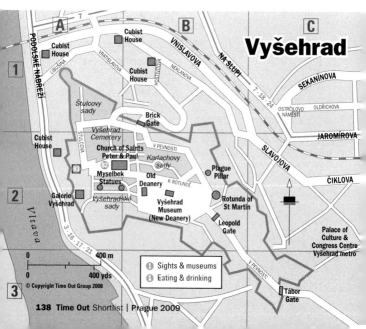

Passepartout p140

Vinohrady & Žižkov

Vinohrady

Only a few minutes' walk from the Old Town, tree-lined Vinohrady, with its stately 18th- and 19th-century architecture, has become the natural home to Prague's more stately set. But it also draws foodies, cocktail-bar fans and more adventurous clubbers from all over the city, offering them more options every season. Once an autonomous town, Vinohrady is named for the wine grapes once grown here. These days it cultivates French and Irish real-estate investors, boutique hotels, gourmet delis and a flourishing gay scene. The heart of the district is **Náměstí Míru**, a round 'square' spiked by St Ludmila's twin spires. Its main artery, Vinohradská, formerly called Stalinova třída, is lined with art-nouveau apartments.

Sights & museums

Church of St Ludmila
Kostel sv. Ludmily
Náměstí Míru (no phone). Metro Náměstí Míru. **Open** No official hours. **Map** p141 A2 ❶
Spooky and opulent, this neo-Gothic church marks a hub of the Vinohrady district, the point from which protesters started the march that brought down communism in 1989.

Eating & drinking

Café Medúza
Belgická 17 (222 515 107). Metro Náměstí Míru. **Open** 11am-1am Mon-Fri; noon-1am Sat, Sun. **Café**. **Map** p141 A4 ❷
An old-hand at the homely café concept, this calming jumble of secondhand tables and Persian rugs makes for a great winter retreat. One of the city's

cosiest, if threadbare, hideout spots, with light snacks but warm service and drinks served on little silver trays. Run by two sisters who serve warming soups and mulled wine to regulars.

Café Sahara

Ibsenova 1 (222 514 987). Metro Náměstí Míru. **Open** 8am-midnight daily. **$$**. **Mediterranean**. **Map** p141 A2 **3**

Capacious rooms with cool sandstone tones and big wicker chairs, and waiters out of a fashion-spread make for a full-on café experience. Throw in the view of Vinohrady's main square and the appealing Italianesque menu and it's a sure hit among the stylish – if not the cheapest option around.

Efes

Vinohradská 63 (222 250 015). Metro Náměstí Míru. **Open** 11am-11pm Mon-Sat. **$**. **Turkish**. **Map** p141 C2 **4**

Not much to look at and easy to miss, but worth the visit for the ample offerings of authentic Anatolian tastes and family atmosphere. *Ayvar*, a red pepper, chilli and garlic paste you spread on fresh sourdough, is a must, as is the garlic-yogurt *cacic* and great vegetarian fare. *Sonbahar kisiri* is a cracked-wheat mix of walnuts and olives, and the *kizartma* of caramelised aubergine and peppers seduces fast.

Kaaba

Mánesova 20 (222 254 021). Tram 11. **Open** 8am-10pm Mon-Fri; 10am-10pm Sat, Sun. **Café**. **Map** p141 A1 **5**

A gem of a café with retro-cool (but never pretentious) decor and ambience and friendly servers who obviously don't mind the smoke. It offers a good range of coffees from around the globe, cult wines from well-known domestic producers and a handy newsstand at one end for reading supplies. Excellent for lazy mornings of page turning and refills.

La Lavande

Záhřebská 24 (222 517 406/www. lalavande.wz.cz). Metro Náměstí Míru. **Open** noon-3pm, 5.30pm-midnight Mon-Thur, 5.30pm-midnight Fri-Sun. **$$$**. **Continental**. **Map** p141 B4 **6**

Another Prague contender for gourmet spot of the moment, this is a Czech restaurateur passion that's growing yearly. Largely, La Lavande brings it off with charm and quietly efficient service in a semi-casual French farmhouse atmosphere. The Spanish-style rabbit, veal with green olive and black truffle, fried anchovies with coriander and beef Rossini are all recommended.

Park Café

Riegrovy sady 28 (no phone). Metro Jiřího z Poděbrad. **Open** 11am-11pm daily. **Café**. **Map** p141 B1 **7**

One of the liveliest beer gardens in the district, this one's always crowded with old-timers, kids, dogs and expats. The beer is cheap and copious, though, and rock bands liven it up for summer. Just watch where you step.

Passepartout

NEW *Americka 20 (222 513 340/ www.passepartout.cz). Metro Náměstí Míru.* **Open** 11am-11pm daily. **$$**. **French**. **Map** p141 B4 **8**

An elegant but casual island of tasty Francophile fare that caters to the French real-estate investors who are redoing Vinohrady. Very reasonably priced bistro food from Moroccan lamb stew to duck confit, all preceded by fresh and varied salads and followed by a tempting dessert cart and espresso.

Passion Chocolat

NEW *Italská 5 (222 524 333). Metro Náměstí Míru.* **Open** 8am-7pm Mon-Sat. **Café**. **Map** p141 A2 **9**

Chocoholics throughout Prague have been whispering the name of this lovely little place, created by French couple Nádine and Jean-Francois, a pastry chef who insists on the best. Top-drawer Valrhona chocolate is a key ingredient in the sweets and pastries – *millefeuille* with espresso is a slice of heaven.

Pastička

Blanická 25 (222 253 228/www. pasticka.cz). Metro Náměstí Míru.

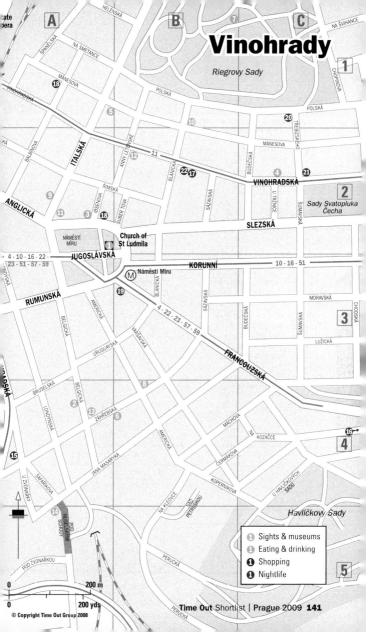

Vinohrady

Riegrovy Sady

Church of
St Ludmila

Náměstí Miru

*Sady Svatopluka
Čecha*

Havlíčkovy Sady

- ❶ Sights & museums
- ❶ Eating & drinking
- ❶ Shopping
- ❶ Nightlife

200 m

200 yds

© Copyright Time Out Group 2008

Open 11am-1am Mon-Fri; 5pm-1am Sat, Sun. **Pub**. Map p141 B1

The 'Little Mousetrap' is a beloved neighbourhood hangout that's always jumping with an eclectic crowd – especially on the summer terrace out back. They go in for gab, pub grub, beer and cigarettes. Lots of 'em.

Popocafepetl

Italská 2 (777 944 672/www. popocafepetl.cz). Metro Náměstí Míru. **Open** 11am-1am Mon-Fri; 4pm-1am Sat, Sun. **Café**. Map p141 A2

A sister café to the one in Malá Strana (p78), this is the quieter, gentler Popo, but not by much. Regulars fill the space till the wee hours. They're not here for fine service or beers, but somehow the place has always got a buzz, with its mix of local bohemians and decadent expats.

Roca

Vinohradská 32 (222 520 060). Metro Náměstí Míru. **Open** 11am-11pm daily. **$$. Italian**. Map p141 B2

Good, homely Italian in a local favourite hideout. The founding owners have moved on, leaving some regulars unhappy, but Roca's still a top draw in the neighbourhood. Hearty pastas in creamy sauces are still plentiful, the shellfish is tender and the meat scallopinis still seduce with sauces like mushroom and nutmeg. Service is attentive and genial, the decor rustic and casual.

Žlutá pumpa

Belgická 12 (no phone). Metro Náměstí Míru. **Open** noon-1am Mon-Fri; 4pm-1am Sat, Sun. **$$$. Continental**. Map p141 A4

The 'Yellow Pump' is a buzzy local pub with reasonably priced Czech-Mex food, the latest trend, it seems, in trying to find new angles on trad pubbing. A colourful, lively joint, but don't expect great service or chow.

Zvonařka

Šafaříkova 1 (224 251 990). Metro IP Pavlova. **Open** 11am-midnight daily. **Bar**. Map p141 A5

Passion Chocolat p140

Patterned on Paris's Shakespeare & Co, Prague's conception is considerably scaled down but features walls of well-chosen new and used books, as well as a calendar of publishing-related events and readings and Bernard beer on tap. Cosy, low-key and comfortable if you can find the backstreet it's on.

Nightlife

Bordo

NEW *Vinohradská 40 (728 229 554/ www.bordo.cz). Metro Náměstí Míru.* **Open** 5pm-2am Mon-Thur; 5pm-4am Fri, Sat; 6pm-2am Sun. **Map** p141 B2 ⓱

Raw, dark and fairly beat-up, Bordo reeks of authenticity and rock, with live acts from the fringe getting everybody to put down their beer glasses and get moving. Prague clubs were once all like this but Bordo's one-of-a-kind now. Head upstairs for Bordo. The gay club Valentino is downstairs.

Le Clan

Balbínova 23 (222 251 226). Metro Náměstí Míru. **Open** 10pm-3am Tue-Fri, Sun; 10pm-6am Sat. **Map** p141 A1 ⓲

With a dimly lit entrance (hit the bell to be buzzed in) and none of the downstairs decadence visible from without, this bar and club feels secretive and daring – which, of course, it is. Red plush interiors, sofas, passable basic cocktails and a lower-level dancefloor that's sometimes open, all add up to a great hideout.

Retro Music Hall

NEW *Francouzská 4 (603 476 747/ www.bordo.cz). Metro Náměstí Míru.* **Open** 5pm-5am Thur-Sat. **Map** p141 B3 ⓳

The latest big-scale club to open in the district, Retro knows how to make the most of its multilevel underground space with loud, packed dance parties led by local DJs. The bold programme also stretches to US hip hop acts, which draw every pretty young thing around.

A stylish bar in a graceful old building that has long generated a buzz among locals in the media scene. Food's on offer, but, apart from the grilled meats on the terrace, there's nothing terribly imaginative or unusual. Still, a fine view of the Nusle valley rewards those sitting outside.

Shopping

Fra

Šafaříkova 15 (274 817 126/www. fra.cz). Metro Náměstí Míru. **Open** 9am-11pm Mon-Fri; 1-11pm Sat, Sun. **Map** p141 A4 ⓯

A bookshop and café specialising in small-press volumes and works in translation by Czech and Central European writers, with a studious crowd of characters who stage readings and occasional poetry nights.

Shakespeare & Sons

Krymská 12 (271 740 839/www.shakes .cz). Metro Náměstí Míru. **Open** noon-midnight daily. **Map** p141 C4 ⓰

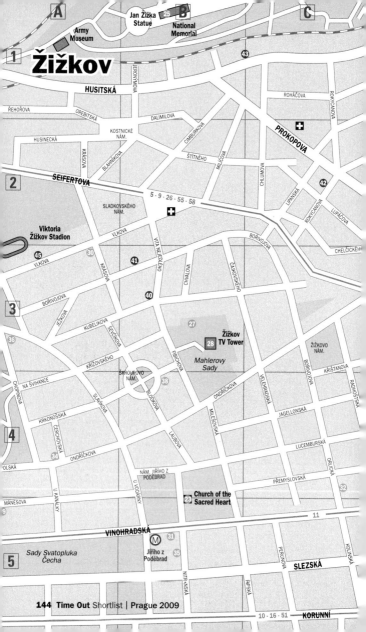

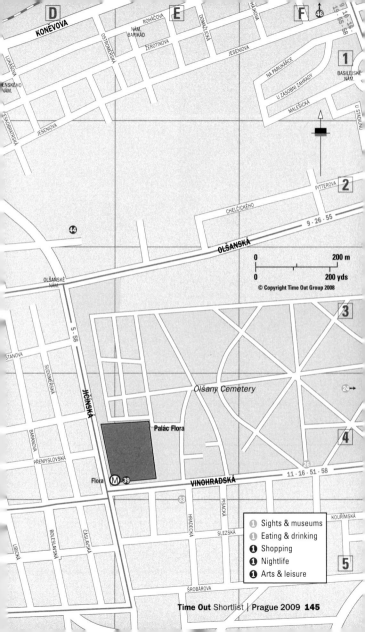

D   KONĚVOVA

E   ROHÁČOVA   NÁM.
BARIKÁD   ŽEROTINOVA   DOMAŽLICKÁ

F   46

JESENIOVA   HAJKOVA   NA PARUKÁŘCE

BASILEJSKÉ NÁM.   1

U ZÁSOBNÍ ZAHRADY

MALEŠICKÁ   U STADIÓNU

OSTROMĚŘSKÁ

LUKÁŠOVA   ENSKÉHO NÁM.   ČESNOBRSKÁ   JESENIOVA

PITTEROVA   2

CHELČICKÉHO

44   9 - 26 - 55

OLŠANSKÁ

0   200 m
0   200 yds
© Copyright Time Out Group 2008

OLŠANSKÉ NÁM.

5 - 58

STANOVA   SUDOMĚŘSKÁ   3

Olšany Cemetery   24→

JIČÍNSKÁ

BARANOVA   PŘEMYSLOVSKÁ

Palác Flora   4

26

Flora Ⓜ 39   VINOHRADSKÁ   11 - 16 - 51 - 58

BOLESLAVSKÁ   ČÁSLAVSKÁ   LIBICKÁ

33   HRADECKÁ   PSÁRSKÁ   SLEZSKÁ   KOUŘIMSKÁ

❶ Sights & museums
❶ Eating & drinking
❶ Shopping
❶ Nightlife
❶ Arts & leisure

5

ŠROBÁROVA

Time Out Shortlist | Prague 2009 **145**

National Memorial

drag, with three floors of fun, two dancefloors, multiple bars and the odd darkroom. So successful it took over the old Gejzeer club on this spot and expanded it massively. There's a giddy atmosphere and highly danceable DJ and theme nights.

Žižkov

Down the hill to the north and east of Vinohrady is Žižkov, which balances Vinohrady's charms with a concentration of pubs that's said to be the world's greatest per capita. Notorious for its artists, indulgers and large Romany population, the district makes for a colourful pastiche of good times and bad behaviour. Always a working-class district, it's also home to the greatest monument to working-class hero Jan Žižka, the one-eyed Hussite horseman general, and an impressive former signal-jamming tower.

Saints

Polská 32 (222 250 326/www.prague saints.cz). Metro Náměstí Miru. **Open** 7pm-4am daily. **Map** p141 C1 ❷⓿
A friendly, casual gay bar and dance club that doubles as an information hub for the community in Prague (the website offers loads of gay accommodation and entertainment listings), run by British owners who excel at cocktails.

Termix

Třebízského 4a (222 710 462/www. club-termix.cz). Metro Jiřího z Poděbrad. **Open** 10pm-5am daily. **Map** p141 C2 ❷❶
A crammed, jammed little bar and dance club with a mixed local and foreign crowd, a bar that's better at beer than anything elaborate and a decorator who likes old car parts. It does swing all night long, however.

Valentino

Vinohradská 40 (222 513 491/www. club-valentino.cz). Metro Náměstí Miru. **Open** 2pm-5am daily. **Map** p141 B2 ❷❷
Prague's biggest and most popular gay disco is located on the district's main

Sights & museums

Church of the Sacred Heart

Nejsvětější Srdce Páně
Náměstí Jiřího z Poděbrad (no phone). Metro Jiřího z Poděbrad. **Map** p144 B4/B5 ❷❸
Ecclesiastical modernism reaches new heights in this fantastic (for 1928-32, of course) church, whose rose window features an unbroken ramp you could ascend on a bicycle. It's one of the most inspiring structures in the city, designed by Josip Plečnik, the pioneering Slovenian architect who also redid Prague Castle to make the mark of the First Republic.

Jewish Cemetery

Židovské hřbitovy
Vinohradská and Jičínská (no phone). Metro Želivského. **Open** 9am-4pm Mon-Thur, Sun. **Admission** 20 Kč. **Map** p145 F4 ❷❹
Not to be confused with the Old Jewish Cemetery (p95) in Staré Město, this

PRAGUE BY AREA

neglected posthumous home to Franz Kafka, founded in 1890, has ivy-covered graves mainly thanks to the Holocaust – few family members remain to care for the graves, while those across the street are lovingly weeded with fresh flowers. For Kafka's grave, follow the sign by the Želivského metro entrance; it's approximately 200m (660ft) down the row by the southern cemetery wall.

National Memorial

Národní památník
U památníku 1900 (222 781 676). Metro Florenc. **Open** times vary (booking required). **Admission** varies. **Map** p144 B1 ㉕
Unless you've got 19 friends to book a party inside, you'll be relegated to the exteriors of this monumental mausoleum for communist big-wigs, where Klement Gottwald was encased in glass for a time. Its façades feature Soviet war heroes and it's topped by the largest equestrian statue in the world, a 16.5-ton (16,764-kg) effigy of Hussite hero Jan Žižka. The view from the top of Vitkov hill's impressive too.

Olšany Cemetery

Olšanské hřbitovy
Vinohradská 153/Jana Želivského (272 739 364). Metro Flora or Želivského. **Open** dawn-dusk daily. **Map** p145 F4 ㉖
The Garden of Rest honours Red Army soldiers who died in Czechoslovakia. To the right of the entrance, is the grave of anti-communist martyr Jan Palach, the student who set fire to himself in Wenceslas Square in 1969.

Žižkov Jewish Cemetery

Fibichova (no phone). Metro Jiřího z Poděbrad. **Open** 9.30am-1pm Tue, Thur. **Admission** 20 Kč. **Map** p144 B3 ㉗
This is all that remains of the cemetery that once covered this square, displaced by the communist regime to make way for its Western signal-jamming transmitter, Žižkov Tower (below). A poignant reminder of the not-too-distant past.

Žižkov Tower

Máhlerovy sady (242 418 784). Metro Jiřího z Poděbrad. **Open** 11am-11pm daily. **Admission** 60 Kč; free under-5s. **Map** p144 B3 ㉘
The huge, thrusting, three-pillared television tower in Žižkov has long been dubbed the Pražský pták, or Prague Prick, by locals. Completed early in 1989 as a foreign signal-jamming transmitter, it now broadcasts reality TV shows to eager Czechs. A lift flies up to the eighth-floor viewing platform; alternatively, take a drink in the fifth-floor café in this 216m (709ft) monstrosity. The intriguing, rather disturbing babies on the side are the work of Czech bad-boy artist and satirist David Černý.

Eating & drinking

Aromi

Mánesova 78 (222 713 222/www.aromi.cz). Metro Jiřího z Poděbrad. **Open** noon-11pm Mon-Sat; noon-10pm Sun. **$$$**. **Italian**. **Map** p144 A5 ㉙
Right from the incredible *antipasti* (buttery mozzarella from Puglia, salt cod, seared scallops), it's clear Aromi's living up to its rep as one of Prague's top Italian dining rooms. Thankfully located off the tourist radar (but definitely book ahead), Aromi makes for a gracious evening of slow dining on delights, with seafood a particular draw. But don't overlook the guinea fowl or veal in morel juice. Authoritative kitchen mastery meets low-key rough wood and brick interiors and homely presentation. Excellent, fairly priced wines are available.

Blind Eye

Vlkova 26 (no phone/www.blindeye.cz). Metro Jiřího z Poděbrad. **Open** 7pm-4am daily. **Bar**. **Map** p144 A3 ㉚
If you're looking to get into a three-hour talk about conspiracy theories or meet a US student doing a semester abroad, this is the place. Once run as a speakeasy, this thoroughly local bar is now legal but still features dark corners

PRAGUE BY AREA

Aromi p147

and well-worn interiors, making for a rough and ready late night hangout.

Černá kočka Bílý kocour

Vinohradská 62 (222 519 773). Metro Jiřího z Poděbrad. **Open** 11am-3am daily. **$**. **Grill bar**. **Map** p144 B5 ③①

A whimsical cellar bar that's become a late-night spot among the district's hip (but not obnoxious) set. Rib tips, chicken wings and burgers go well with the warm yet fleeting staff – these two qualities rarely meet in Prague restos; 'Black Cat White Cat' is the exception.

Hapu

Orlická 8 (222 720 158). Metro Jiřího z Poděbrad. **Open** 6pm-2am Mon-Sat. **Bar**. **Map** p144 C4 ③②

Not easy to find, yet invariably full, this one-room cellar with beaten-up sofas and a small bar has been a living-room bar to the neighbourhood for years. That's because it whips up the best cocktails around but mixes in none of the pretense of the usual cocktail bars in Prague. Always filled with a fun crowd of international raconteurs.

Infinity

Chrudimská 7 (272 176 580). Metro Flora. **Open** 6pm-2am daily. **Bar**. **Map** p145 E4/E5 ③③

Mellow and smoky, Infinity hosts regulars around its cellar long bar and offers a light menu of salads, lamb carpaccio and suchlike. Brick and red-washed interiors make for mellow sipping, with DJ action (of varying quality) after 10pm.

James Bond Café

Polská 7 (222 733 871). Metro Jiřího z Poděbrad. **Open** 6pm-2am daily. **Café**. **Map** p144 A4 ③④

This 007-inspired café hasn't held back when it comes to mod seating and bar surfaces, but its cocktails don't quite live up to 'licensed to kill' – although service is a notch up from many bars.

Mozaika

Nitranská 13 (224 253 011). Metro Jiřího z Poděbrad. **Open** 11.30am-midnight Mon-Fri; 4pm-midnight Sat, Sun. **$**. **World**. **Map** p144 B5 ③⑤

A consistent fave among locals, this friendly, casual place offers solid value and above-average comfort food like the hamburger with fresh mushrooms.

Homemade pâté, duck breast and Philly cheesecake are all well done and served with speed and cheer.

Rossini

Chopinova 26 (222 729 041). Metro Náměstí Míru. **Open** 11am-11pm daily. **$$. Italian.** Map p144 A3 ㊳
This rustic room serves up gorgeously done pastas, carpaccio, mortadella and well-chosen regional Italian wines. Book well ahead for one of the sought after, but surprisingly affordable, tables on any weekend. The place is located on a quiet side street well worth finding.

Sonora

Radhošťská 5 (222 711 029). Metro Flora. **Open** 11am-midnight daily. **$. Mexican.** Map p145 D4 ㊲
Some of the city's best Mexican food, complete with mole sauce, salsa, taco salad, beef burritos and tasty quesadillas. All complemented perfectly by cheap Czech beer – and a handy wall-sized map of Indian tribes.

U Sadu

Škroupovo náměstí 5 (222 727 072). Metro Jiřího z Poděbrad. **Open** 10am-2am daily. **$. Czech.** Map p144 B4 ㊳
Bustling with students and locals, and also cheap and Czech, with well-located outside seating in the summer and a friendly, smoky and packed interior the rest of the year.

Shopping

Palác Flóra

Vinohradská 151 (255 741 700/www. palacflora.cz). Metro Flóra. **Open** 8am-midnight daily. Map p145 E4 ㊴
Yet another major installation in the tidal wave of Czech malls. This one's admittedly handy, and attracts young couples who love to hang out in its cafés and bars. You can also pick up another winter layer or two or catch a movie.

Nightlife

Akropolis

Kubelíkova 27 (296 330 911/www. palacakropolis.cz). Metro Jiřího z

Žižkov Tower p147

Poděbrad. **Open** *Divadelní Bar* 7pm-5am daily. *Malá Scéná Bar* 7pm-3am daily. *Concerts* 7.30pm. Map p144 B3 ㊵
The city's most respected shrine to indie and world music, theatre and art bar culture, Akropolis is dear to the heart of Praguers. With three bars and a performance hall and two full calendars of simultaneous events, the club covers a lot of ground. United Colours of Akropolis and Jazz Meets World promote a rich array of artists and avant-garde acts (the new Internet radio, www.radioakropolis.cz, provides a taste). The downstairs bars host free DJs and MCs, and the street-level restaurant serves until late.

Bukowski's

Bořivojova 86 (222 212 676). Metro Jiřího z Poděbrad. **Open** 6pm-midnight daily. Map p144 B3 ㊶
Fast turning into a local insider's scene, this homely British pub-style (but with pure Prague ambience) room is the latest venture from longtime expat barman/former lumberjack Glen Emery and friends. The promised kitchen's yet to materialise, but the original cocktails, cool soundtrack and agreeable crowd

Pub heaven

Drinkers go to Vinohrady when they die; serious drinkers go to Žižkov. Classic Czech pubs are still more common in this district than minimarts, thank goodness, and, although money's flowing in, the old-time grotty, lively, smoke-filled *hostinec* is alive and well.

Pastička (p140) is a local hangout that's both cosy and rollicking, with well-primed beer taps and pickled cheese on the menu. **Žlutá pumpa** (p142), meanwhile, has expanded the trad offerings to throw in Mexican food, invariably a magnet for younger, well-travelled Czechs. **U Sadu** (p149) is a jumble of junkyard finds, with half a dozen good beers and a gathering of footie fans when there's a match. **Park Café** (p140) and **Parukářka** (p151) offer the same ethic but in a sylvan setting, making for better breathing possibilities. **Zvonařka** (p142) has views just as grand, plus considerably better decor and cuisine (there's little beyond crisps at most trad Czech pubs so the beer effects build up fast).

Proper bars are hardly in short supply, of course. One of the most buzzy is **Popocafepetl** (p142), while **Blind Eye** (p147) stays up later, attracting an American crowd with its student-friendly vibe. **Bordo** (p143) has the same comfortably rundown feel, but with live bands amping things up at weekends.

Le Clan (p143) is an insider's secret (ssshhh), hidden down stairs barely visible from its front room, where only brave souls dare enter by buzzing. For all that build-up, though, it's pretty innocent inside, though definitely decadent. **Černá kočka Bílý kocour** (p148; pictured) is a fine addition, handily located and with tasty grill food, decent cocktails and corner niches.

Hapu (p148) is just a tattered room but serves the best mixed drinks in the district; nearby **Bukowski's** (p149) is providing competition, however, with more space and a supercool soundtrack.

Akropolis (p149) is a survivor of the early 1990s and worth a visit for the weird surrealist decor, concerts and late hours. *Na zdraví!*

of local bohemians add up to enough laughs that no one seems to mind much.

Klub XT3

Rokycanova 29 (222 783 463/ www.xt3.cz). Metro Jiřího z Poděbrad. **Open** 6pm-5am daily. **Map** p144 C2  ❷

Difficult to find and with a programme that ranges from jazz fusion to punk and dancehall, XT3 is worth the trouble on a good night. Check the website first but Saturday nights are a good bet and the pace has picked up significantly in the last year.

Matrix

Konêvova 13 (731 411 355/www. matrixklub.cz). Metro Florenc. **Open** 8pm-4am Tue-Sat. **Map** p144 B1/C1 ❸

With a growing list of live rock and DJ nights, this former meat refrigerating facility is coming along nicely as a party hotspot. Still a rough and ready dance hole that draws local teens, it also features a decent sound system and, naturally, rivers of cheap beer.

Parukářka

Olšanská & Prokopova (no phone/ www.parukarka.cz). Metro Flora. **Open** *Pub* 7pm-2am daily. *Club* varies. **Map** p145 D2 ❹

This rustic old pub atop a grassy hill is an attraction indeed, with occasional live bands and a dedicated crowd of characters, but it's the club in the old bunker, deep inside the hill, that's the real attraction. Normally open at weekends, you descend down spiral stairs once you find the curved lead-filled fallout shelter door above Prokopská street.

Sedm Vlků

Vlkova 7 (222 711 725/www.sedm vlku.cz). Metro Jiřího z Poděrad. **Open** 5pm-3am Mon-Sat. **Map** p144 A3 ❺

An old-style scene of beer-stained, backroom decadence, the 'Seven Wolves' is refreshingly unchanged (if that's the word) and comfortable being a cigarette-burned meeting spot for insomniacs with the need to jump around the tiny dancefloor and order another round. Cruisy as hell with a distinct lack of inhibitions.

Arts & leisure

Karlín Studios

Divadlo Na Vinohradech

Křižíkova 34 (no phone/www.karlin studios.cz). Metro Křižíkova. **Open** *Public gallery* noon-6pm Tue-Sun. **Map** p145 F1 ❻

Recently renovated but still a wonderfully industrial art space, this vast complex of studios now hosts year-round shows by some of the best Czech creatives and holds regular open days for them. It's also the traditional home of the Prague Biennale, the much-anticipated modern art event of the summer of 2009.

Akropolis p149

National Gallery

Holešovice

The city's most up-and-coming quarter, Holešovice – with its sprawling public parks, 19th-century apartments and hip but unpretentious drinking venues and galleries – is well worth exploring. Quietly beckoning from across the Vltava river to the north of Old Town, this area is rapidly being transformed after years of industrial neglect into a new centre of expat and Bohemian living. The process might be happening fast (very characteristic of Prague), but there are still striking juxtapositions of grimy façades and smart cafés, marginal shops still hanging on somehow and plugged-in theatres, sports centres and art spaces. Those arriving by train may well enter the city here: the area is host to one of Prague's two international train stations, Nádraží Holešovice, which, having been badly neglected, remains a stunning example of the old Holešovice. The new can be seen in fit climbers at Boulder Bar and at **Stromovka park** and **Letná**, where young families and skaters vie for control of the paths.

Holešovice's main drag, Dukelských hrdinů, features a sleek constructivist building, **Veletržní palác**, a modern art mecca of the National Gallery. Výstaviště, up the street, is an appealingly rundown exhibition ground with a lapidarium and aquarium that houses the original saints from Charles Bridge and a funfair – Lunapark – behind its glorious main hall. Stromovka, a park to the west, laid out by Rudolf II in the 16th century, provides green space, as does **Letná** to the south. In between these are lifestyle-conscious places like **Fraktal** and **La Bodega Flamenca**. **Mecca**, on the eastern side of the district, is a classic club for thirtysomethings, while **Misch Masch**, to the west, is big, young disco central.

A ten-minute walk north of Stromovka via the bridge (or by bus No.112 from Metro Nádraži Holešovice) brings you to **Zoo Praha**, which continues to expand its facilities and programmes yearly, and makes for a great family day out.

Sights & museums

Lapidárium
Výstaviště (233 375 636/www.nm.cz).
Metro Nádraži Holešovice. **Open** noon-6pm Tue-Fri; 10am-6pm Sat, Sun.
Admission 40 Kč; 80 Kč family.
Map p155 D1 ❶
Don't go looking for the original stone saints from Charles Bridge on the bridge itself. They're all resting peacefully here, along with outstanding Czech stone sculptures from the 11th to 19th centuries.

National Gallery Collection of 19th-, 20th- & 21st-Century Art
Sbírka moderního a současného umění
Veletržní palác, Dukelských hrdinů 47 (224 301 122/www.ngprague.cz).
Metro Vltavská. **Open** 10am-6pm Tue-Sun. **Admission** 200 Kč; family 300 Kč; half-price after 4pm. *Temporary exhibitions* 50 Kč; free under-10s.
Map p155 D2 ❷
This functionalist building, designed by Oldřich Tyl and Josef Fuchs and opened in 1929, houses the National Gallery's collections of modern and contemporary art, including paintings by Karel Purkyně and 19th-century symbolists like Max Švabinský and František Bílek. The groundbreaking abstract artist František Kupka is well represented here as well, along with Czech Cubists.

Letná park

Výstaviště
Za Elektárnou 49 (220 103 111/ www.incheba.cz). Metro Nádraži Holešovice. **Open** *Grounds* 9am-9pm daily. *Water World* 10am-7pm daily.
Admission *Grounds* free. *Water World* 240 Kč; 145 Kč under-12s; free under-4s. **Map** p154 C1 ❸
Filligree exhibition hall towers mark this out as a retro gem of the district; it was built for the Jubilee Exhibition (circa 1891), and signalled the birth of the new architectural form in Prague. The grounds around it, alas, are sleepy except during the midwinter carnival Matejsky pout, when high-tech German and Dutch attractions and rides are rolled in. The area also features a time-worn fountain with a musical light show and a new aquarium, Water World, that draws the kiddies. The Lapidárium hall contains fantastic Baroque stone statuary by masters like Matthias Braun and Jan Brokoff.

Zoo Praha
U Trojského zámku (296 112 111/ www.zoopraha.cz). Metro Nádraži Holešovice. **Open** *Mar* 9am-5pm daily.

Holešovice

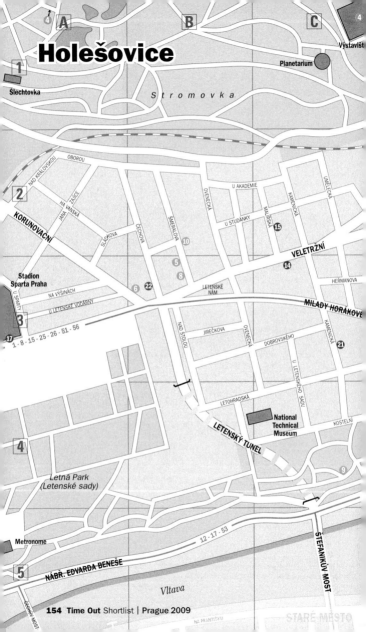

A **B** **C**

Výstaviš⁴

Planetarium

1
Šlechtovka

S t r o m o v k a

2

KORUNOVAČNÍ

NAD KRÁLOVSKOU
OBOROU
HÁ JALICE
JANA ZAJÍCE
SLAVÍČKOVA
ČECHOVA
ŠMERALOVA
10
 OVENECKÁ
U AKADEMIE
U STUDÁNKY
MALÍŘSKA
KAMENICKÁ
UMĚLECKÁ
15
VELETRŽNÍ
14
HERMANOVA
5
8
6   22
LETENSKÉ
NÁM.

Stadion
Sparta Praha

NA VÝŠINÁCH
U LETENSKÉ VODÁRNY
U SPARTY

3
17
1 · 8 · 15 · 25 · 26 · 51 · 56

MILADY HORÁKOVÉ

NAD ŠTOLOU
JIREČKOVA
OVENECKÁ
DOBROVSKÉHO
U LETENSKÉHO SADU
KAMENICKÁ
21

LETOHRADSKÁ

National
Technical
Museum
KOSTELNÍ

4

Letná Park
(Letenské sady)

LETENSKÝ TUNEL

9

Metronome
12 · 17 · 53

ŠTEFÁNIKŮV MOST

5
NÁBŘ. EDVARDA BENEŠE

Vltava

STARÉ MĚSTO

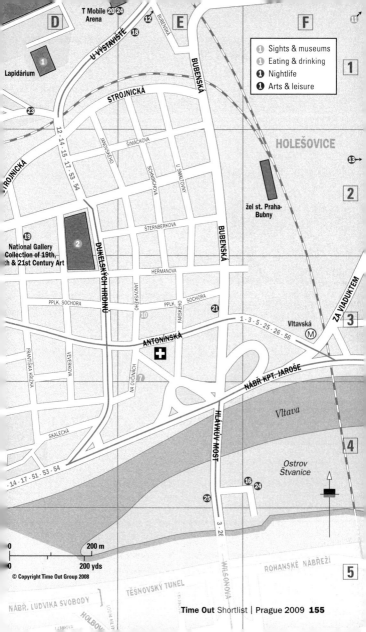

D

T Mobile 🟠20 🟠24 Arena

U VÝSTAVIŠTĚ

🟠18

🟠12 BUBENSKÁ

E

BUBENSKÁ

F

🟠11

Lapidárium 🔵1

STROJNICKÁ

🔵1 Sights & museums
🟢1 Eating & drinking
🔴1 Nightlife
🟠1 Arts & leisure

1

23

ŠIMÁČKOVA

HOLEŠOVICE

STROJNICKÁ

12 · 14 · 15 · 17 · 53 · 54

JANOVSKÉHO

ŠMIDROVA

U SMALTOVNY

🟣13→

BUBENSKÁ

žel st. Praha-Bubny

2

19

National Gallery
Collection of 19th,
th & 21st Century Art

🔴2

ŠTERNBERKOVA

DUKELSKÝCH HRDINŮ

HERMANOVA

PPLK. SOCHORA

JANOVSKÉHO

PPLK. SOCHORA

FARSKÉHO

🟠21

🟠10

1 · 3 · 5 · 25 · 26 · 56

Vltavská Ⓜ

ZA VIADUKTEM

3

FRANTIŠKA KŘÍŽKA

VEVERKOVA

ANTONÍNSKÁ

✚

NA OVČNÁCH

🟠7

NÁBŘ. KPT. JAROŠE

Vltava

SKALECKÁ

HLÁVKŮV MOST

4

14 · 17 · 51 · 53 · 54

Ostrov
Štvanice

🟠16 🟠24

🟠25

3 · 26

0   **200 m**
200 yds

© Copyright Time Out Group 2008

ROHANSKÉ NÁBŘEŽÍ

5

NÁBŘ. LUDVÍKA SVOBODY

HOLBOV

TĚŠNOVSKÝ TUNEL

WILSONOVA

La Bodega Flamenca

Apr, May, Sept, Oct 9am-6pm daily.
June-Aug 9am-7pm daily. *Nov-Feb* 9am-4pm daily. **Admission** 150 Kč; 450 Kč family; free under-3s. **Map** p154 A1 ④
Praguers have rallied round their newly remodelled zoo, which now hosts 652 species and nearly 5,000 animals (at last count), including rare snow leopards. Scientists here also conduct important research on breeding. The children's area is a hit, as is the new outdoor exhibition grounds for Sumatran orangutans. There's a list of feeding and exercise times (in English) posted on the website.

Eating & drinking

La Bodega Flamenca
*Šmeralova 5 (233 374 075/www.
labodega.cz). Metro Vltavská.* **Open** 4pm-1am Mon-Thur, Sun; 4pm-3am Fri, Sat. **$. Spanish. Map** p154 B3 ⑤
The Serrano ham is the first tip-off that the owners of La Bodega are true Hispanophiles, dedicated to doing up the best tapas bar selection in the city – and keeping it affordable for all their artist/student friends. Often packed to the rafters, it's worth finding the nondescript entrance two doors north of Fraktal. Bacon-wrapped plums and marinated peppers kick off the perpetual salsa party. Bench-style seats line the walls and fill up fast and things start hotting up after 1am.

Un Chien Andalou
*Korunovační 4 (no phone). Metro
Hradčanská, then tram 1, 8, 15.* **Open** 7pm-5am daily. **Bar. Map** p154 B3 ⑥
Cool, dark and sofa-filled, this plush little place is a local secret, where live bands occasionally perform, usually as iconoclastic as the bar staff. Decent cocktails and with a wall-to-wall decadent atmosphere.

La Creperie
*Janovského 4 (220 878 040/www.
lacreperie.cz). Metro Vltavská.* **Open** 9am-11pm Mon-Sat; 9am-10pm Sun.
$. Crêperie. Map p155 E3 ⑦
This dim and cosy French-owned spot, complete with a reliable Edith Piaf soundtrack, still serves large crêpes, both sweet and savoury, for a pittance. But it's also been updated with Wi-Fi, a non-smoking area and children's play

corner. There's a nicely expanded wine list as well and crispy fresh croissants.

Fraktal

Šmeralova 1 (777 794 094/www.fraktal bar.cz). Metro Vltavská. **Open** 11am-midnight daily. **Café**. **Map** p154 B3 ⑧
Voted home of the best burger in Prague by the *Prague Post*, this funky cavern of carved logs and hammered copper is a good deal more than this, with Wi-Fi, the district's most popular brunch, strong bloody marys and beat-up charm that draws bohemian types, both local and expat, year-round. The Czech-Mex dishes are done well (pesto quesadillas recommended).

Letenský zámeček

Letenské sady 341 (in Letná Park) (233 375 604/www.letenskyzamecek. cz). Metro Hradčanská. **Open** *Beer garden* Apr-Oct 11am-11pm daily. *Restaurants* 11am-11.30pm daily.
$$. Czech. **Map** p154 C4 ⑨
This leafy enclave on the hill above the Vltava is arguably the city's finest summer beer garden. A local crowd gathers under the chestnut trees for cheap beer in plastic cups late into the evening, every evening that it's warm enough to sit out (above freezing seems to qualify). The adjoining Brasserie Ullmann and Restaurant Belcredi provide the upscale counterbalance to the ruddy benches outside, with modern designer interiors, a dressy crowd and excellent Bernard beer on draught.

Ouky Douky

Janovského 14 (266 711 531/ www.oukydouky.cz). Metro Vltavská. **Open** 8am-midnight daily. **Café**. **Map** p155 E3 ⑩
A bookstore café without much to read for English speakers, this place is the original location of the Globe Bookstore and Coffeehouse (p135). The owners tried to copy its formula, but haven't been too successful.

Pivovar U Bulovky

Bulovka 17, Libeň (284 840 650/ www.privovarubulovky.cz). Metro Palmovka, then tram 10, 15, 24, 25. **Open** 10am-midnight daily.
Pub. **Map** p155 F1 ⑪
Though it's well off the beaten track (and beyond the Holešovice district borders), critics from the *New York Times* have tracked down František Richter's pub, known to beer afficionados far and wide for its excellent microbrew beers, homemade sausage and unique flavouring inspirations. The Friday night blues bands play irregularly but add a jolt.

Nightlife

Cross Club

Plynární 23 (736 535 053/www. crossclub.cz). Metro Nádraží Holešovice. **Open** 2pm-3am Mon-Fri; 4pm-5am Sat, Sun. **Map** p155 E1 ⑫
It may resemble an auto-parts store but don't be taken in as you hike north from the metro station to find it. This magnet for arts types is a centre for music, film, dance and drink and every surface has been welded or molded, gallery-style, into the city's edgiest art bar. And a raw and laidback one at that; not for pretentious scenesters.

Mecca

U Průhonu 3 (283 870 522/www. mecca.cz). Metro Vltavská. **Open** *Club* 10pm-5am Wed, Fri, Sat. *Concerts* 10pm; call for days. **Map** p155 F2 ⓭
Recently taken over by the management of Duplex club (p136) across the river, Mecca is still a comfortably cool space in semi-industrial Holešovice, with two levels, three bars and hundreds of loyal house and techno fans, who turn out in style to catch their fave DJs. The place was an early bastion of clubbing in this part of town, and it's never slackened its pace.

Misch Masch

Veletržní 61 (603 222 227/www. mischmasch.cz). Metro Vltavská. **Open** 8pm-4am Thur-Sat. **Map** p154 C3 ⓮
These days, the former Disco Letná is as over-the-top as ever, with endless wacky and intensely local theme parties dedicated to loud pop-dance tracks and everything from wet bikinis to somewhat dubious fashion creations. Local celebrity DJs who are fond of shouting pep talk at dancers on the MC form the mainstay here.

Wakata

Malířská 14 (233 370 518/www.wakata. cz). Metro Vltavská. **Open** 5pm-3am Mon-Thur; 5pm-5am Fri, Sat; 6pm-3am Sun. **Map** p154 C2 ⓯
Bar stools here are made of motorcycle seats, and a stoned crew of servers and DJs comprise the staff, but Wakata is open late and has a truly anarchic neighbourhood feel.

Arts & leisure

I. ČLTK

Ostrov Štvanice 38 (222 316 317/www. cltk.cz). Metro Florenc or Vltavská. **Open** 7am-midnight daily. **Map** p155 F4 ⓰
Ten outdoor clay courts, three of which are floodlit, plus sparkling indoor facilities (four hard courts, two clay courts) all make for tennis facilities up to scratch for Czech players who take the game deadly seriously. Booking essential.

AC Sparta Praha

Toyota Arena, Milady Horákové 98, (220 570 323/www.sparta.cz). Metro Hradčanská. **Admission** *European games* 400-900 Kč. *League games* 50-230 Kč. **Map** p154 A3 ⓱

Výstaviště p153

PRAGUE BY AREA

Sweat it off

Though it's only a good javelin toss across the Vltava river from Old Town, the Holešovice district offers so many sport and fitness options that you'd think it was in the remote suburbs. The area has probably benefited from the neglect it suffered after 1989, when its by-and-large useless factories and warehouses shut down, leaving clean air and relatively open spaces. The other handy legacy from the bad old days is the number of arenas, stadiums and tennis courts so loved by the central planners who put great stock in Czech Olympic wins; there are more places to work off your sausage and beer overdose in Holešovice than in any other quarter.

If you're just up for a stroll, **Stromovka** (p160) has you covered. The gentle slopes, lakes and glens of this park beckon on nice days, and people of all ages can be seen gliding its paths on rollerblades. **Zoo Praha** (p153), on the north side, also has plenty of long, hilly paths to go with its incredible collection of fauna. In the district's other great green space, **Letná** (pictured) there's a good five miles of paved paths perfectly suited to a jog or a skate, with views of the spires of Old Town as your backdrop – and the leafy **Letenský zámeček** (p157) beer garden awaiting the end of your workout. Within a short walk of both parks is the **Skala Sport** shop (p160), well stocked with rental skates, boards and bikes.

One of the best tennis complexes in town is on the island halfway between Holešovice and Old Town; it still sports the classic communist-style name **I. ČLTK** (p159). Don't be fooled though – serious facilities are to be found here, and it's unlikely you'll get a court without an advance reservation. The same island offers a taste of the old regime in **Zimní stadion Štvanice** (p160), where bizarre hours and nary a word of English await those brave enough to try ice skating here.

An perhaps easier workout is on offer at the more friendly **Boulder Bar** (p160), where you can witness the Czech love of crawling up cliff faces. Just remember: climbing first, *then* beer.

Sparta is the team to beat in Czech football. It's comparatively poor in Europe, but this hasn't stopped it from pulling off some mighty upsets against wealthier opponents. Their 18,500-capacity stadium, aka Letná, is the country's best.

Boulder Bar

NEW *U výstavište 11 (233 313 906/ www.boulder.cz). Metro Nádraží Holešovice, then tram 5, 12, 17.* **Open** 8-11pm Mon-Fri; noon-11pm Sun. **Map** p155 E1 🔞

Having moved from their original location downtown, the rock is back, with 300 square metres of climbing wall space, some surfaces 4.3 metres high. Rallies, training, a gear shop, friendly pros and an easygoing café-bar out front.

Divadlo Alfred ve Dvoře

Františka Křižka 36 (233 376 997/ www.alfredvedvore.cz). Metro Vltavská. **Open** *Box office* 1hr before performance. **Map** p155 D2 🔞

With a progressive programme that runs from 'physical concert' to 'industrial haiku', this small but important theatre in a modern building constructed in a residential courtyard is known nationwide. Non-verbal, experimental theatre, as well as dance, tends to dominate.

HC Sparta Praha

T-Mobile Arena, Za Elektárnou 419 (266 727 443/www.hcsparta.cz). Tram 5, 12, 14, 15, 17. **Open** *Box office* 1-6.30pm Mon-Fri; 1-5.30pm Sun. **Map** p155 D1 🔞

Sparta's home ice rink was state-of-the-art when it was built; today it's showing signs of wear and tear. The team itself, though, is well-financed and always competitive. The large arena doesn't really come alive till the play-offs. Tickets can be bought in advance from the box office at the entrance, or online through the Ticketpro agency (p186).

Hunt Kastner Artworks

Kamenická 22 (233 376 259/www. huntkastner.com). Metro Vltavská. **Open** *Sept-July* noon-5pm Thur, Fri or by appointment. **Map** p154 C3 🔞

This private gallery was established to nurture the careers of a stable of over a dozen Czech contemporary artists like Tomáš Vanik and Michael Thelenová, while at the same time helping to find collectors for their works and encourage development of the fledgling art market.

Skala Sport

NEW *Čechova 3 (605 258 670/ www.skalasport.wz.cz). Metro Vltavská.* **Open** 10am-6pm Mon-Fri; 10am-4pm Sat. **Map** p154 B3 🔞

Rent inline skates or bikes by the hour or the day to be kitted out for nearby Stromovka or Letná parks. Skis, boating, climbing and camping gear can be hired as well and the canny staff can do repairs on your gear.

Stromovka

U Výstavište & Dukelských hrdinů. Metro Nádraží Holešovice, then tram 5, 12, 17. **Map** p155 D1 🔞

Just 15 minutes from downtown but with nary a hint of the city about it, this former royal hunting ground draws runners, strollers, lovers, kids and dogs. After the initial sprint to avoid the Výstavište crowds, you can have the meadows to yourself. See if you can hear the language of birds that alchemist John Dee claimed to understand here.

T-Mobile Arena

Výstaviště, Za elektárnou 319, Holešovice (266 727 411). Metro Nádraží Holešovice. **Map** p155 D1/E1 🔞

A skating rink when not a concert hall, this barn has all the acoustics you'd expect from such a place. But it's the only indoor spot in Prague that can accommodate thousands.

Zimní stadion Štvanice

Ostrov Štvanice 1125 (602 623 449/ www.stvanice.cz). Metro Florenc or Vltavská. **Open** 10am-noon, 2.30-4.15pm Mon; 10.30am-noon, 3-5.30pm Tue, Thur; 10am-noon, 3-4.30pm Wed; 10.30am-noon, 3-5.30pm Fri; 9am-noon, 2-5pm, 8-10pm Sat; 9am-noon, 2-5pm Sun. **Map** p155 E4 🔞

This rickety-looking structure houses two rinks, with generous, if seemingly random, opening hours, on an island in the Vltava. Bring a Czech friend – little English is spoken.

Essentials

Ventana Hotel p175

Hotels

Prague's boom in hotels means more competition and choice than ever before and, fortunately, it's coming in at all price ranges. Boutique stays are classier than ever, with a new confidence visible in service and more thoughtful (and useful) amenities, from Wi-Fi, which is everywhere now, to bigger bathtubs and hotel bars that are attractions in themselves. Still, the learning curve is steep and many new establishments have not yet worked out all the bugs (refunds do not readily come to mind with most Czech entrepreneurs as an option just yet). That said, young managers are eager to please and more imaginative and gracious than ever. The **Icon** hotel is a good example of affordable style, while the **Ventana** is a welcome addition

to the top-range choices. Backpackers, meanwhile, will likely forget that the **Czech Inn** is a hostel, while the **Rosemary Hostel** is nearly as well appointed and customer friendly.

Opulence still resides at the **Hotel Mandarin Oriental**, but the Alchymist group has expanded into the buzzing genre of residence hotels, having taken over and totally redone the **Alchymist Residence Nosticova** with taste, character and style. Great deals are still best found on the web pages of hostelries, especially in off-peak seasons. (Many think Prague is loveliest in autumn and winter, anyway.) More adventurous travellers, of course, can always scare up a spare room with a family or in basic pensions, which agencies like Stop City

ESSENTIALS

(www.stopcity.cz) specialise in, while a newer generation of apartment bookers such as www.pragueapartment.cz carries more homely places with cooking facilities and services like laptop and mobile phone rental.

Also remember that you can often score an arched room in a restored palace, evocative villa or 17th-century inn for about the same rate as the Best Western if you book ahead, taking full advantage of the city's stunning architecture. Family facilities are better than ever too, with babysitting services or free rates for kids who share your room more and more common.

Money matters

Many hotels quote their rates in euros and, though the Czech Republic is not yet in the euro zone, will happily take them. Note that if you pay in Czech crowns, the price often won't be calculated at the official exchange rate and you'll take a hit. Many places, however, offer discounts for cash, so it may be worth proffering euro notes if you don't mind carrying them.

Many hotels quote room prices exclusive of VAT. Always check.

Hradčany

Dům U velké boty
Vlašská 30, Malá Strana (257 532 088/www.dum uvelkeboty.cz). Metro Malostranská. **$$**.
The Rippl family won back their 1470 house (situated on the border of Malá Strana and Hradcany) from the state after 1989 and, fortunately for their writer and artist regulars, opened the 'House at the Big Boot' to guests to fund restoration. Now it's a prime bargain and the most rewarding place to stay in the area. There's no sign, just a buzzer marked 'Rippl', and rooms decked out in period furniture.

Family suites may include a kitchen. Breakfast is an extra 200 Kč and there's Wi-Fi connection.

Golden Horse House
Úvoz 8 (777 130 286/www.gold horse.cz). Tram 22, 23. **$**.
Prime location meets low price in these 11 rooms, all en suite. Service is amiable, breakfast is available for an extra 120 Kč and it's next door to a hip pub (U zavěšenýho kafe), where veteran Prague musos, scribes and actors hang out. You can cook on site and Wi-Fi's available.

Hotel Neruda
Nerudova 44 (257 535 556/www. hotelneruda.cz). Metro Malostranská. **$$$$**.
In a cosy 1348 building, old-world charm has been meshed with an open, airy feel. Czech star designer Bořek Šipek oversaw the expansion that has brought the total of rooms from 20 to 43. Service is attentive and friendly and you're smack bang on the main lane to Prague Castle. The terrace restaurant has Wi-Fi.

Hotel Questenberk
Úvoz 15 (220 407 600/www. questenberk.cz). Tram 22, 23. **$$$**.
Converted in 2002 from a neglected monastery (there's still an imposing stone crucifix at the entrance), the 30 rooms of this quaint Baroque building, just 500 metres from the Castle, are a good bit too comfortable for monks and now come with Wi-Fi. They're not as posh as you'd expect for the price, though, and staff, while enthusiastic, are sometimes a bit flustered. An only-in-Prague feel.

Hotel Savoy
Keplerova 6 (224 302 430/www. hotel-savoy.cz). Tram 22, 23. **$$$$**.
First impressions are of quiet, traditional competence, as evidenced by the library, fireplace and gliding service. Then you notice Robert Palmer in the elevator and spot a Hollywood star in the breakfast room (or, if you're lucky, in the hot tub). The plush, if not huge, 61 rooms keep the biz and showbiz crowds coming back.

ESSENTIALS

Romantik Hotel U raka

Černinská 10 (220 511 100/
www.romantikhotel-uraka.cz).
Tram 22, 23. **$$$**.
Booking well ahead is the only way to
land one of these six rooms, which date
back to 1739. It's a small, rustic pen-
sion suited to couples with time to
spare, on a quiet Hradčany backstreet
within earshot of the bells of the Loreto.
Unique but also backed by polished
service. Enchanting breakfast/reading
room with brick hearth. No children
under 12 allowed.

U Červeného Lva

Nerudova 41 (257 533 832/www.
hotelredlion.com). Metro Malostranská.
$$$.
There are few small hotels on the Royal
Route leading up to the Castle that can
boast such authentic 17th-century
decor, including colourful hand-painted
vaulted ceilings. This reconstructed
burgher's house of just eight rooms
provides guests with a sense of
Renaissance Prague but service more
adequate than standout.

U krále Karla

Úvoz 4 (257 532 869/www.romantic
hotels.cz). Metro Malostranská. **$$$**.
Solid oak furnishings, painted vaulted
ceilings, stained-glass windows and
Baroque treasures lend this 19-room
inn the feel of an aristocratic country
house, even though it was once owned
by the Benedictine order. There are
discounts for cash payments and a
Bohemian restaurant on site.

Malá Strana & Smíchov

Alchymist Hotel Residence

Tržiště 19, Malá Strana (223 920
118/www.alchymisthotel.cz). Metro
Malostranská. **$$$$**.
Humbly ensconced in the Baroque U
Ježíšek Palace, the Alchymist works its
magic on more than just your wallet.
Mottled walls, vaulted ceilings, frescoes,

Best new
- Alchymist Residence Nosticova (p167)
- Czech Inn (p177)
- Icon Hotel (p176)
- Ventana Hotel (p175)

Best for hipsters
- Hotel Savoy (p164)
- Maximilian Hotel (p174)

Best palace stays
- Pachtův Palace (p174)
- Le Palais (p179)

Most stellar restaurants
- Four Seasons: Allegro (p100)
- Hotel Savoy: Restaurant Hradčany (p66)

Best for families
- Dorint Don Giovanni (p177)
- Mövenpick Hotel (p169)

Cheap as chips
- Pension Accord (p174)
- U Šuterů (p176)

Most charming atmosphere
- Hotel U páva (p168)
- Residence Řetězová (p175)

Superior pensions
- Dům U velké boty (p164)
- Romantik Hotel U raka (p165)

Happening hostels
- Hostel Rosemary (p172)
- Miss Sophie's Prague (p179)

Best budget style
- 987 Prague Hotel (p175)
- Hotel Anna (p177)

All-round winners
- Aria Hotel (p167)
- Floor Hotel (p172)
- Hotel Elite (p176)
- Julian (p169)

ESSENTIALS

four-poster beds and spoiling service are complemented by one of Prague's hottest new wellness centres, with Balinese massage and pool. The US embassy is right next door.

Alchymist Residence Nosticova

Nosticova 1, Malá Strana (257 312 513/www.nosticova.com). Metro Malostranská. **$$$.**
Completely made over in one of the city's most talked-about boutique hotel developments, this Baroque 'residence', on a quiet lane just off Kampa Island, now features the latest in everything. The ten suites range from ample to capacious and come with antique furniture, huge bathrooms and fully equipped kitchenettes. Two have working fireplaces and one a rooftop terrace. If you don't feel like cooking your own, continental breakfast is served for an extra nine euros. Sushi bar, massages and sauna add to the decadence.

Aria Hotel

Tržiště 9, Malá Strana (225 334 111/ www.ariahotel.net). Metro Malostranská. **$$$$.**
The Aria has broken new ground and set the standard for luxe boutique hostelry in Prague, with its amenities, service and location. The oddly shaped rooms (the building was previously a post office) are classically designed and jammed with audiophile toys; computers, DVD players and serious speakers are standard, and each room is dedicated to a musician, whose biog and songs are on your hard drive, and there's a music library (great books and DVDs too) in the lobby. The roof terrace may offer the best view afforded anywhere in the city. Request a room facing the Baroque gardens. Free airport shuttle, gym and a much-lauded lobby piano café/bar are additional draws.

Best Western Kampa Hotel

Všehrdova 16, Malá Strana (271 090 847/www.euroagentur.com/cz/ best-western-hotel-kampa). Metro Malostranská. **$$$.**

Located on a quiet backstreet in Malá Strana, the Kampa Hotel has retained its 17th-century architecture and style through recent renovations, and rooms are elegantly arranged. The vaulted 'Knights Hall' dining room and adjacent pub will be a huge hit with frustrated knights. Fret not for lack of the grail, the 60 Kč beers are barely worth it anyway.

Hostel Sokol

Nosticova 2, Malá Strana (257 007 397/www.sokol-cos.cz/hostel.html). Metro Malostranská. **$.**
Find Hostel Sokol (the entrance is via the yard behind the Sokol sports centre) and you've found the starving student travel nerve centre of Prague. It has a great terrace for beer-sipping with a view. Many bunks are located in the large gymnasium. Not far from Prague Castle and the Charles Bridge. Breakfast is not included. Book ahead by telephone, or email hostelsocool @seznam.cz.

Hotel Hoffmeister

Pod Bruskou 7, Malá Strana (251 017 111/www.hoffmeister.cz). Metro Malostranská. **$$$$.**
Filled with original images by Adolf Hoffmeister, an inveterate chronicler of the Jazz Age in Prague, this hotel offers suitably decadent and classy rooms, a fine terrace restaurant with an impressive wine cellar, and a wellness centre that's won praises among demanding travellers. Book well ahead for the best deals.

Hotel Mandarin Oriental

Nebovidská 1, Malá Strana (233 088 888/www.mandarinoriental.com/ prague). Tram 6, 9, 12, 20. **$$$$.**
The hotel event of 2006 was the opening of this 99-room gem in a wonderfully quiet spot just three blocks from Charles Bridge. The former 14th-century monastery has been handsomely renovated with custom rooms, a spa with holistic treatments and a grand restaurant with fine Asian and continental fare. Rooms are modern and high-tech yet cosy, with royal blue

Romantik Hotel u raka p165

accents and retaining many original features; those on the upper floors have magical views across Prague. Excellent service.

Hotel U Kříže
Újezd 20, Malá Strana (257 313 272/ www.ukrize.com). Tram 6, 9, 12, 20, 22, 23. **$$**.
Quaint enough, with 22 pleasant rooms, and great value for money, the Hotel U Kříže is strategically located across the street from Petřín hill. It's a quick walk from Kampa Island, one tram stop to the National Theatre and two stops to Malostranská náměstí. Ask for a room facing the atrium; those facing the hill tend to get rattled by the street trams. Free coffee and cake can be taken in the lobby bar from noon to 6pm. The place is also pet friendly.

Hotel U páva
U Lužického semináře 32, Malá Strana (257 533 360/www.romantichotels.cz). Metro Malostranská. **$$$**.

The dark oak ceilings and crystal chandeliers don't synthesise as well here as at U krále Karla (p165; also owned by Karel Klubal), where the elegance is seamless, but the location is ideal, in a serene corner of Malá Strana. Suites 201, 301, 401 and 402 look on to the Castle. Some rooms are not accessible by lift, so if you need it, say so when booking. An old-world restaurant, massage service, sauna and no-smoking rooms have kept the 'Peacock' on the veteran travellers' lists for years.

Hotel U Zlaté Studně
U Zlaté studně 4, Malá Strana (257 011 213/www.zlatastudna.cz). Metro Malostranská. **$$$**.
The 19-room inn is nestled on a secluded street on a Malá Strana hill below the Castle. Rooms feature wood floors and ceilings and stylish furniture. If you could use a soak, ask for one of the rooms with a huge tub. Breakfast on a terrace goes with a stellar view of the city. The view from the indoor dining area is tremendous.

Hotel William

Hellichova 5, Smíchov (257 320 242/
www.euroagentur.com/cz/ea-hotel-
william). Tram 6, 10, 12, 20. **$$**.
Opened in 2001, this inconspicuous
hotel of 42 rooms has a great location,
a quick walk from the funicular up
Petřín hill, and just one tram stop from
Malostranské náměstí, the main square
of the district. Decorators went a wee bit
overboard trying for a 'castle feel' but
rooms are comfortable and good value.
Ask for one on the back side of the hotel,
away from the noise of the trams.

Janáček Palace Hotel

Janačkovo Nabřeži 19, Malá Strana
(775 168 611). Tram 6, 9, 22, 23. **$$$**.
This 17-apartment 'palace' has an
impressive riverside location and gabled
exterior but rooms don't really live up to
the name, comfortable and airy as they
are. More spent on design and decor
would make this exceptional building
more exceptional but it still offers a taste
of living well in Bohemia and the three-
bedroom apartments have Jacuzzis.

Julian

Elišky Peškové 11, Smíchov (257
311 150/www.julian.cz). Tram 6, 9,
12, 20. **$$**.
A bit of luxury in Smíchov, the Julian
features a drawing room with fireplace
and library and a non-smoking lobby
bar, a rarity in Prague. Room decor is
light and understated and there are
apartments with kitchenettes as well
as a family room, complete with toys.
Not quite in the centre, but an easy
tram or metro ride away from Old
Town. Airport/railway station shuttle,
gym, sauna, whirlpool, massage and
Wi-Fi all feature.

Mövenpick Hotel

Mozartova 1, Smíchov (257 151 111/
www.movenpick-prague.com). Metro
Anděl/tram 4, 7, 9. **$$**.
The not so easily accessible location is
more than set off by the surrounding
beauty and excellent Mövenpick-stan-
dard service. Actually two buildings
(the executive wing is accessible only
by cable car), it's family-friendly and

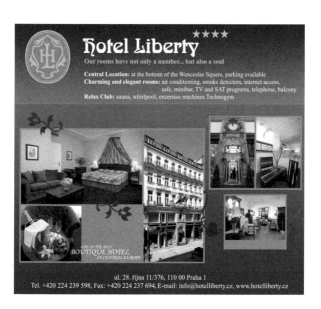

has fine dining restaurants frequented by many Praguesters. Rooms are fairly standard-issue, but deep discounts are available off-season and a verdant park is next door. Good concierge and business services plus babysitting.

Pension Dientzenhofer

Nosticova 2, Malá Strana (257 311 319/www.dientzenhofer.cz). Metro Malostranská. **$$**.
This always-booked inn facing Kampa Island has a quiet courtyard and back garden that offer a lovely respite in the midst of Malá Strana. The ten rooms are not tremendously posh, but are bright, and the staff are friendly – something still not standard in Prague. Baroque architect star Kilian Ignaz Dientzenhofer was born in the 16th-century building and his work fills this quarter of the city.

Rezidence Lundborg

U Lužického semináře 3, Malá Strana (257 011 911/www.lundborg.se). Metro Malostranská. **$$$**.
With a prime view of Charles Bridge, and on the site of the old Juditin Bridge, this Scandinavian-owned hotel of 13 suites exudes luxury and charm. A prime example of the executive residence/hotel hybrid that's spread throughout Prague, Lundborg pampers stressed guests with apartments that successfully blend reconstructed Renaissance with business amenities. A major splashout, but every need is anticipated, from wine cellar to arranging golf programmes in Karlštejn or Konopiště resorts during summer.

Riverside Hotel

Janáčkovo nábřeží 15, Malá Strana (234 705 155/www.riversideprague.com). Metro Malostranská. **$$$**.
A luxe little retreat that's already a favourite with actors seeking an escape from the bright lights while shooting in Prague. This gem of the MaMaison group is ensconced in a lovely Baroque townhouse whose east-facing rooms overlook the Vltava river. Wooden floors, spacious bathrooms, Wi-Fi in the lobby, a DVD library and other extras helped make the hotel an award-winner in its first year of opening.

U Karlova mostu

Na Kampě 15, Malá Strana (257 531 430/www.archibald.cz). Metro Malostranská. **$$**.
Formerly named Na Kampě 15, 'At the Charles Bridge' affords fine views of the bridge and Old Town, yet it's situated at a sufficient distance to offer peace and quiet. The former 15th-century tavern that brewed one of the city's pioneering beers still has homely rooms with wood floors, exposed beams and garret windows but with modern furnishings. The two cellar pubs and beer garden out the back offer Czech trad grub and well-tapped beer.

Staré Město

Cloister Inn

Konviktská 14 (224 211 020/www.cloister-inn.com). Metro Národní třída. **$$**.
Resting behind the cheaper Pension Unitas, the Cloister Inn has attentive staff, a great location, good prices and a nearby house full of nuns should you need redemption. Bright, cheery rooms and a lobby computer with free internet, plus free coffee and tea and a lending library all feature. The prices have risen of late, but the website often offers good deals.

Euro Agentur Hotel Royal Esprit

NEW *Jakubská 5 (224 800 055/www.euroanentur.com/cz/ea-hotel-royal-esprit). Metro Náměsti Republiky.* **$$$**.
Until recently known as the Hotel Mejstřík, this hotel, handily located in the heart of Old Town, was founded in 1924. Now chain-licensed, it still features individually decorated rooms that are a hybrid of ubiquitous modern hotel decor and 1920s style. Art deco elements and wood trim are a nice touch and corner rooms offer great vantages for spying on streetlife and gables. No-smoking

ESSENTIALS

Aria Hotel p167

be hard-pressed to catch even a whiff of musty history. Of course, there's no shortage of that just outside the walls, so you might as well enjoy the luxurious surroundings and service. Vista seekers will want to reserve the top-flight rooms with sweeping views of Prague Castle and Charles Bridge. In-room massage and pedicures go a long way to restoring Castle-worn lower extremities.

Hostel Rosemary

NEW *Ružová 5 (222 211 124/www.praguecityhostel.cz). Metro Můstek.* **S**.
Far cleaner and better run than you might expect for a hostel, the Rosemary is the latest generation, offering some private rooms with en-suite baths starting at 38 euros and twins at 19 euros per person with nary a curfew. Breakfast isn't included, but free internet is, credit cards are fine and the location can't be beat, just off Wenceslas Square. A good new option for backpackers, with more beds available at sister hostel U Melounu.

Hotel Černý Slon

Týnská 1 (222 321 521/www.hotel cernyslon.cz). Metro Staroměstská. **$$**.
With an incredible location in the shadow of the Tyn church, just off Old Town Square, this cosy 16-room inn is ensconced in a 14th-century building that's on the UNESCO heritage list. Gothic stone arches and wooden floors go with the smallish, but comfortable rooms laid out with basic amenities. Windows look out on the cobbled mews in the quieter part of Old Town, but there's still a constant parade of characters.

Hotel Josef

Rybná 20 (221 700 111/www.hoteljosef. com). Metro Náměstí republiky. **$$$**.
With a recently renovated fitness centre and sauna, the Josef remains one of the hippest designer hotels in Old Town, starting a trend when it opened in 2002. Flash modernist interiors and unique fabrics and glass bathrooms (superior-class rooms only) are the work of London-based designer Eva

and disabled-adapted rooms are available, and there's a reasonable traditionally Czech restaurant.

Floor Hotel

Na Příkopě 13 (234 076 300/ www.floorhotel.cz). Metro Můstek. **$$**.
An affordable addition to Prague's marquee shopping promenade, but the venture capitalists kept it simple with 43 rooms over four storeys, half of which offer traditional luxury, the other half sleek and modern decor (Jacuzzis optional). The upscale fusion eaterie has an impressive menu, and there's a large, crystal chandeliered conference room for the business crowd.

Four Seasons Hotel Prague

Veleslavinova 2A (221 427 000/ www.fourseasons.com/prague). Metro Staroměstská. **$$$$**.
The only fault to be found with the Four Seasons is that it's perhaps too perfect. While it's a seamless melding of restored Gothic, Baroque, Renaissance and neo-classical buildings, guests will

Jiřičná. All this in the thick of the historic centre, with the top-floor rooms in the 'Pink House' having the best views. There's no real designer bar, alas, just the overlit lobby one, but you do feel sleek here. Kids under six are free.

Hotel Paříž Praha

U Obecního domu 1 (222 195 195/ www.hotel-pariz.cz). Metro Náměstí Republiky. **$$$**.

If any hotel captures the spirit of Prague's belle époque, it's this one. Immortalised in Bohumil Hrabal's novel *I Served the King of England* (the film version of which was released in 2006) the Paříž is ageing with remarkable grace. Those weary of cookie-cutter hotels will appreciate the patina of the historic rooms and carefully preserved Jazz-Age dining room and café. Money no object? Try the Royal Tower Suite, with its 360-degree view of the city. Nice wellness-spa centre too; see box p178.

Hotel U Prince

Staroměstské náměstí 29 (224 213 807/www.hoteluprince.cz). Metro Staroměstská. **$$$**.

An authentic slice of history smack in the centre of Old Town Square. The hotel, which opened in 2001, is a reconstruction of a 12th-century estate and boasts huge rooms with antiques and individually designed canopy beds and armoires. Marble bathrooms are nicely decadent too. There are several eateries, including a seafood cavern and a rooftop café with a dazzling view of Prague landmarks. Neighbouring restaurants offer better value and privacy, but U Prince is still good for breakfast or a cocktail.

Hotel U Tří Bubnů

U radnice 10 (224 214 855/www. utribubnu.cz). Metro Staroměstská. **$$**.

Just 50 metres from Old Town Square, this is another place out to prove you can just about sleep within the landmark sights of Prague. Well-appointed rooms have been updated of late and feature a rustic vibe, thanks to the wood furniture and ceilings. The attic suites are huge – perfect for a family

Slick sleeps

Prague now thinks of itself as something of a specialist in boutique hotels, with the trumpeting of new 500-room hostelries heard less and less often. Sometimes, frankly, this means little more than pseudo-*moderne* furniture and a colour scheme out of art school 101, but a few places take trendsetting seriously and have backed up their slick looks with thoughtful high-tech amenities, dining and chillout options as cool as the decor, and warm and helpful staff.

The **Icon** (p176), with its earth-and-chartreuse palette, is a hit in all these areas, offering Balinese massage and appealing in-room media toys. Its partnership with one of the hippest cafés in town, Jet Set (p82), results in a lobby bar that's open late, equipped with all the necessary lattes, wines and olive paste; it's the perfect spot for a meeting with your film crew/brand manager.

The **Ventana** (p175), the other new hit venture in the genre, goes in for diffuse natural light and a library that appeals to more bookish media types. Its lines are, however, just as clean and rooms as refreshingly designed – a breakthrough for this part of Old Town, where tradition normally dominates.

The **Aria Hotel** (p167), across the river in Malá Strana, has won rave reviews from day one, with Condé Nast plaudits for its integrated avant-garde style and music theme, including its expertly curated media library and fabulous, airy piano bar.

ESSENTIALS

Maximillian Hotel

– and the place is quiet, despite the location, due to thick ancient walls. Service is worthy of the days of old as well. Wi-Fi access available.

Inter-Continental Praha

Náměstí Curieovych 5 (296 631 111/www.icprague.com). Metro Staroměstská. **$$$$**.

Prague's flagship for decadence for 32 years, the Inter-Continental Praha may at last be getting it right. While visual traces of communist design were expunged during a $50-million refurbishment in the 1990s, only recently does the transformation seem to have taken hold in earnest, with courteous service and no reminders of the C-word in sight. All 372 rooms have a dataport for your laptop and the entire hotel has Wi-Fi. The negatives? One side of the hotel faces a garish neon-lit casino, and you have to pay an extra 40 euros or so for a room facing the river. Kids eat for free, however, and the fitness centre, Jacuzzi and sauna attract Prague's elites.

Maximilian Hotel

NEW *Haštalská 14 (225 303 111/www.maximilianhotel.com). Metro Náměstí republiky.* **$$**.

With 71 sleek but hardly antiseptic rooms, this design entry has won a following since it opened and offers great value, especially in the off-peak season. With all the mod cons, from free Wi-Fi to massive showerheads, plus the Asian wellness centre, which a place like this simply must have these days, the Maximilian is worth seeking out.

Pachtův Palace

Karoliny Světlé 34 (234 705 111/ www.pachtuvpalace.com). Metro Národní třída. **$$$$**.

With 50 deluxe, just-modernised apartments, and country managers already moving in, you'll be in powerful company here. The former residence of Count Jan Pachta is a swank stay, where showbiz amenities, a classy bar and babysitting go along with the timbered rooms and, well, palatial public areas.

Pension Accord

Rybná 9 (222 328 816/www.accordprague.com). Metro Náměstí republiky. **$$**.

With a convenient location just three blocks from Old Town Square, and spring and summer double rates of 103 euros including breakfast (30 less

ESSENTIALS

in winter), this clean, basic place follows the Central Europe efficiency model. But for budget travellers who won't be in their rooms much, you could do far worse.

Residence Řetězová

Řetězová 9 (222 221 800/www. residenceretezova.com). Metro Staroměstská. **$$$**.

A beautiful labyrinth of restored Renaissance rooms, some with timbered ceilings and lofts, make up this easy-to-miss Old Town gem. Genial service, an incredible location and a homely feel make it easy to imagine retiring to this abode to live a quiet life. The significant spread in rates reflects, aside from deep seasonal discounts, a variety of room sizes – all tastefully appointed charmers.

Travellers' Hostel

Dlouhá 33 (224 826 662/www. travellers.cz). Metro Náměstí Republiky. **$**.

No lock-out nonsense, all branches open 24 hrs, dorm rooms starting at 300 Kč per person, breakfast included, and, at this location, the hottest club in Old Town (the Roxy, p114) right next door. There's a romantic suite with beamed ceilings, plus free Wi-Fi. Both apartments and the suite feature kitchens but book ahead. This is also the booking office for a network of hostels (www.czechhostels.com), many scattered around Prague. The seventh night is free of charge.

U Medvídků

Na Perštyně 7 (224 211 916/www. umedvidku.cz). Metro Národní třída. **$$**.

The iron doors on some rooms recall Gothic dungeons, while the rudimentary bathrooms evoke the benighted years of communism. The traditional inn's a pub – one of the first to serve Budvar – that keeps a constant stream of tourists and locals fed on roasted pig, beer-basted beef and dumplings. Damn handy for carousing.

U zlaté studny

Karlova 3 (222 220 262/www.uzlate studny.cz). Metro Staroměstská. **$$**.

Arcanery abounds in this 16th-century building named for the well in its cellar. Exquisitely furnished with Louis XIV antiques and replicas, the four suites and four doubles are cavernous by Old Town standards. The UNESCO heritage building is halfway between Charles Bridge and Old Town Square on the Royal Route.

Ventana Hotel

NEW *Celetná 7 (221 776 600/ www.ventana-hotel.net). Metro Staroměstská.* **$$**.

From the Italian marble-filled lobby onwards, it's clear this new entry in Old Town hostelry is a classy indulgence. A design hotel for grown-ups, the genteel Ventana features a five-storey atrium and understated but plush rooms, many with exposed beams and Philippe Starck bathtubs. Its bar and library are elegant, if not as conducive to lingering.

Nové Město & Vyšehrad

987 Prague Hotel

Senovážné náměstí 15 (255 737 100/ www.designhotelscollection.com). Metro Hlavní nádraží. **$$**.

987 Prague Hotel was transformed by Philippe Starck from a 19th-century apartment building, the façade of which is the only aspect unchanged. Interiors are infused with contemporary brightness and have a sleek, comfortable 1960s/'70s feel. A good option for late rail arrivals.

Andante

Ve Smečkách 4 (222 210 021/ www.andante.cz). Metro Muzeum/IP Pavlova. **$$$**.

A fairly spartan modern exterior hides a warm, welcoming interior. A recent renovation improved the decor and infrastructure and it's still clean and simple. The excellent service and super staff are the main draws here. The 32 rooms are small, but you're a block from the most lively street in town. A bookish retreat it ain't, though rooms are quiet. Concierge and airport transit available.

Carlo IV

Senovážné náměstí 13 (224 593 111/ www.boscolohotels.com). Metro Hlavní nádraží. **$$$**.

The locale, a well-placed but not picture-pretty street, makes this palace look out of place. Boscolo Hotels made over the former bank with unrestrained Italian opulence, complete with cigar bar, pool, gym, wooden floors and a colour-palette of sage, gold and mahogany, but the service is classic Mediterranean, alas. There's also a spa and wellness centre.

Hotel Adria Prague

Václavské náměstí 26 (221 081 111/ www.hoteladria.cz). Metro Můstek. **$$**.

In olden times a nunnery for the Carmelites, the Adria now sits in sin city central on Wenceslas Square, the only sign of the virtuous days being the placid Franciscan Gardens. Newly modernised, like so much of Prague, the place has young and (mostly) eager staff, plus a memorable restaurant (in a faux grotto) and a bar with fairly standard-issue offerings. Concierge, sauna, massage and a summer garden are further draws.

Hotel Elite

Ostrovní 32 (224 932 250/www.hotel elite.cz). Metro Národní třída. **$$**.

Elite is part of the Small Charming Hotels group, and fits perfectly into this brand's specs. The 14th-century building, carefully renovated to retain its character, is protected by the Town Hall as a historical monument and the former barracks is right downtown with loads of hip restaurants and bars nearby.

Hotel Palace Praha

Panská 12 (224 093 111/www.palace hotel.cz). Metro Můstek. **$$$$**.

Just off Wenceslas Square, yet still close to everything, especially the city's tonier high street, Na příkopě. The Palace seems a world apart with understated,

old-style formal service and solid credentials among business travellers. Along with its award-winning Gourmet Club restaurant, there's a meeting centre with interpreting services, no-smoking floors and a sauna.

Ibis Praha City

Kateřinská 36 (222 865 777/www. hotelibis.cz). Metro IP Pavlova. **$$**.

For familiarity and reliability (read predictability?) in travel, the Ibis does offer deals on clean, new rooms in good locations – and at the time this guide went to press, it was planning another 430-room branch on handy Na Poříčí just east of Old Town. Unlike many wannabe exclusive places in Prague, it also knows its customer service. There's disabled access, a gym and an all-night restaurant.

Icon Hotel

NEW *V jámě 6 (221 634 100/ www.iconhotel.eu). Metro Můstek.* **$$**.

One of the best successes among Prague's crop of new designer hotels, the Icon stands apart for its service, amenities and thoughtful touches, which go far beyond copper and fuschia colour schemes. With the attached Jet Set bar, a cousin of this cool scene setter originally installed in Smíchov, even the lobby makes for a good hangout in which to catch the latest wave. There's a pampering wellness centre, of course.

Radisson SAS Alcron

Štěpánská 40 (222 820 000/www. radisson.com/praguecs). Metro Muzeum. **$$$$**.

Originally known as a jazz hotel when built in 1930, the Alcron celebrates the heritage of Duke and Satchmo, who both passed through, with art deco motifs. It's also kept up its rep as one of the city's first luxe hotels and has the finest seafood restaurant in the country off the lobby. The higher up you go, the better the views, but the high ceilings and period appointments make every room a classic. Lobby jazz bar, concierge, gym and no-smoking floors are further draws.

U Šuterů

Palackého 4 (224 948 235/www.
usuteru.cz). Metro Můstek **S**.
A winner for seekers of small and cosy
in the Wenceslas Square area. The
building dates back to 1383, but rooms
were last renovated in 2004. Yet the
whole interior is a time trip back to pre-
World War II days, and the formal but
solid service highlights this. The pub
restaurant downstairs is popular
throughout the city for its cheap and
classic Czech fare and venison goulash.

Vinohrady & Žižkov

Arcotel Hotel Teatrino

Bořivojova 53, Žižkov (221 422 211/
www.arcotel.at). Metro Jiřího z
Poděbrad. **\$\$\$**.
Rough and ready Žižkov is rapidly
being turned into Prague's Greenwich
Village, largely down to places like this
big shrine to nationalist art. Austrian
designer, architect and painter Harald
Schreiber is to blame for the interiors –
the lobby sports his epic, a giant rendering of about 100 Czech heroes,
which contributes much to the odd
mixture meant to 'animate the hotel's
guests for a journey through the art
and history of the city'.

Clown & Bard

Bořivojova 102, Žižkov (222 716 453/
www.clownandbard.com). Metro Jiřího
z Poděbrad. **S**.
Something of a free-for-all, this hostel's bar is well known in Prague
among the party-hearty set. Located
in the always colourful Žižkov district, it's a good choice if you're after
some after-dark action. No lock-out,
no reservations and no hassles, and
there's also a free vegetarian breakfast and laundry service. No credit
cards accepted though.

Courtyard by Marriott

Lucemburská 46, Žižkov (236 088
088/www.marriott.com). Metro
Flora. **\$\$**.
Adjacent to a green line metro stop and
the city's trendiest shopping mall, this
surprisingly solid-value spot is a good
option for families or those on biz
trips, with the usual Marriott service
standards. With 161 rooms, it's a good
backup if there's no room at the inn.
Disabled access and non-smoking
rooms available.

Czech Inn

NEW *Francouzska 76, Vinohrady*
(267 267 600/www.czech-inn.com).
Metro Náměstí Miru. **S**.
It almost seems wrong to call this spot-
less, designer accommodation a hostel,
but that it is. Private ensuite rooms are
available, as well as dorms, and no
membership is required (don't even
ask about curfews). With a glitzy cocktail bar, tasty breakfasts, internet café
and free booking of your next hostel
down the road, word's spreading fast
about Czech Inn.

Dorint Don Giovanni

Vinohradská 157A, Žižkov (267
031 111/www.dorint.de). Metro
Želivského. **\$\$\$**.
Not in the livelier west end of Žižkov,
but this 397-room mammoth makes up
for it with a borderline sci-fi lobby and
rooms that could almost be described
as whimsical. Dependable top-notch
Dorint service and it's a good option for
families – up to two kids free and an
indoor and outdoor playground factor
in. Deep discounts can shave loads
from the price as well – check the website. There's a concierge, disabled-
adapted rooms, a gym, a sauna and
massages available.

Hotel Abri

Jana Masaryka 36, Vinohrady
(222 515 124/www.abri.cz). Metro
Náměstí Miru. **\$\$**.
This small but lovely hotel is well-
situated in a quiet Vinohrady neighbourhood, about five minutes from the
metro station, and just two minutes
from a tram stop. The staff here are
unflappable, the rooms are large, the
lobby is spacious and the terrace
entices in warm weather. A restaurant
serving modern Czech food is also to
be found on site.

ESSENTIALS

Well, well, well

Hotel Hoffmeister

The fact that Prague's historic **Hotel Pařiž Praha** (p173), with its ornamental belle époque interior, now offers Ayurvedic massage in its wellness spa surely shows that the city has finally seen beyond the orthodoxy of servile tradition. The hotel is clearly aware that guests these days aren't going to be impressed by chocolates on their pillows and shoe polishing; and with its promises of treatments aimed at finding 'individual harmony and equilibrium in the physical, psychic and spiritual spheres,' it seems it does not intend to miss the wellness centre bandwagon sweeping through the industry.

And, when going up against the stone baths of the **Hotel Hoffmeister** (p167), the Caribbean elixirs of **Le Palais** or the Balinese

massage offered by the **Alchymist Hotel Residence** (p165), it's hard to blame the venerated Pařiž.

The **Four Seasons** (p172), of course, is no trend chaser, and seems to win praises enough with its in-room massage and pedicures, while the **Inter-Continental Praha** (p174) has been famous for years for its fitness facilities, with the heads of corporations and Radio Free Europe spotted there on a regular basis.

But even fabulous athletic and sauna facilities aren't really enough to set you apart these days, as **Carlo IV** (p176) clearly understands. This luxe rococo pile has been visionary enough to invite local journalists around to try its 'Roman baths'.

Of the many hotels offering everything from hot stones to detox aromatherapy, **Le Palais** (p179) seems to be one of those to watch: its spa offers 'well-being massages for relaxation of the body and soul, and luxury procedures for ultimate radiance using the finest natural cosmetic Ligne St Barth, made in St Barthélemy – French Caribbean.'

As if that weren't enough, the place also throws in five separate treatments, soft pack, hammam bed, a couple's room and, naturally, professional massage until 9pm.

And to think the Czech literary lion Bohumil Hrabal, in his descriptions of the Hotel Pařiž before the war, thought that drinks and good-time girls constituted the height of indulgence. If he could only see the services they offer the body now.

Hotel Anna
Buděčská 17, Vinohrady (222 513 111/ www.hotelanna.cz). Metro Náměstí Míru/tram 4, 10, 16, 22, 23. **$$**.
The Anna, with modernised amenities but an art nouveau interior and wall-to-wall warmth, is a Prague veteran-visitor trump card. Simply but classily furnished, its 24 rooms, some admittedly a squeeze, feature Wi-Fi internet access.

Hotel Tříska
Vinohradská 105, Žižkov (222 727 313/www.hotel-triska.cz). Metro Jiřího z Poděbrad. **$**.
Whitewashed Baroque meets Czech murals, art deco and imperial style, but it's a dead bargain and the owners have lovingly designed each room individually. It's also in the heart of the district, with great bar and club offerings nearby. If possible, request a courtyard-facing room; the street gets noisy.

Miss Sophie's Prague
Melounova 3, Vinohrady (296 303 530/www.miss-sophies.com). Metro IP Pavlova. **$**.
Dorms, private rooms and apartments, all in uptempo style in an uptempo district. Recently opened, Miss Sophie's has fitted its apartments with full kitchens, the dorm rooms with wooden floors and the private rooms with elegant marble bathrooms. A helpful vibe prevails. The more elegant end of the budget hotel scale, with a terrace and a cellar lounge.

Le Palais
U Zvonařky 1, Vinohrady (234 634 111/ www.palaishotel.cz). Metro IP Pavlova/ Náměstí míru/tram 4, 16, 22, 23. **$$$$**.
This gorgeous belle époque palace was once a meat-processing plant, but that's now hard to imagine in this idyllic corner of Vinohrady. It was originally decorated by 19th-century Czech artist Luděk Mařold in exchange for rent, and many of his touches remain, including the frescoed ceilings and staircase. Service is excellent and the rooms are classically posh (mind the movie crews). A well-equipped fitness centre, a buzzing restaurant and a lovely summer terrace, plus massage services, add appeal.

Prague Hilton
Pobřežní 1, Karlín (224 841 111/www. hiltonprague.cz). Metro Florenc. **$$$$**.
This glass box behemoth is very un-Prague like from the outside but hides an airy atrium and the trademark five-star luxury inside. You won't want for much, except for Prague charm, but it's just east of the old centre so an escape is easy to make. The lauded Czech House restaurant is another plus, and there are disabled-adapted rooms.

Holešovice & north

Diplomat Hotel Praha
Evropská 15, Dejvice (296 559 111/ www.diplomatpraha.cz). Metro Dejvická. **$$$$**.
On the city end of the airport road (20 minutes from Ruzyně), the Diplomat's still close enough to downtown (ten minutes by metro) to be considered central. Business-like, with serious meeting rooms, it's also big with families and has regular specials. Accommodating and helpful staff plus disabled-adapted rooms, a gym, no-smoking floors and interpreting services are further draws.

Hotel Schwaiger
Schwaigerova 3, Bubeneč (233 320 271/www.villaschwaiger.cz). Metro Hradčanská. **$$$**.
The former villa of a 19th-century Bohemian painter, the Schwaiger is located in a quiet, leafy part of town close to Stromovka park (a ten-minute taxi ride from downtown). It was recently redone in what could be described as Tuscan-meets-zen style. Staff are pleasant and there's a lovely back garden and sauna.

Sir Toby's Hostel
Dělnická 24, Holešovice (283 870 635/ www.sirtobys.com). Metro Vltavská or Nádraží Holešovice. **$**.
Friendly, accommodating staff make Sir Toby's a winner, with 70 beds in an art nouveau building that's been stylishly done over so that you nearly forget you're in a hostel. Also in the heart of a happening neighbourhood, with handy galleries and youth-orientated nightlife.

ESSENTIALS

Getting Around

Arriving & leaving

By air

Ruzyně Airport

*239 007 576/www.czechairlines.com/en.
About 20 km (12.5 miles) north-west
of central Prague, off Evropská.*
There's no metro access to Ruzyně;
the quickest way into town is by
ČEDAZ shuttle (220 114 296,
www.cedaz.cz) to the Dejvická
metro station and Náměstí Republiky,
which takes 20 minutes and runs
from 6am to 9pm daily. Singles
cost 90 Kč to Dejvická, and 120 Kč
to Náměstí Republiky.

The **Prague Airport Shuttle**
(602 395 421, www.prague-airport-
shuttle.com), with English-speaking
staff, runs daily, providing door-to-
door transport. Transport to your
hotel is 600 Kč for up to four people,
900 Kč for 5-8 passengers, 1,500 Kč
for 9-12 passengers. Book online.

The **Public bus** (www.dp-praha.cz)
service runs between Ruzyně and the
Dejvická metro, with the 119 running
every 20 minutes from 4.16am to midnight daily. It takes about 15 minutes
and costs 26 Kč for a single, with
tickets available from the machine
at the bus stop but not onboard.

AAA Taxi (14014, www.
aaataxi.cz) charges about 450 Kč
for a ride to the centre and, to the
relief of many passengers, now has
a rank outside the arrivals hall. Just
be careful to avoid the other taxis
waiting at the airport, which are
likely to rip you off.

By rail

Czech Rail

Trains run everywhere and are
highly affordable; they're generally
threadbare but reliable. For info in
English on train times, call 221 111

122 or visit www.cd.cz. For ticket
prices, call 840 112 113. The website
www.idos.cz also gives timetable
info for all buses. You cannot buy
tickets online but staff at the train
stations speak English. All the major
train stations are served by the metro.

Mainline stations

Hlavní nádraží

*Main Station, Wilsonova, Nové Město
(972 241 100/www.idos.cz). Metro
Hlavní nádraží.*
Most international trains arrive at
Hlavní nádraží, two blocks north of
Wenceslas Square, situated on the red
metro line C.

Nádraží Holešovice

*Holešovice Station, Vrbenského,
Holešovice (220 806 790/www.idos.cz).
Metro Nádraží Holešovice.*
A few international trains stop only at
Nádraží Holešovice, in the Holešovice
district and on the red metro line C, a
ten-minute metro ride north of the centre of Prague. However, many more
stop at Nádraží Holešovice then continue on to the main station, Hlavní
nádraží, so be sure not to hop off early.

Smíchovské nádraží

*Smíchov Station, Nádražní (221 111
122/www.idos.cz). Metro Smíchovské
nádraží/tram 12.*
Some trains arriving from the west
stop at Smíchovské nádraží, which is
situated on the yellow metro line B, but
usually also at Hlavní nádraží.

By coach

Florenc station

*Křižíkova 4, Prague 8 (infoline 900
144 444/www.csad.cz). Metro Florenc.*
International buses arrive at Florenc, a
grimy and unprepossessing station.
However, it lies a ten-minute walk east
of hotels on the much more civilised Na
Poříčí street on the edge of Old Town.

ESSENTIALS

Public transport

Prague public transport – its metro, trams, buses, night trams, night buses and funicular – is run by Prague Public Transit, or **Dopravní podnik**, whose website (www.dpp. cz) provides maps and information that can be downloaded and printed. Services generally run from 5am to midnight daily, with night trams and buses running at other times. At the information offices below, employees usually have at least a smattering of English and German and provide free information, night transport booklets and individual tram and bus schedules and sell tickets (cash only). You can also find maps for sale from agents and the routes posted in metro stations. Tram stops, meanwhile, have posted schedules but not handy route maps for the taking. At tram stops, the times posted apply to the stop where you are – which is highlighted on the schedule. If your destination is listed below the highlighted stop, you're in the right place. Call 800 191 817 for more information, 7am-9pm daily, or check www.dpp.cz.

Information offices

Anděl metro station *Smíchov (222 646 055)*. **Open** 7am-6pm Mon-Fri.
Můstek metro station *Nové Město (222 646 350)*. **Open** 7am-6pm Mon-Fri.
Muzeum metro station *Nové Město (222 623 778)*. **Open** 7am-9pm daily.
Nádraží Holešovice metro station *Holešovice (222 646 055)*. **Open** 7am-6pm Mon-Fri.
Ruzyně Airport *(220 115 404)*. **Open** 7am-10pm daily.
Ruzyně Airport Terminal North *(296 669 652)*. **Open** 7am-10pm daily.

Prague Card

The **Prague Card** is a four-day sightseeing admissions card that comes with an optional transport pass good for all modes of public transit for the same period. The Prague Card (www.praguecard.biz), sold at the offices of Čedok (p186), the state tourism company, covers entrance to some 55 museums and attractions, including Prague Castle and the Astronomical Clock in Old Town, for a fee of 790 Kč for adults or 530 Kč for students. Add on the transport card for a further 330 Kč for three days. If you're planning to take in several museums and galleries it's worth the price, but note that the Jewish Museum and some excellent galleries like the Rudolfinum are not covered. The travel pass is good no matter how many journeys you make and valid for the entire centre. The Prague Card is available at travel information centres and at the office of the Prague Information Service on Old Town Square (www.pis.cz), though not at metro stations.

To use the transport pass with your Prague Card, fill out your name and sign it (they're non-transferable), and just keep it with you while you ride – no need to pass it through card readers.

Travelcards

Day or multi-day travelcards are also available from the metro stations. Rates are 100 Kč for a 24-hour pass, 330 Kč for a 72-hour pass and 500 Kč for a 120-hour pass, and they cover all travel on public transport in the centre of the city, including metro, trams, buses and the funicular on Petřín hill in Malá Strana. They're good for any time of day or night and also cover night trams and night buses.

Travelcards start to save you money with the three-day version, if you plan to be on the road a lot. One-day and three-day travelcards come as standard printed tickets that you insert into the slot in

ESSENTIALS

metro station entry gates, or in the yellow ticket boxes on trams or buses, which time-stamp your pass. To validate a short-term pass, fill in your full name and date of birth on the reverse. The dates go into effect from the time you first put down. Once that's done, you can ride any bus or tram and only need show your pass to a driver or inspector if asked.

Metro

The Prague metro, constructed during the evil days of Soviet 'normalisation', is one of the old regime's best achievements. It's fast, clean, reliable and roomier than most in Europe, probably because it was built so late in the city's history. Stations are deep underground and the city's three colour-coded lines are a cinch to sort out. The system, heavily subsidised by the state, is also cheap, with a 26 Kč ticket getting you anywhere you'd need to go, including transfers – just remember to stamp it as you enter the metro or board surface transport, lest you face the wrath of the city's generally unpleasant inspectors, who may fine you 700 Kč, cash only, on the spot.

Using the system

A one-day travelcard or **Prague Card** is the best way to pay for your metro transport if you're going to make more than four round trips or travel on an unpredictable schedule. Otherwise, single tickets can be purchased from a ticket office or machine in the metro station (annoyingly, they're almost never installed at tram or bus stops).

Metro timetable

The metro runs daily from around 5am. Generally, you won't have to wait more than ten minutes for a train, and during peak times

services should run every six to eight minutes. But they can slow to every 20 minutes on weekends and holidays. Last trains are usually around midnight daily.

Fares

A 26 Kč ticket is valid for 75 minutes at any time or on any day of the year, allowing unlimited travel throughout Prague, including transfers between metros, buses and trams.

Buses & trams

The Prague bus and tram systems require you to buy a ticket before boarding. Do so: there are inspectors about, who can fine you 400 Kč. You can buy one (or a one-day pass) from ticket machines, though, frustratingly, they're usually only located in metro stations.

Night buses & trams

The latest-running regular trams and buses operate only until about 20 minutes after midnight, so night trams and buses, which are popular with a party-loving crowd, can be a lifesaver. They generally run from around 11.30pm to 5am, seven days a week, but come less frequently on weekends and holidays. Night trams have numbers in the 50s and night buses are numbered in the 500s. Most services run every 30 to 45 minutes so it may serve you well to check the schedule before going out for the night, especially in winter.

Taxis

Prague taxis have a well-deserved reputation for rip-offs and, despite frequent campaigns announced to clean them up, you still face a pretty good risk of being ripped off if you use any but a handful of reputable companies. Fortunately you can now find these drivers at taxi ranks in central areas of town, which until recently were considered the turf of the opportunists. Taxis with a yellow rooftop sign switched on are available but you really should call an established company and order a cab, which will generally be able to fetch you in five minutes or so. Starting rates are 30 Kč plus 22 Kč per kilometre and 4 Kč per minute waiting.

To book an honest taxi, call **AAA** (14014), **ProfiTaxi** (844 700 800) or **Halo Taxi** (244 114 411). They generally don't take credit cards, but you'll pay nothing extra for the call-out service.

Water transport

There are no commuter boat services in Prague, but for leisure cruises, see Jazz Boat (p116).

Driving

Parking

Driving can be a nightmare in Prague. The city has one of Europe's highest accident rates, combined with narrow, cobbled streets, trams (which always have right of way and use special traffic signals of their own) and frequent rain, ice and snow. Street parking in the centre without a residents' permit is not permitted either, and is likely to end up getting you clamped with one of Prague's infamous yellow boots (call the number on the boot or 158 to pay up and get yourself freed).

Blue zones are reserved for local residents and companies. Orange zones are for stops of up to two hours and cost a minimum of 10 Kč for 15 minutes and 40 Kč for one hour; and green zones are for stays of up to six hours and cost 15 Kč for 30 minutes, 30 Kč for an hour and 120 Kč for six hours.

You'll need to pay at coin-operated parking meters, which dispense tickets that must be displayed face up on the dashboard, visible through the windscreen.

There are increasing numbers of underground private car parks of paid parking in central Prague but they are expensive, often short-term and usually full.

Vehicle removal

If your (illegally parked) car has mysteriously disappeared, chances are it's been taken to a car pound. Penalty and release fees are stiff. To find out where your car has been taken and how to retrieve it, call 158, 24hrs daily.

Vehicle hire

Alimex (800 150 170, www.alimex.eu) offers competitive rates, just so long as you don't mind driving a branded car around town. Otherwise, try **Europcar** (224 811 290, www.europcar.cz), **Czechocar** (800 321 321, www.czechocar.cz) or **Budget** (235 325 713, www.budget.cz).

Cycling

Pedalling in Prague is hellish: no cycle lanes, drivers oblivious to your presence and pedestrians who yell at you if you ride on the pavement. If you must, bikes can be hired, and tours taken, from the following organisation:

City Bike

Královdvorská 5, Staré Město (mobile 776 180 284, www.citybike-prague.com). Metro Náměstí Republiky. **Open** *Apr-Oct* 9am-7pm daily. *Hire* 290-490 Kč for two hours. Cycle tours of the city, leaving from this address three times a day (10.30am, 1.30pm and 4.30pm), and with reasonable bike rental fees.

ESSENTIALS

Resources A-Z

Accident & emergency

Prague's general emergency phone number is 112.

The following hospitals have 24-hour emergency facilities.

Canadian Medical Care *Veleslavínská 1, Dejvice (235 360 133/ emergency 724 300 301). Metro Dejvická.*

Medicover Clinic *Pankrác House, Lomnického 1705, Pankrác (234 630 111/emergency 603 555 006). Metro Pražského povstání.*

Motol Hospital *(Fakultní nemocnice v Motole) V Úvalu 84, Smíchov, Prague 5 (224 431 111/emergency 224 438 590). Anděl Metro, then tram 7, 9, 10, 58, 59.*

Na Homolce Hospital *(Nemocnice Na Homolce) Roentgenova 2, Smíchov, Prague 5 (257 271 111, emergencies 257 273 191). Anděl Metro, then tram 7, 9, 10, 58, 59.*

Credit card loss

American Express *222 412 241*
Diners Club *267 197 450*
JCB *0120 500 544*
MasterCard/Eurocard/ Visa *800 111 055.*

Customs

For allowances, see www.cs.mfcr.cz.

Dental emergencies

Dental Emergencies *Palackého 5, Nové Město (224 946 981). Metro Můstek.* **Open** 7pm-6.30am Mon-Fri; 7am-6.30pm and 7pm-6.30am Sat, Sun.

European Dental Center *Václavské náměstí 33, Nové Město (224 228 994). Metro Můstek.* **Open** 8.30am-8pm Mon-Fri; 9am-6pm Sat. Sunday and later hours at a premium.

Disabled

Prague is a difficult city for disabled visitors, though legislation is gradually improving access. Some buses are getting more wheelchair-accessible and trams with wheelchair access are being phased in, but the metro is mostly escalator-dependent. A free guide to stations with lifts is available from ticket offices.

Electricity

The Czech Republic uses the standard European 220-240V, 50-cycle AC voltage via continental three-pin plugs.

Embassies & consulates

Also refer to the *Zlaté stránky* (or Yellow Pages), which has an index in English at the back.

American Embassy *Tržiště 15, Malá Strana (257 022 000/emergency 257 532 716/www.usembassy.cz). Metro Malostranská*

Australian Trade Commission & Consulate *Klimentská 10, Nové Město (251 018 350). Metro Náměstí Republiky.*

British Embassy *Thunovská 14, Malá Strana (257 402 111/www. britain.cz). Metro Malostranská.*

Canadian Embassy *Muchova 6, Dejvice (272 101 800/www.canada.cz). Metro Hradčanská.*

Irish Embassy *Tržiště 13, Malá Strana (257 530 061/www.embassyofireland.cz). Metro Malostranská.*

New Zealand Consulate *Dykova 19, Vinohrady (222 514 672). Metro Náměstí Míru.*

Internet

There are lots of cybercafés around town, and many bars, such as Jáma

(p129), feature free Wi-Fi. For more, check www.cybercafes.com. For locations, check with your provider or visit www.wi-fihotspotlist.com.
Internet Café Pl@neta *Vinohradska 102, Vinohrady (267 311 182/ www.planeta.cz). Metro Jiřího z Poděbrad.* **Open** 8am-11pm daily. **Terminals** 60.

Opening hours

Banks 8am or 9am-5pm or 6pm Mon-Fri.
Businesses 9am-5pm Mon-Fri.
Shops 10am-6pm Mon-Sat; some to 8pm. Many are also open on Sunday, usually 11am-5pm or noon-6pm.

Pharmacies (Lekárna)

Belgická 37 *Vinohrady (222 519 731). Metro Náměstí Míru.* **Open** 24hrs daily.
Palackého 5 *Nové Město (224 946 982). Metro Můstek.* **Open** 24 hrs daily.

Police

The main police station (Na Perštýně and Bartolomějská streets, Staré Město, Metro Náměstí Republiky) should have an English-speaking person available to help, but many visitors have found this lacking and police to be generally unhelpful. The emergency number is 158.

Post

Post offices are usually open 9am to 5.30pm Monday to Friday and 9am to noon Saturday, although the main Post Office on Jindřišská street is open from 2am-midnight daily, shutting only for two hours. For general post office enquiries, call the central information line on 800 104 410 or consult www.ceskaposta.cz.

Main post offices

Hybernska 15 *Nové Město (224 219 714). Metro Náměstí Republiky.*

Jindřišská 14 *Nové Město (221 131 111). Metro Můstek.*
Kaprova 12 *Staré Město (224 811 587). Metro Staroměstská.*

Public phones

Public payphones take coins or pre-paid cards, available at newsstands in denominations of 50-100 units, or credit cards (sometimes both). Local calls cost 10 Kč for five minutes during peak hours. Note that most public phones in the city centre are in a poor state of repair, however, because Czechs have embraced mobile phones with a passion.

Operator services

Call 800 123 456 for the operator if you have difficulty in dialling or for help with international person-to-person calls. Dial 155 for the international operator if you need to reverse the charges (call collect) or if you can't dial direct.

Directory enquiries

For help in finding a number, dial 1180 or the international operator at 1181. Online, many of the most useful contacts for visitors are at www.expats.cz and www.prague.tv.

Safety

Prague is not a particularly dangerous city for visitors, but its crowded spots – buses, busy streets, metro trains and stations – attract the usual complement of petty crooks. Keep valuables in your hotel or room safe and make sure the cash and cards you carry with you are well tucked away in your bag.

Smoking

In 2006, a law banned smoking in restaurants during peak times, but permitting it at others. It also bars smoking at tram stops, the area of which the law fails to define. At press time the scuffle to amend the vague law was continuing. Many hotels offer smoking rooms.

Telephones

The Czech Republic's dialling code is 420. If you're calling from outside the country, dial your international access code, then this number, then the full Prague number. To dial abroad from the Czech Republic, dial 00, then the country code.

Tickets

With the exception of the major cultural institutions, which have in-house box offices and offer phone and web ticketing services at no significant premium, most venues subcontract their ticket sales out to agencies. To find out which, consult the venue's website. Between them, Ticketpro and Bohemia Ticket International represent most venues, but note that Bohemia Ticket accepts no credit cards.

Bohemia Ticket International

Malé náměstí 13, Staré Město (224 227 832/www.ticketsbti.cz). Metro Můstek. **Open** 9am-5pm Mon-Fri; 9am-1pm Sat.

Ticket Pro

Old Town Hall, Staré Město (224 223 613/www.ticketpro.cz). Metro Staroměstská. **Open** 9am-6pm Mon-Fri; 9am-5pm Sat-Sun.

Time

The Czech Republic operates on Central European time, which is one hour later than Greenwich Mean Time (GMT), and six hours ahead of the US's Eastern Standard time. In spring clocks go forward by one hour. In autumn they go back to CET.

Tipping

Tip in taxis, restaurants, hotels, hairdressers, bars and pubs. Ten per cent is normal, but some restaurants add as much as 15 per cent.

Tourist information

Čedok is the city's official tourist information company. There is also a Prague Information Service office on Old Town Square.

Čedok

Na Příkopě 18, Nové Město (800 112 112/www.cedok.cz). Metro Náměstí Republiky. **Open** 9am-7pm Mon-Fri; 9.30am-1pm Sat.

Prague Information Service

Staroměstké Náměstí, Staré Město (no phone/www.pis.cz). Metro Staroměstská. **Open** *Nov-Mar* 9am-6pm daily. *Apr-Oct* 9am-7pm daily. **Other locations** *Main Station (Hlavní nádraží)*

Visas

EU citizens do not require a visa to visit the Czech Republic nor do those of the USA. At press time citizens of Canada, Australia, South Africa and New Zealand require a visa, which cannot be obtained at an entry point but must be arranged with a Czech consulate or embassy abroad. Use www.ukvisas.gov.uk to check your visa status well before you travel.

What's on

Numerous free listings magazines are distributed around town and with newspapers, but *The Prague Post* (www.praguepost.com), out on Wednesdays, is the best reference. Good online sources are www.expats.cz and prague.tv. For gay listings, look out for www.gayguide.net.

Vocabulary

Pronunciation

a – as in gap; **á** – as in father;
e – as in let; **é** – as in air;
i, y – as in lit; **í, ý** – as in seed;
o – as in lot; **ó** – as in lore;
u – as in book; **ú, ů** – as in loom;
c – as in its; **č** – as in chin;
ch – as in loch; **ď** – as in duty;
ň – as in onion; **ř** – as a standard
r, but with a forceful buzz like ž;
š – as in shin; **ť** – as in stew;
ž – as in pleasure; **dž** – as in George

The basics

Czech words are always stressed
on the first syllable.
hello/good day *dobrý den*
good evening *dobrý večer*
good night *dobrou noc*
goodbye *nashledanou*
yes *ano*
no *ne*
please *prosím*
thank you *děkuji*
excuse me *promiňte*
sorry *pardon*
help! *pomoc!*
attention! *pozor!*
I don't speak Czech
nemluvím česky
I don't understand *nerozumím*
do you speak English?
mluvíte anglicky?
sir *pán*
madam *paní*
open *otevřeno*
closed *zavřeno*
I would like... *chtěl bych...*
how much is it? *kolik to stojí?*
may I have a receipt, please?
účet, prosím
can we pay, please?
zaplatíme, prosím
where is... *kde je...*
go left *doleva*
go right *doprava*

straight *rovně*
far *daleko*
near *blízko*
good *dobrý*
bad *špatný*
big *velký*
small *malý*
no problem *to je v pořádku*
rip-off *zloděJina*

Street names etc

avenue *třída*
bridge *most*
church *kostel*
embankment *nábřeží* or *nábř*
gardens *sady* or *zahrada*
monastery, convent *klášter*
square *náměstí* or *nám*
station *nádraží* or *nádr*
street *ulice* or *ul*

Numbers

0 *nula*; 1 *jeden*; 2 *dva*; 3 *tři*; 4 *čtyři*;
5 *pět*; 6 *šest*; 7 *sedm*; 8 *osm*; 9 *devět*;
10 *deset*; 20 *dvacet*; 30 *třicet*;
40 *čtyřicet*; 50 *padesát*; 60 *šedesát*;
70 *sedmdesát*; 80 *osmdesát*; 90
devadesát; 100 *sto*; 1,000 *tisíc*

Days & months

Monday *pondělí*; **Tuesday** *úterý*;
Wednesday *středa*; **Thursday**
čtvrtek; **Friday** *pátek*; **Saturday**
sobota; **Sunday** *neděle*

Pick-up lines

What a babe! *To je kost!*
What a stud! *Dobrej frajer!*
Another drink? *Ještě jedno?*

Put-down lines

Give me a break! *Dej mi pokoj!*
Kiss my arse! *Polib mi prdel!*

Menu Glossary

You'll find that Czech menus generally list two categories of main dishes: *minutky*, cooked to order (which may take ages), and *hotová jídla*, ready-to-serve fare. The usual accompaniments to these dishes are rice, potatoes or the fried béchamel dough known as *krokety*, all of which should be ordered separately. When dining in pubs, the closest thing served to fresh vegetables is often *obloha*, which is a garnish of pickles, or a tomato on a single leaf of cabbage. Tasty appetisers to try are Prague ham with horseradish or rich soups (*polévka*), while a dessert staple is *palačinky*, filled pancakes.

Meals (jídla)

snídaně *breakfast*; oběd *lunch*; večeře *dinner*

Preparation (příprava)

bez masa/bezmasá jídla *without meat*; čerstvé *fresh*; domácí *home-made*; dušené *steamed*; grilované *grilled*; míchaný *mixed*; na roštu *roasted*; pečené *baked*; plněné *stuffed*; smažené *fried*; špíz *grilled on a skewer*; uzené *smoked*; vařené *boiled*

Basics (základní)

chléb *bread*; cukr *sugar*; drůbež *poultry*; karbanátek *patty of unspecified content*; máslo *butter*; maso *meat*; ocet *vinegar*; olej *oil*; omáčka *sauce*; ovoce *fruit*; pepř *pepper*; rohlík *roll*; ryby *fish*; smetana *cream*; sůl *salt*; sýr *cheese*; vejce *eggs*; zelenina *vegetables*

Drinks (nápoje)

čaj *tea*; káva *coffee*; mléko *milk*; pivo *beer*; pomerančový džus *orange juice*; sodovka *soda*; víno *wine*; voda *water*; slivovice *plum brandy*; Becherovka *herbal liqueur*; Fernet *bitters*; červené vino *red wine*; bílé vino *white wine*; perlová *carbonated*; neperlová *still*

Appetisers (předkrmy)

boršč *Russian beetroot soup (borscht)*; chlebíček *meat open-sandwich*; hovězí vývar *beef broth*; kaviár *caviar*; paštika *pâté*; polévka *soup*; uzený losos *smoked salmon*

Meat (maso)

biftek *beefsteak*; hovězí *beef*; játra *liver*; jehně *lamb*; jelení *venison*; kančí *boar*; klobása, párek, salám, vuřt *sausage*; králík *rabbit*; ledvinky *kidneys*; slanina *bacon*; srnčí roebuck; šunka *ham*; telecí *veal*; tlačenka *brawn*; vepřové *pork*; zvěřina *game*

Poultry & fish (drůbež a ryby)

bažant *pheasant*; husa *goose*; kachna *duck*; kapr *carp*; křepelka *quail*; krocan *turkey*; kuře *chicken*; losos *salmon*; pstruh *trout*

Main meals (hlavní jídla)

guláš *goulash*; řízek *schnitzel*; sekaná *meat loaf*; smažený sýr *fried cheese*; **svíčková** *beef in cream sauce*; **vepřová játra na cibulce** *pig's liver stewed with onion*; **vepřové koleno** *pork knee*; **vepřový řízek** *fried breaded pork*

Side dishes (přílohy)

brambor *potato*; **bramborák** *potato pancake*; **bramborová kaše** *mashed potatoes*; **hranolky** *chips*; **kaše** *mashed potatoes*; **knedlíky** *dumplings*; **krokety** *potato or béchamel dough croquettes*; **obloha** *small lettuce and tomato salad*; **rýže** *rice*; **salát** *salad*; **šopský salát** *cucumber, tomato and curd salad*; **tatarská omáčka** *tartar sauce*; **zelí** *cabbage*

Cheese (sýr)

balkán a saltier *feta*; **eidam** *hard white cheese*; **hermelín** *soft, similar to bland brie*; **Madeland** *Swiss cheese*; **niva** *blue cheese*; **pivní sýr** *beer-flavoured semi-soft cheese*; **primátor** *Swiss cheese*; **tavený sýr** *packaged cheese spread*; **tvaroh** *soft curd cheese*

Vegetables (zelenina)

česnek *garlic*; **chřest** *asparagus*; **cibule** *onion(s)*; **čočka** *lentils*; **fazole** *beans*; **feferonky** *chilli peppers*; **hrášek** *peas*; **kukuřice** *corn*; **květák** *cauliflower*; **mrkev** *carrot*; **okurka** *cucumber*; **petržel** *parsley*; **rajčata** *tomatoes*; **salát** *lettuce*; **špenát** *spinach*; **žampiony** *mushrooms*; **zelí** *cabbage*

Fruit (ovoce)

ananas *pineapple*; **banány** *banana*; **borůvky** *blueberries*; **broskev** *peach*; **hrozny** *grapes*; **hruška** *pear*; **jablko** *apple*; **jahody** *strawberries*; **jeřabina** *rowanberries*; **mandle** *almonds*; **meruňka** *apricot*; **ořechy** *nuts*; **pomeranč** *orange*; **rozinky** *raisins*; **švestky** *plums*; **třešně** *cherries*

Desserts (moučník)

buchty *traditional curd-filled cakes*; **čokoláda** *chocolate*; **dort** *layered cake*; **koláč** *cake with various fillings*; **ovocné knedlíky** *fruit dumplings*; **palačinka** *crêpe*; **pohár** *ice-cream sundae*; **šlehačka** *whipped cream*; **zákusek** *cake*; **závin** *strudel*; **žemlovka** *bread pudding with apples and cinnamon*; **zmrzlina** *ice-cream*

Useful phrases

May I see the menu? *Mohu vidět jídelní lístek?* **Do you have…?** *Máte…?* **I am a vegetarian** *Jsem vegetarián/vegetariánka (m/f).* **How is it prepared?** *Jak je to připravené?* **Did you say 'beer cheese'?** *Říkal jste 'pivní sýr'?* **Wow, that smells!** *Páni, to smrdí!* **Can I have it without…?** *Mohu mít bez…?* **No ketchup on my pizza, please** *Nechci kečup na pizzu, prosím.* **I didn't order this** *Neobjednal jsem si to.* **How much longer will it be?** *Jak dlouho to ještě bude?* **The bill, please** *Účet, prosím.* **I can't eat this and I won't pay for it!** (use with extreme caution) *Nedá se to jíst a nezaplatím to.* **Takeaway/to go** *S sebou.* **A beer, please** *Pivo, prosím.* **Two beers, please** *Dvě piva, prosím.* **Same again, please** *Ještě jednou, prosím.* **What'll you have?** *Co si dáte?* **Not for me, thanks** *Pro mě ne, děkuji.* **No ice, thanks** *Bez ledu, děkuji.* **He's really smashed** *Je totálně namazaný*

Index

ESSENTIALS

ESSENTIALS